Bomber
Pilot

Captain Philip Ardery

Bomber Pilot

A Memoir
of World War II

BY PHILIP ARDERY

The University
Press of Kentucky

To the officers and men
of the 564th Bomb Squadron,
the 389th Bomb Group
and the Second Combat Wing

Copyright © 1978 by The University Press of Kentucky

Scholarly publisher for the Commonwealth,
serving Bellarmine College, Berea College, Centre
College of Kentucky, Eastern Kentucky University,
The Filson Club Historical Society, Georgetown College,
Kentucky Historial Society, Kentucky State University,
Morehead State University, Murray State University,
Northern Kentucky University, Transylvania University,
University of Kentucky, University of Louisville,
and Western Kentucky University.

Editorial and Sales Offices: The University Press of Kentucky
663 South Limestone Street, Lexington, Kentucky 40508-4008

03 02 01 00 99   5 4 3 2

Library of Congress Cataloging-in-Publication Data

Ardery, Philip, 1914–
   Bomber pilot.

   Includes index.
   1. World War, 1939–1945—Aerial operations, American.
2. World War, 1939–1945—Personal narratives, American.
3. Ardery, Philip, 1914–   4. United States. Air
Force—Biography. 5. Air pilots, Military—United
States—Biography. I. Title.
D790.A86   940.54'49'73   77-92919
ISBN 0-8131-1379-2
ISBN 0-8131-0866-7 (pbk.: acid-free paper)

This book is printed on acid-free recycled paper meeting
the requirements of the American National Standard
for Permanence of Paper for Printed Library Materials

♾ ✪

Manufactured in the United States of America

Contents

Illustrations follow page 164

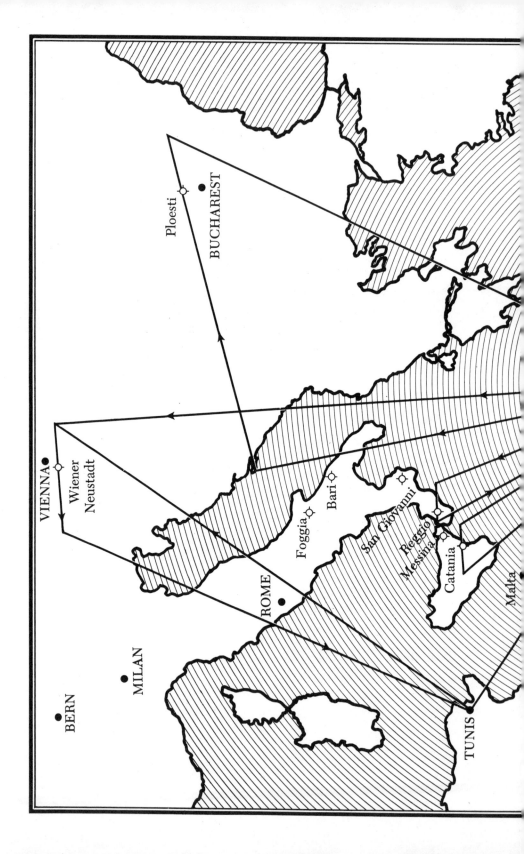

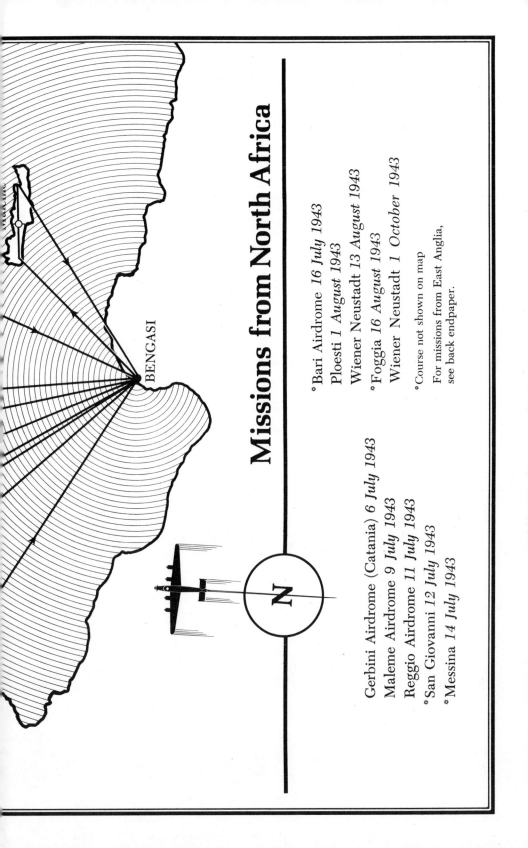

Missions from North Africa

BENGASI

Gerbini Airdrome (Catania) 6 July 1943
Maleme Airdrome 9 July 1943
Reggio Airdrome 11 July 1943
*San Giovanni 12 July 1943
*Messina 14 July 1943

*Bari Airdrome 16 July 1943
Ploesti 1 August 1943
Wiener Neustadt 13 August 1943
*Foggia 16 August 1943
Wiener Neustadt 1 October 1943

*Course not shown on map

For missions from East Anglia,
see back endpaper.

Foreword

A man who goes to war takes part in an event which the merger of national effort and individual experience makes more profound than any other he may ever know. His nation may rise or fall and, if he sees combat, his own life is at stake. The awesome spectacle, the horror, the pain, the heroism, and the cowardice are etched in his mind. For some, these leave more grievous wounds than those which scar the body. While many might suppress their memories or select only the easier, lighter moments to recall, other survivors feel compelled to tell what they saw—to describe those moments of intensity so starkly different from the ordinary course of events.

In American history, the combination of a high level of literacy and an interest in the common man has resulted in a wealth of soldier accounts from the Civil War to the present. The fact that newly discovered Civil War diaries appear in print at a time when the first wave of Vietnam memoirs are coming out shows the continuing interest in what those who fought have to say.

There are World War II memoirs which have set a high standard. Among them the reminiscences of two infantry officers (Charles MacDonald, *Company Commander*, and Harold Bond, *Return to Cassino*) and that of a B-17 Fortress co-pilot Bert

Stiles whose *Serenade to the Big Bird* was published after his death in the air war over Europe. Although not intended as a memoir, J. Glenn Gray's beautiful philosophic study *The Warriors: Reflections on Men in Battle* includes letters, journal notes, and fragments of memory of his service with infantry divisions in Europe. His emphasis, however, is on the universal rather than the individual experience.

Philip Ardery's account belongs in this group of first-rate books. Older and better educated than most who fought, he possesses a fortunate combination of sensitivity and maturity as well as a talent for writing. From the beginning of flight training in 1940 through the several schools as student and instructor to the end of his combat tour in 1944, he describes not only the actions but also the sensations he experienced. As a B-24 squadron commander, then group and later wing operations officer in the Eighth Air Force, he was in the midst of the great bomber offensive. He went on the famous Ploesti raid and flew over the great D-day armada. After the former he remembered: "The sky was a bedlam of bombers flying in all directions, some actually on fire, many with smoking engines, some with great gaping holes in them or huge chunks of wing or rudder gone." And he cannot forget: "The noise a bomber pilot hears. . . . The horrible screaming . . . of the enemy radio jamming apparatus. It is like the death cry of the banshees of all the ages." He saw some friends die in flames and others lose "the youthful facade which tears so easily in combat." He describes the effects of fear and how he mastered it for, as he put it, "no matter how fast things happened, I always had time to get scared." Off duty he moved in a select circle. He knew Edward R. Murrow and talked with T. S. Eliot and Harold Laski. There are brief characterizations of them and of his fellow pilots—Jimmy Stewart among them.

This is a book which answers well the comprehensive question—what was it like? It is also a fascinating story. I have never met Philip Ardery but I feel as if I know him after reading these pages. And he is, to use an old fashioned term, a worthy.

EDWARD M. COFFMAN, Professor of History
University of Wisconsin at Madison

Acknowledgments

I would like to acknowledge the patience and constructive assistance of the following, who read the manuscript and made suggestions: Robert Ardrey, Mr. and Mrs. William B. Ardery, Robert A. Thornbury, Joy Bale Boone, John Ed Pearce, and Alan U. Schwartz.

Brigadier General H. J. Dalton, Jr., and the Office of the Secretary of the Air Force/Office of Information have been very helpful.

Prologue:
On the Shoulders
of the Dead

It was the early spring of 1944 and I had just completed a combat tour of heavy bombardment missions. I was a wing operations officer. I was standing on the control tower of one of the air-dromes in our wing in East Anglia near Norwich waiting for the ships to return from a mission. There was a haze in the air which made visibility very poor, and a combat wing of B-24s (Liberators) was flying over. (The Liberators and the B-17 Flying Fortresses were America's heavy bombers in the European theater.) This was a new wing practicing formation flying with a full complement of bombs and fuel, getting ready for its first encounter with the enemy.

The formation, constituted of three groups flying together, numbered about forty-five heavy bombers. It was extremely compact; the whole occupied less space than some single groups I'd seen. As it flew over, several officers standing with me in the control tower commented. "They're flying closer than the B-17s do," said one. "They can't do that. No Lib outfits have been able to do it. They'll make our wing look sick if they go into combat flying that way."

"Don't worry," said another. "As soon as they hit any rough going they'll start running into each other and blowing up. Look at that leader of the low left element of the lead squadron jockey-ing his position in and out. He's too close for comfort and he knows it. You can tell it to look at him. So is the rest of the for-mation."

The sentence was hardly out when we saw a formation of Flying Fortresses nosing through the haze from the east, return-ing from a mission. The big bunch of Libs was flying north and it was apparent that neither formation leader saw the other un-til they were about to meet over the field. The formation of For-tresses was slightly smaller and a little looser than the Libs. It was also flying a little lower. They were almost above us when an officer standing beside me shouted, "Watch out!" All heads turned up. Two WACs right in front of me leaned against the tower rail. At that moment apparently the Fortress leader saw himself running a collision course with the other unit; he dived his formation earthward.

The leader of the Libs was hard put to do anything, for his large, tight formation was unwieldy. The purpose of such for-mations is for the guns of the planes to provide mutual support against enemy fighter attacks. But when that many airplanes fly that close the leader has to be extremely careful not to make any erratic movements. The Liberators' leader tried to climb his formation a little and turn it slightly to the right. It was evident that the pilots of a number of ships in his formation saw the Forts about the same time he did and individually tried to avoid them. That must have been the cause of the tragedy.

One Liberator pulled up to one side and too close under another. The wings of the two airplanes touched and crumpled; for an instant neither plane seemed to change its direction of flight. Then the wings began to come off both ships. All the other airplanes in the immediate vicinity began getting out regardless of formation. Suddenly a flame shot up. The two bombers were right up against each other now and coming apart. Another in-stant and that whole part of the sky was aflame as the gasoline and bombs exploded. One big fire gently descended. Falling from it could be seen engines, props, wheels, bits of wings, and some bundles that might have been men.

The collision occurred at about eight thousand feet almost directly over the field. By the time the fire reached the ground there was almost nothing left. The few bits that had not been consumed had fallen clear of the flames. Where the collision had occurred the sky was black with smoke. Bombers, both B-17s and B-24s, were still flying out of the cloud headed in all directions.

And as I looked back into the sky I saw one lone parachute coming down. It looked too small to carry a man suspended from it. I found later that the chute carried a portable dinghy radio used in air-sea rescue. It landed without a scratch.

One of the WACs leaning on the rail looked like she was about to vomit. The other had no expression at all. They had just seen twenty men killed and they knew as I did that the only way any member of those crews could be identified would be by checking the fillings of his teeth.

I was sick too, but not at my stomach. Here were twenty men, trained arduously for years, who had at last reached the combat zone and who would never help their country. Could the others of their wing have succeeded without the loss of them? Was such an incident essential to the hardening and forming of a combat unit? I recalled that our group had also had a fatal accident nearby while we were getting ready for combat. And I knew of one group that lost two squadron commanders in mid-air collisions before it became operational.

I had flown all the combat the Air Corps required for the time being. I had flown inches above the chimneys of the oil refineries of Ploesti, Romania. I had been over the guns of Berlin on a bright day when Berlin raids were at their worst. I had attacked Norway, Austria, Crete, Italy, France, Belgium, Sicily, Holland, and practically every other country where there was a target to be found in our war on Nazis and Fascists. I wondered how many of my class at pilot training school were still alive. I thought of those who stood naked in line with me at Fort Knox in September, 1940, to take the physical exam for pilot training. How many were now living graduate pilots?

Behind that I thought about Frankfort, Kentucky, where I

had practiced law from 1938 to 1940. I thought of Bill Young, a neophyte lawyer with me in Frankfort who won wings more than a year after I did. He had already been shot down in Germany and reported a prisoner of war. And so of the two members of the Franklin County Bar who eventually became pilots in the Air Corps it seemed I had drawn 100 percent of the luck.

1
The
Gadget

In the summer of 1940 I was a lawyer in active practice, twenty-six years old, two years out of Harvard Law School, and five years out of the University of Kentucky. My parents' home was in Bourbon County, just outside of Paris, Kentucky, on the road to Lexington. That was where I had lived most of my life. I went some forty miles west of my home to Frankfort to hang out my shingle. I chose Frankfort because it was nearby, it was a small town, it was the state capital, filled with politics, and at that time it didn't seem quite so overcrowded with lawyers as other small towns in the Bluegrass. I had almost no clients for six months. But things slowly began to change, until by that summer of 1940 I had quite a practice. It was about three-fourths charitable, but quantitatively it stood fair comparison to the practices of several other lawyers in town.

I was a reserve officer on the active list and had been presented with orders to attend the Second Army maneuvers in Wisconsin. I had received a commission as a second lieutenant, Infantry Reserve, along with my bachelor of arts degree from the University of Kentucky in 1935. I had kept up my training and in the summer of 1940 was a first lieutenant. I was young, healthy, and unmarried, and in the forefront of those called to the maneuvers. It was evident America was perking up a bit to the sounds of war in Europe. France had fallen that spring. In about a month the air blitz of London would begin.

And so I went to Wisconsin in July. It rained every day except one during the maneuvers. The confusion and general awkwardness of our war machine just beginning to unlimber itself were frustrating. Beer cans were used as simulated mortar ammunition and stovepipes as simulated mortars. During the height of maneuvers trucks dashed about carrying signs which read TANK or PROPELLED GUN. We sat in the mud and rain not knowing whether the spectacle was tragic or funny. In the downpour of rain beans floated over the side of my messkit before I could eat them. Between battle problems I tried futilely to rest on a cot in my one-man pup tent. The level of water almost reached the point where I lay, and more water dripped dismally from the roof. I blamed what I didn't like about those maneuvers on the Infantry.

I had always wanted to fly. A friend who owned a Cub airplane had been trying to sell me flying lessons for a long time. I didn't have the time or the money for flying lessons, and so I had declined. Now it crept into the back of my mind that I might learn to fly at government expense and at the same time break clear of the Infantry. In war the men of the Air Corps got back to warm beds and hot meals, if they got back at all. The men of the Air Corps didn't have to stand out in the rain all day counting the beans that floated out of their messkits. The men of the Air Corps stood around big open fireplaces singing, with glasses in their hands, and when they stopped singing they turned and broke their glasses in the fire. I was twenty-six and the age limit for student pilots was twenty-seven. I wrote out my application for pilot training and sent it off.

When I got home from maneuvers I found a letter notifying me to come to Fort Knox to take a physical exam for the Air Corps. I took the exam immediately and returned to Frankfort. I was trying to get ready for the September term of Circuit Court, and at the same time trying to visualize what it might be like to cover the shingle for a couple of years and be off to the Air Corps. Everything seemed a maze of important detail until two weeks later when the news came that I had passed the physical and would soon receive assignment to a class in flight training. I scurried around making an effort to leave the affairs of my clients in proper hands.

Within an hour of the time the mail arrived bearing the notice ordering me to flight training I was packing my Ford convertible. My orders were to report to Fort Knox for induction and then to Lincoln, Nebraska, for primary flying school. I would miss Frankfort, but I hoped I would soon be coming back to take up where I had left off when I might be secure in the knowledge that I could concentrate the rest of my life on law.

I took my belongings to the home of my parents. Mother was away at the time visiting her sister in Virginia, which gave me a pang of conscience about her. I hadn't told her I was hoping to go into the Air Corps because I had felt there was such a strong chance I would be rejected. Now I realized it was a bad conclusion. My father was surprised. "There are some hazards a man can't escape," I told him. "I have a commission and I must choose what I want now or lose my chance to choose." He nodded sadly but understandingly and waved as I got in the car and drove off.

I arrived in Lincoln, Nebraska, on a Friday night. It was a fairly large town, comparable to Louisville but newer and laid out in a more orderly fashion on ground as flat as the country around it. I questioned a policeman and was directed to a small building on the edge of town toward Omaha. It was a house currently rented by the Lincoln Airplane and Flying School, a private institution conducting primary flight training under contract to the Air Corps. I went in and found a bed. I was delighted to discover that the upper-class cadets lived downtown in the YMCA, so I would not see much of them except at the flying line.

Next day I woke early, dressed and breakfasted, and was first in line waiting for the bus to take us to the field. Already I could see I was going to like the life of a flying cadet. The meals were good, the beds were soft, we even had maid service to give us the same freedom from chores that we might expect as officers. I was quite conscious of the fact that I was no longer a first lieutenant Infantry, but a flying cadet. As such my status was that of an enlisted private.

Our airport's huddle of buildings appeared to be temporary structures. The big hangar had Lincoln Airplane and Flying School painted across the top of its doors. That morning as we drove up, what first caught our attention was the line of parked airplanes. They were brilliantly painted Stearman PT13As. There must have been twelve or fifteen of them lined up wingtip to wingtip on the ramp facing the hangar. They were two-seater biplanes with yellow wings and blue fuselages and looked as warlike as anything I had ever seen outside of the movies. I walked up to the end airplane. It had a big Lycoming radial engine which I had been told developed 225 horsepower and it obviously weighed three times as much as the Cub I knew back in Kentucky. Just as I was inspecting the ship, the upperclassmen came piling out of the flight room donning their flying gear. They scattered themselves among the planes and in a moment engines were sputtering and props were sending little whirlwinds of dust back under the wings.

Our class was called into the flight room, lined up according to height, and broken up into groups of three. Two fellows named Steinemann and Jensen, blond Nordic men, were put with me, and all of us were presented to an instructor. He was a rather tough-looking, stubby, blond fellow named Lowe, and I learned that he had been an old-time barnstormer. He looked the part and talked in an offhand manner slightly out of the corner of his mouth, his eyes glittering like a bird's. Lowe chatted a minute or two about inconsequential things, and then disappeared into the flying instructors' room. I hoped I would like Lowe and that Jensen and Steinemann wouldn't excel as pilots, which might cause me to get washed out.

In the bus on our way back to town we had a loud discussion about flying and why we were in the Air Corps. I don't think I said why I was in the Air Corps, but I do remember many of the fellows saying that they were confident there wasn't going to be a war. The United States was just concentrating on national defense to prevent war. Most of my classmates declared they were taking pilot training to be of use if the need ever arose, but they were confident it never would. They wanted to get pilot training and then get good jobs with the airlines. That theme was so predominant it surprised me, though an expansion of the airlines appeared certain. The air blitz of London was beginning, but the ocean between us and London made it seem far away.

When I got back to the house I had lunch in the cadets' big dining room. While I was eating I saw a car outside the house with a Kentucky license plate bearing a number from Jefferson County. After lunch I found the owner, a cadet named John S. Petot, Jr., and introduced myself. John was a blond, wavy-haired fellow with the sort of smooth look of an operator who knew his way about. I was convinced he did when he suggested that we set out to explore the town for college girls. He thought we might drop by the Kappa Kappa Gamma house for a call.

We headed toward the campus of the University of Nebraska, drove up to the sorority house, and went in. In the front room were two pretty girls seated at a table playing double solitaire. Before they could jump and run John slid quietly into one of the extra chairs at the table and I into the other. He picked up a new deck, quickly dealt out a hand of bridge, and bid. The whole maneuver was so quick that the girls' possibility of withdrawal seemed cut off, and without much comment the game proceeded. We played bridge for an hour or so and then persuaded our companions to accept a dinner invitation. Our evening was quite enjoyable and at the early hour of collegiate curfew John and I delivered the girls back to their sorority and went home.

We drove back to our quarters in a high state of amusement over apparently having succeeded in "going college" again. As we walked up the steps to the cadet house we were shouting out the supposedly tender notes of "I Love You Truly, K.K.G." Though the lights were out we gave no thought to the noise we were making until a bull-necked, pajama-clad figure appeared in the hallway to growl at us. We recognized Cadet Chester Tucker, our section marcher. Tucker sharply ordered us to shut up and go to bed. John faced our interrupter with complete calm. He realized that in numbers we were an even 100 percent stronger than Tucker. "Listen, Tucker," he said. "I suggest you forget the point you just made and go back to bed before you get batted right between those beady eyes of yours." Tucker growled again and went to bed.

On Monday flying began. I had been up a number of times before and so the sensation wasn't exactly new, yet there was enough novelty to be exciting. I had a feeling of freedom as the plane cleared the ground, and I recall turning around in the rear seat to look back at the field and seeing the rudder move slowly, like the tail of a fish, as we climbed a few hundred feet. We flew around the area where we were to confine our training activity and Lowe pointed out the checkpoints of the boundaries. Every little while he would ask me to point out the direction back to the field, which I did with some difficulty.

After the first flight I found myself almost immediately in the thick of flying. The troublesome thing was that my progress in those early stages seemed so terribly slow I could hardly see any improvement at all. I was told to do "coordination exercises" by the hour. These were rolling movements of the ship from one side to the other which were accomplished by simultaneous pressure on stick and rudder first in one direction and then in the other. When the exercise was done properly the ship would roll from a little less than a vertical bank in one direction to the same amount of bank in the other direction. The nose of the plane theoretically should remain centered on the same spot on the horizon. I then had serious doubt about the value of this maneuver, and after five thousand flying hours I still do. But it may help a new pilot to get the "feel" of an airplane.

We also did gentle, medium, and steep turns, climbing and gliding turns, and stalls. Precision in turns comes slowly to a beginner and certainly did to me. The very idea of unbounded freedom of movement on all sides seems to militate against precision. The traction of automobile tires holds a car in one exact course. But an airplane has no such traction to give it exactitude. And yet my instructor seemed to think that exactness and precision could be and should be attained. He felt I should be able to make a steep turn to the right, roll the plane into a certain degree of bank, hold exactly that degree of bank all the way around, and roll out smoothly to level flight on precisely the same level at which I had begun the turn. If a steep turn is done perfectly and without gain or loss of altitude, a second or two after rolling out the ship will hit an air bump formed by the "propwash" or turbulence laid down during the turn. Hitting that bump is supposed to indicate the turn completed was nearly perfect. But in reality it is possible to hit an air bump after rolling out of a turn even though the altitude has been varied during the maneuver if the airplane enters and leaves the turn at the same altitude.

I was told the stalls I practiced were for the purpose of teaching me how to land the plane. Maybe they were. At that time I practiced stalls because I was told to do them, not because I could see much connection with landings. Later, of course, I did see that a landing includes a stall—that is the transition stage between the time air control is lost and ground control is acquired as the wheels of an airplane touch the ground. It is in that transition that real piloting ability shows up in good landings.

My landings, though safe, weren't good. My instructor seemed to feel a good deal more confidence in my flying than I did. I wasn't satisfied with momentary successes which I could neither understand nor be sure of repeating. But after I had about seven hours of flying time my instructor decided I was ready to solo. I shall never forget that day.

A number of other students of my class were up for their first solo flights. You could cast one glance at the field and see that there were a bunch of "dodos" up for their first solos. Just before I went up Lowe tried to solo Jensen, who at least started out with a good takeoff. He flew the traffic pattern around and made his approach for landing. Initially it looked good, but after a few seconds with his wheels on the ground one wing went down and the ship spun around violently in what is commonly known as a "ground loop." Jensen walked away from the landing and the plane wasn't damaged much. I learned then that the Army didn't take the simple view that the test of a good landing is whether the pilot is able to walk away from it.

When my turn came Lowe was already visibly disturbed by Jensen's experience—as, indeed, I was. Lowe and I were in the airplane together. We had made one or two dual landings which were not particularly good, but which he appeared to consider satisfactory. He told me to taxi the ship over to the center part of the field, where he got out.

I taxied out into position, checked everything carefully, and gave the plane the throttle. In a moment I was speeding down the field. In another I was in the air. The front cockpit looked horribly vacant. I realized with something of a shock that either I was flying this airplane or it was flying itself, and my lack of confidence was appalling. I thought it would be the greatest accident of the age if I were to come down to a good landing. Then I remembered that these ships land so slowly and are so safe that there is little danger of a pilot hurting himself no matter what he does wrong, but I was very worried that a mistake now might cause me to be washed out.

I climbed two hundred feet and made my first turn. So far so good. I kept climbing until I reached five hundred feet and leveled out. Then I turned again to fly a reciprocal heading to the direction of takeoff, known as the "downwind leg." In a few more seconds I turned onto the "base leg" and then cut throttle. Then I turned from the "base leg" into the "final approach." I established a pretty good glide, which the instructors say is 75 percent of a good landing. Just as I was picking my spot to set her down, a cadet in a parked airplane—a "dodo" also out for his first solo—gave his ship the throttle and taxied right in front of me. One always should go around for another try when in doubt, but as a beginner would, I decided not to. It appeared the ship on the ground was going to get clear of my landing approach before I touched down.

Had I concentrated on my landing I don't think I would have had any trouble. But my mind was occupied with thoughts about the need to avoid the other airplane and to get my own ship on the ground. Just as my wheels touched, the other plane cleared across in front of me. I had unconsciously given a little rudder to get away from the obstructed spot, causing my ship to set down a little crosswind. It touched down easily the first moment I felt the ground, but I failed to make the proper correction on the rudder to straighten out the forward roll. The little airplane spun to the left with the force of a carnival crack-the-whip. The outside wing went down and dug into the ground, causing the plane to reverse action suddenly and start spinning to the right. It turned out I had committed the prize boner of the day.*

When I came to a stop I couldn't see much visible damage to the plane but couldn't understand why not. I looked to the side of the field where the instructors were standing. Most of them were laughing at me, but Lowe had thrown his helmet on the ground and was stomping on it. Finally he waved me over to where he stood. I taxied over and picked him up. He taxied the ship up to the hangar, killed the engine, and got out. "Write up in the form one you ground-looped and drug a wing," he said disgustedly. Jensen was there with a camera to take my picture getting out of the cockpit as I managed a silly grin.

For several days after my disastrous attempt at solo flying the weather was bad. I didn't get a chance to make up for that terrible day and I was nervous about it. I was facing my first and most serious check ride, and it was entirely possible that it would come before I had a chance to get the thing straightened out in my mind. Several days later I saw on the board in the flight room that I was up for the all-important check ride, and to make matters worse I was up for a violation of hours from the evening before.

John Petot had been having trouble with his flying, too. We had discussed what we would do in case we were eliminated. We both decided Canada was in greater need of pilots than the United States. Consequently, their standards of training must be lower, and so we would go to Canada. From that decision I took some comfort. But when I looked to see who was to be my check pilot grim despair closed in on me. I was assigned the toughest one of the lot.

The only way I could get my spirits up at all was to say to myself: "You're already washed out. There is just a matter of form to be accomplished—so worrying about how you do is absolutely needless. You've already made up your mind to go to

---

*Today's aircraft are almost all designed with tricycle landing gear; that is, two main gears under the wing and a nose gear under the nose. It is almost impossible to ground-loop such a plane. But the old configuration with a tail wheel in place of the one under the nose made ground looping a distinct possibility, which I conclusively proved.

Canada; therefore you might profit something from this ride if you try to get as much out of it as you can."

With that thought in mind I got into the airplane relaxed and almost completely at ease. Following the direction of the instructor I taxied into position and took off. It was a smooth, straight, almost perfect takeoff. I saw the check pilot in the front seat raise his right hand and join his thumb with his forefinger in a circle indicating he thought it was okay. And I knew I was going to fly the wings off the airplane. We went out some distance from the field and at his direction I went through my stalls, spins, and turns, and then returned to enter the traffic pattern. I made a fairly good entry into traffic, turned on the base leg, cut the throttle and made a gliding turn into my final approach for landing. The glide was good. Just before it seemed the wheels were about to touch I came back firmly on the stick. As the nose of the ship rose and the tail settled we floated just an instant within inches of the ground and then touched down as gently as a feather. "Keep on flying it," I said to myself. I watched the nose for the slightest tendency to veer off course and corrected with the rudder carefully and quickly to keep my ship rolling straight ahead. It rolled to a stop, and I felt better than I had since my arrival at flying school. Proudly, I taxied into the line and cut the engine. I hopped out and waited while my instructor slowly got out of the front seat and jumped off the wing. He stood and smiled at me a minute and said, "I bet that was the first good landing you've made." I nodded. "Damn good time to make it," he said and walked away.

From that time on flying went along much easier. I did my first really successful solo flight and progressed through several "accuracy stages." These were tests of precision landings which gave me the first real confidence I had about flying. My good friend Petot fared otherwise. His instructor said he "lacked coordination." Whenever an instructor felt a student wasn't material to go on—for any reason whatever—the reason always given was that he "lacked coordination." Petot was on his way out. He made application to navigators' school, as others had done. I knew he would stick around for ten days or so until his application could be passed on, and then he would be gone.

With my newly found security in flying school, and enjoying the last days of a good companionship with John, my life became gayer than before. I took dinner out nearly every night and even made a couple of trips to Omaha, where I went to see Katheryn "Kak" Hosford. Kak was a naturally beautiful girl and the smartest in appearance I had seen in many a day. Two days before the final withdrawal of the departing Petot, we made one last trip to Omaha. Our day seemed filled with political arguments. I was for Roosevelt, and John and Kak were for Willkie. Kak did have a good sense of humor and told a story I liked. One of her sister Junior Leaguers, braving a pair of tight shoes on hot pavements all day to give out Willkie buttons, accosted a laboring man. "May I give you a Willkie button?" she asked. The man looked her in the eye, shook his head slowly, and replied, "Lady, you ain't got a thing I want." Kak's friend said of the episode, "I never was so insulted in M-Y life!"

Flying now became more fun than ever as I took up many new maneuvers. The first of these were chandelles. A chandelle is a steep, climbing turn which leaves an airplane on a course 180 degrees from its original heading. It was developed in dog-fights in World War I. Each pilot tries to gain the maximum altitude on his adversary. To do that concurrently with making sharp turns requires perfect knowledge of the handling of the airplane. And that knowledge in turn results in getting the feel of the craft, so that the pilot can sense an approaching stall well before it occurs.

We did pylon eights, eights over a road junction, and S turns over a road, all of which were to teach us the effect of wind drift on the path of flight. These maneuvers were all done at low altitudes and with reference to ground markings. The substance of what I learned was the principle of "steepen the turn downwind, shallow it out upwind." Thus I was able to make S turns over a road in a heavy crosswind in such a way that the loops of the S on the upwind side of the road were approximately the size of the loops on the downwind side. Three years later I found the wind-drift principle applicable with extreme importance in forming up a unit of heavy bombers over an overcast. In England we would take our bombers off one at a time, climb individually through the overcast and, upon breaking out, form up circling over a radio beacon. Frequently the problem was made more difficult by strong winds. It was surprising how many pilots had come that far along and still appeared not to know the wind-drift principle.

Some of the other maneuvers we did at that time were to teach us the increasing effect of engine torque as the plane approaches a stall. Though not applicable to most modern aircraft, all the maneuvers were what every airman needed to know and remember if he flew reciprocal-engined prop types. The maneuvers to increase precision gave way to acrobatics. In the early stages of flying the only maneuvers we did that might have been classed as acrobatics were spins and spin recoveries. Spin practice was to protect us against the danger of failing to understand recoveries in case of accidental spins. The real acrobatics we did later served mainly to give us added confidence. I gained a lot of confidence after I learned a little about how to control a ship flying on its back. I loved acrobatics. When I got so I could do a good slow roll, snap roll, and Immelmann turn I thought I was about the best pilot I had ever known. That confidence in my ability to handle the ship in any attitude of flight did a lot for my general flying proficiency.

It might have been a bit too much of this confidence that almost put me in a hole. Though I didn't rate highest in my class as a pilot, I did have the distinction of being the only one who had never overshot the field, and I was determined to preserve that distinction. One day I was returning to the field to land after having practiced maneuvers on a solo flight of about an hour. When I took off there was a fairly strong wind blowing from the south and without taking pains to check it, I supposed the wind for my landing would be about the same. I noticed the traffic was landing to the south. I made my entry into traffic and turned on the base leg, cut my throttle and turned in on the final approach. Almost immediately I saw I had misjudged the wind, for I was much too high and my takeoff wind had died down. For the wind then prevailing I should have put the base leg farther back from the field, giving the speed more time to kill and the glide a little more space to the boundary of the landing strip.

Actually when I crossed the boundary fence I seemed to have the same 500 feet of altitude I had had on the base leg. The field wasn't long enough to permit a landing coming in that high. Should I give it the throttle and go around, or should I try to land? I knew I could lose altitude by "slipping"; to do that you hold the nose up and throw the plane into a steep bank which results in loss of altitude without increasing forward speed. But we weren't permitted to slip an airplane because that was considered a Navy stunt, though it is the easiest way to lose excess altitude for landing.

But I had learned another trick, based on the principle that the slower the gliding speed, the shorter the landing. I decided to slow up my glide to the point of stalling my airplane. I would let it fall a little, then make a recovery and land. Immediately I pulled the stick back and the nose of the plane rose. We were not allowed airspeed indicators in those days, but I could feel the airplane slow up gradually until finally the aileron pressure, controlled by sidewise movement of the stick, became wobbly. I knew the wings were stalled, but there was still a measure of rudder control. The nose of the ship fell in the stall, and I prevented a possible spin by kicking rudder one way and then the other in anticipation of the ship's tendency to "fall off." I looked at the ground and saw that it was coming up toward me fast. I shoved the stick forward. After a moment the nose dropped sharply toward the ground. The landing strip was only about a hundred feet below me as I felt the airspeed pick up slightly. The stick pressure returned a bit, telling me the wings were out of the stall and were flying again. In another instant I would hit the ground. The nose of the plane was pointed down at a dangerous angle, but before the wheels touched I came back quickly with the stick. The nose of the craft rose up and up. I pulled the stick back now all the way into my lap. As it happened I had just enough forward speed to cushion the landing. All three points touched gently and simultaneously, and the ship rolled only a little way to a stop.

I was almost as exultant over the success of this landing as I had been about the landing on my first check ride. I taxied into the line thinking that I would corner some of the boys standing around and ask them if they'd seen that landing. I parked the ship, filled out the form one, and rushed into the flight room. Lowe met me with an exceedingly mean gleam in his eye. "Who the hell do you think you are? I seen that landing. That airplane just fell in from 500 feet, that's what it did—just fell in! And the next time any student of mine gets smart enough to try that, if he don't break his damn neck he'll be out of here within twenty-four hours." I believed him. Since that time I've seen a few complete wrecks resulting from pilots trying the same thing. I wasn't good—just lucky—because in such a stall it is impossible to tell exactly what a plane will do. All the fun was gone out of my prize landing.

My last few days of training at Lincoln were happy. Upon expectation of moving out I traded my Ford convertible for a fine looking black Buick sedan. This transaction was by dint of a small but steady income enjoyed from the old law practice accounts receivable. I bought the car with the idea of making it a Christmas gift to my mother, but I made the mistake of telling that to my friends, who seized on it as a running gag.

We weren't given the time off we had expected after finishing at Lincoln, and so instead of traveling to Paris, Kentucky, I loaded "mother's car" up with cadets and struck out for our assigned base at Randolph Field, Texas. Jake Greenwell, Chuck Kruck, Harry Cerha, and Ray Williams were with me. We had about one day and night to spare if we went straight to Texas and made good time. We decided to spend the extra day in Houston because everyone wanted to hear a famous boogie-woogie pianist named Peck Kelly. My mother's car arrived in San Antonio with its load of new cadets about ten o'clock the night after we left Houston. We stayed at the Saint Anthony Hotel because we heard most of the Randolph Field cadets frequented the Gunter, and we wanted no premature meetings with our upperclass.

In the morning we drove out to Randolph. It was about fifteen miles northeast of San Antonio. Known as "the West Point of the Air," Randolph was laid out with the exactness of an octagonally cut gem. I had seen its tall administration building many times in pictures. Coming in the front gate I felt a welling pride in the Air Corps and in being a part of it.

Basic school was like a plunge into a pool of ice water. We had been so unbridled in training at primary school that we were amazed by the change. I thought the system was horrible. I was older than most of my classmates and I had been a first lieutenant in the Infantry Reserve. But in the early winter of 1940 that made absolutely no difference; I was merely a cadet. I learned from the upperclass that here I was "just another lousy dodo, lower than whaleshit," who had to "reach up to touch bottom." I drilled gladly all the time we were supposed to drill, but when not assigned to duty I stayed in my room. I acquired an intense dislike for my upperclassmen. About the only thing they did or said to me I didn't mind was when they called me "Kentucky," which I liked.

The flying was great. Our planes were the North American BT-14s, successors to the BT-9s. They were wonderful craft, and to us they seemed extremely complicated and powerful monsters. They had 450-horsepower engines, two-way radios, variable pitch propellers, and many complexities entirely new to us.

On my first ride with Lieutenant Watkins, my instructor, we flew around to look over the area and then dropped down low to do figure eights over a road. The plane seemed very low to me, but I was confident Lieutenant Watkins knew what he was about. After a few figure eights he told me to take over and try some, but he warned me not to gain altitude. The thought struck me that he cared as much for his neck as I did for mine, and he wouldn't let me get low enough to hit anything. So I made a figure eight or two and then gradually began letting down until I was below the level of some of the trees. Some weeks later I was outside the instructors' room and heard Watkins comment to another instructor about my almost knocking the tops out of some of the trees on the first day's flying. I discovered that one of the first tests given students in those days was carrying any maneuver down to a very low altitude to ascertain whether a student was ground shy. My flying perhaps wasn't great, but at least that was one test I passed.

At that time, in the early winter of 1940, the United States was looking to major expansion of our air garrison in Hawaii and the Philippines, as well as the pilot training program at home. The crying need for pilots was obviously the reason I didn't feel in danger of washing out. Indeed, it might well have earned me my wings, for orders had gone out to the training center that all students who could possibly make the grade were to be passed. This is not to say that students were not being eliminated; only about 35 to 40 percent of my original class finally graduated. But in other times this might well have been 10 to 15 percent. Many of those who were eliminated from my original group survived to do service as bombardiers or navigators. Giving a washed-out pilot a shot at navigating or bombardiering has its faults. I lived to see in the combat zone the frustration of a would-be pilot relegated to a bombsight or a navigator's computer. It was a problem with no adequate answer.

One night in the early stages of night flying I did royally mess things up. I suppose my own nervousness was the main cause. I forgot to relax. As soon as I took off that night I began having trouble with my radio. I couldn't get it tuned properly to the tower frequency. I had been called in to land several times but had not heard the calls. When the tower operator saw that his radio calls to me did no good he flashed me a green light with the "biscuit gun," a signal spotlight used to give directions from the tower when radio communications fail. I had been completely checked out on dual night landings and the whole night procedure several nights before. I knew what a green light from the tower meant, but I was paying so much attention to tuning my radio that I never thought to look at the tower.

All the other ships had been called out of their zones for their last landing and there I was still a circling lone companion to the stars. Finally it occurred to me that they must have tried to get me to land. I made my approach, all the time continuing to twist the dial furiously in an attempt to get contact with the tower. Just as I was making my glide into the field I caught a scrap of a radio message, obviously meant for me: "Go around, you fool, you're too damn high." I had committed again that grave error of dividing my attention. Sure enough, now I did notice I was too high—but then I was an expert at losing excess altitude. I would simply slow up my glide a little and come in shorter. Then I remembered what a narrow escape that last stall-in landing of mine was. I also remembered that I had been given a specific direction to go around. I did.

I made only one landing that night to three or four for each of the other students. When flying was called off I went to the flight building to learn that the flight commander directed that I stay there until he came down from the tower. He came down shortly and gave me more concentrated hell than I'd had since I entered flying school. He made all sorts of the meanest personal references garnished with a little knife-edged profanity. When he finished shouting I would have gladly strangled him—except for the fact that I had promised myself a pair of wings. That was my narrowest squeak at Randolph. The next night I went out to fly again and I had no trouble at all. Maybe the screaming I got was just what I needed.

Almost before I felt well settled at Randolph, I saw the announcement on the bulletin board that certain members of my class were to report to stand an extra inspection. It was apparent, though not announced, that we were being looked over as the prospective cadet officers to take over upon the departure of the upperclass. It came as something of a surprise to me, despite my previous military training. I supposed I had just come to think of myself as being unmilitary. We marched out single file and demonstrated one at a time our ability to give commands. Shortly thereafter appointment of the new cadet officers was announced. Chet Tucker became the "big dog," otherwise known as the first captain, or battalion commander. I was selected second captain, and given command of our beloved C Company. That suited me fine, as Tucker and I had become good friends.

Quickly on the heels of the announcement came the departure of our upperclass. Then a new class of dodos arrived. I never bothered the lower classmen except insofar as I had to run an orderly company. I felt their business at Randolph was to learn to fly and not to be hassled by me. I had had genuine affection for C Company before I ever came to command it, and my feeling grew substantially. It had been said for many years that the basic school should properly be called "Randolph-by-the-C." While I was in command the company didn't win all the parades, but it was a fine organization, well drilled, smart looking, and proud, with magnificent spirit.

As an upperclassman I had much more time to make acquaintances in the town of San Antonio and to see my friend Buck Harding, cousin of the beautiful Kak Hosford of Omaha and a flight instructor at Kelly Field. Buck planned to take leave to go home to Omaha for Christmas, but said he would see to it that I got put on some of the party lists during the season. I suppose he must also have told his friend Jean Browne to look after me. I saw myself building up to a grand holiday. Jean took me to three or four Christmas parties and introduced me to most of the season's group of young ladies of San Antonio. I was a little shocked to find that none of them seemed to think there was anything romantic in being a flying cadet. I discovered that cadets were called "gadgets" and that I had better parade as a visiting easterner rather than a local gadget, since gadgets continually overran the town. They were generally looked upon as a pack of drunks who hung out at the cadet club of the Gunter Hotel entertaining a group of perennials known as "cadet widows," girls who accepted the attentions of each succeeding class of cadets.

As my time at Randolph came to an end I was given some warning that I was to go to Kelly Field for advanced training, which pleased me very much. Kelly was an old Army field; most of the old timers since the days of World War I had gone there. In addition to the break I felt I was getting in my assignment, I learned that at advanced school I was to be the big dog. Tucker was going to Brooks Field. This would leave me the ranking officer of my class at Kelly Field and in command of the biggest contingent from Randolph. I left Randolph with no regrets.

Kelly Field was located almost directly across town from Randolph on the southwestern edge of San Antonio, much closer in than Randolph. The best thing about the advanced school was the flying. We had North American AT-6s and BC-1s. They were very fine airplanes, about half again as powerful as our 450-horsepower basics. They had constant speed propellers, retractable landing gear, and many refinements that made us think they were almost the latest type of pursuit craft.

Shortly after I arrived I met my instructor, a pint-sized Pennsylvanian named Richard Herbine. He was then a second lieutenant, in spite of the fact that he had more flying experience than almost any other instructor on the field. He had graduated from West Point a number of years before, had gone through the flying school, and had resigned his commission to go into civil aviation. As a civilian pilot he had flown for Eastern Airlines and had later become the director of the Division of Aeronautics for the state of Pennsylvania under Governor Earle. Lieutenant Herbine met more my idea of what a pilot should be than anyone I had ever known. He had a backlog of flying experience sufficient to carry him through any kind of emergency. He had all the daring necessary to do anything he needed to do, but he was not foolhardy. From him I learned that a pilot should have infinite coolness in emergencies, but also the caution to ensure that the only emergencies he ever meets are those not of his own making. A good Army pilot will perform a suicide mission in combat if need be, but he will not kill himself doing acrobatics low to the ground, buzz the house of his best girl, or take an airplane into bad weather if it is not a good ship to fly on instruments.

By the strong rule of the alphabet, I found my closest associates among my classmates were Cadets Amend, Andrews, Couvrette, Crabtree, and Crewes. Frank Amend was from Stillwater, Oklahoma. Andy Andrews was a long-nosed, keen-witted lad from El Dorado, Arkansas. Couvrette hailed from San Diego. Crabtree was another Oklahoman from a little town named Ada. Johnny Crewes was from Columbia, South Carolina. Naturally we became a well-knit group within the larger organization of our class. We flew together and saw each other all day long. One of the main things which stimulates such friendship is formation flying. We had to fly on each other's wings from time to time and that requires complete reliance upon each other. We thought we were the best group of six on the field. We could put up two nice close-flown Vs of three aircraft. We loved formation flying in the same way that an infantryman loves good close-order drill. But it is really not the same thing at all. When I hit combat it didn't take me long to learn that in those days a pilot's life absolutely depended upon his ability to fly good formation, because its purpose was mutual protection.

In trying to judge myself as a big dog, I can see that my failing was that I prized the friendship of my classmates too much to be a cadet captain of the strictly military type. I knew if the boys didn't like me I could "gig" them into line by depriving them of their time off. That seemed to be the traditional way. I gigged the boys hard sometimes, but then on more than one occasion I gigged myself after I had intentionally violated the rules and went out to "pound the ramp" with the rest of the guys walking off tours.

I became more and more absorbed in flying. I found that Lieutenant Herbine had a great deal more to give his students than most of the new pilot instructors had, as a result of his experience with the airlines. I was fascinated with the business of learning to fly a radio beam. Lieutenant Herbine went into all the mechanics of how a beam works with four open quadrants in each of which a code letter A or N can be heard. These quadrants are bounded by four legs of the beam formed where the quadrant letters overlap each other. Since the signal for an A is a dot and then a dash, and the signal for an N is a dash and then a dot, the natural result of superimposing one over the other is the transmission of a steady hum over your radio receiver.

I started taking beam procedure on our Link trainers before we ever had it scheduled. The Link was a little mock airplane, mounted on a pedestal, which by a thousand ingenious electric motors simulated the action of an airplane and recorded its action by an inked track on graph paper. The pilot using it was under a hood, operating flight instruments like those in an airplane. Great as we thought it was, it was strictly stone age compared to modern simulators.

My early beam-flying instruction helped me a great deal when we were making our first night cross-country flight to

Corpus Christi, Texas, which was about an hour south of Kelly Field. There was a light line leading to Corpus, but there were also several other light lines leading in different directions from the south part of San Antonio. I picked up the light line that seemed to coincide with the proper compass heading and set forth merrily. But after I had flown about fifteen minutes a suspicion entered my mind that I was off course. I couldn't find any reference that would assure me that I was where I ought to be. The lights of the city of San Antonio were now too far behind to help. I looked at the map in my lap and noticed that the south leg of the Kelly Field radio range ran directly down to Corpus Christi. Heading south from the field, the quadrant on the left side of the beam was an A and the one on the right was an N. I read off the frequency of the range and started trying to tune it in. After a moment I got what I thought was it—the monotonous "dit-daah, dit-daah, dit-daah" signal of the A quadrant. I listened intently for a few seconds waiting for the station identification signal to come on. Finally there was a pause in the "dit-daahs" and then came "daah-daah dit-dit—daah-dit." That was it! Those were the letters ZN which identified the Kelly range. I knew then that I must be in the south A quadrant and I turned to a compass heading of due west. After a few minutes I passed through the on-course of the south leg and over into the N quadrant. Then I turned due south again and flew along the right-hand side of the beam. I didn't even look for lights any more.

When I got back that night I learned that three cadets had gotten themselves lost by taking the wrong light lines. Another flew past Corpus Christi and out into the gulf; he had turned back just in time to make it into the Corpus airport before his gas gave out. If it hadn't been for Lieutenant Herbine's early instruction in beam procedure I might have been as badly lost as any of them.

A week or so before graduation at Kelly a man representing a San Antonio paper was scouting the cadet corps for feature material about various cadets who were following in their fathers' footsteps at the time of their entry into the Army. Some of the boys told him I had acted as county judge of Franklin County,

Kentucky, and that my father was a circuit judge. When the feature came out there was a bit about me with a cartoon, giving my name and a few particulars on the judge angle. A few days later I got a note from a man named Robert Ardrey running something like this: "I saw the bit in the paper about you. Your name and mine are sufficiently unusual to make me wonder which of us had an ancestor too stupid to know how to spell his name. Would you come to dinner?" The note explained that he was a writer who had come to San Antonio to have a quiet place to work on a play.*

Shortly after I got the note I called him and fixed a time to see the Ardreys. On the evening of our dinner engagement I put on my slightly fast-track garb of tweeds and flannels. Adding what I thought was a particularly glossy point, I had a pocket watch in my breast pocket with my Phi Beta Kappa key dangling carefully from my lapel—I had seen Roosevelt wear his key in such a fashion. I also wore a Roosevelt type hat, brim turned up all around and creases in the side. I found Bob Ardrey and his wife, Helen, to be delightful. Helen told me later when I knew her better that Bob detested the wearing of Phi Beta Kappa keys. He had thrown his own away, but had forgiven me for what he considered a sin, and we got on well from the beginning.

I recall on one visit Helen offered to do any sewing I might need done. I confided to her that I had a theory about darning socks: that when a sock wears through in one place it is usually so thin in others there is little use to darn it. I did not buy fine socks, and I never had them darned. When they wore through, I threw them away.

I had this "theory" of mine thrown back in my face some time later. I was frequenting the Anacacho Room of the Saint Anthony as often as I could get out to go dancing. I was in the final throes of cadet life and putting on a burst of effort to see each spare moment packed with the proper amount of celebration. Emil Coleman and his musicians were pouring out their lush tangos, rhumbas, and Viennese waltzes at the Anacacho

---

*Robert Ardrey, playwright, screen writer, novelist, and anthropologist is possibly best known for his play *Thunder Rock* and one of his books on anthropology, *The Territorial Imperative*.

Room, and on the evening of my embarrassment I was spinning around with a lovely blond lady named Lydia Hickox. Lydia was visiting in San Antonio and causing quite a stir, partly because she was charming and partly because she was from New York and a product of Miss Chapin's School. She loved to take off her shoes to dance, and had been dancing shoeless for a while when I decided I would be sporting and take mine off too. Together we spun around in big circles trying to do the Wiener Waltz in a manner as continental as possible when I noticed snickers spreading among the guests at the tables. I looked down and caught sight of a toe peeking out of one of my black socks.

At the Kelly Field graduation exercises several speakers talked about our duty to go out and show the world, and said these were the days when "so many owed so much to so few." I noted that most of the speakers evidently thought we were preparing for war. We were not merely engaged in a large pilot training program to enable the class to shift to civilian jobs with the airlines. As first captain, I also was called on to make remarks. I don't remember much of what I said, but it was something like this: "In the United States we have come to consider ourselves the immaculate protectors of what we call liberty. Whether we actually are would bear a great deal of discussion. But now we meet a great challenge to our system and are fast plunging toward a chaos which engulfs much of the rest of the world. We shall fight and what we fight for may be right, and some of it doubtless is wrong. We may win, though that is by no means certain. Let us only hope that, win or lose, those things which are undeniably good within us will survive in a new world of peace." I couldn't express what I felt, and when I finished I felt I had botched it.

The evening of graduation day we had a party for the class at the Gunter Hotel. Earlier in the day Helen Ardrey had pinned a pair of silver wings on my proud breast and that evening I had Bob and Helen as my guests at a table where many of my friends and classmates were seated. I had decided this party was solely for the enjoyment of the brand new crop of shavetails. We would pay no attention to the brass. But shortly after the party was under way, Colonel Harmon, commandant of Kelly Field, got up from his table and came over to ours. I got up with some surprise as he said, "Lieutenant Ardery, I just wanted to tell you how much I enjoyed those splendid remarks you made at the graduation ceremony this morning." I must have looked embarrassed and awkward, because when the colonel left I noticed that Bob and Helen were laughing at me.

After graduation we had several days to wait around Kelly Field for the orders to come out directing us to our next duty. We were given slips to fill out giving our first, second, and third choices. I asked first to be sent to the Philippines. My second choice was Hawaii and my third, Puerto Rico. I felt those in the Philippines would be the first to see action. And I asked to be assigned to pursuit-type aviation rather than heavy, medium, or light bombardment or observation.

After about three days the orders began coming in. I was not on any of the first lists directing groups to the Philippines and Hawaii. Perhaps I was to be on a later order sending still more of our group to one of those places. But then came the lists of those assigned to instruct. I was designated to go to Goodfellow Field, San Angelo, Texas, where a basic training school had just opened. Of all places I did not want to go, San Angelo was about tops. If I had to instruct—which I did not fancy in the least—I wanted to stay in San Antonio, preferably at Kelly Field. But a man's personal preference apparently did not enter the picture at all. Lieutenant Herbine commiserated with me over the sad lot of instructing. But there was a twinkle in his eye which let me know he had deliberately recommended me to instruct after my asking him so many times not to, and after his virtually promising me he wouldn't. When I asked him about it he said, "You'll get in the scrap soon enough. If you get an extra thousand hours of flying experience under your belt before you do, you may have a chance to come through. Otherwise your chances will be slim."

I was ordered to San Angelo and to San Angelo I would go. I might just as well take myself in hand and adjust my attitude about it to be happy if I could. Again I loaded mother's car with as many classmates as it would carry and set forth to our first assignment as full-fledged pilots. I might have to be an instructor, but I would never again have to be a lousy dodo, or a dumbjohn, or a gadget. I was a second lieutenant with shiny gold bars and the silver wings of a pilot.

2

The Merry-Go-Round

San Angelo was then a town of about 30,000 in the eastern beginning of what is called West Texas. It is about 225 miles northwest of San Antonio. The land is high and cool. Less of the moisture-laden gulf air gets over this part of Texas than over San Antonio. The temperatures are not so mild, but since the weather is drier the heat of summer is not particularly oppressive nor the cold of winter so penetrating. It is good ranch country and produces cattle, sheep, and goats; it is a substantial wool and mohair market. There is something here of the old West as it is depicted in the movies. For a time I continued to chafe at being relegated to flying "maytag messerschmitts," and instructing "gadgets" instead of going out to conquer the sky and the enemy in a fast pursuit ship. But I liked San Angelo.

A day or two after we arrived we were given routine check rides by the ranking instructors. Only a few classes of cadets had gone through the school before our arrival, and it was just beginning to expand. So the process of preparing us to instruct was hastened. Our basic trainers were the new Vultee BT-13s and BT-13As. They flew almost like the North American basics we had at Randolph, but we had forgotten a lot about flying basic trainers, and by the time we were faced with our first class of students we had hardly learned how to make proper landings in them.

In those days the life of an instructor was easy. Usually three or four students were assigned to each instructor. That meant that ordinarily there were only three or four hours of flying per day for each of us. After some of the students checked out solo we would fly even less. Frequently one student of the group would be eliminated, lightening the instructor's burden. Aside from the duty of flying there was little for most of the flying officers to do. Occasionally each of us would come up on the roster for post officer of the day, or airdrome officer. There were a few extra duties, but generally speaking the life was unbelievably simple. As soon as duty hours were over we would change to civilian clothes and go to the officers' club or to town.

I decided that since life was so easy, the least I could do was to get all my students through. I believed there wasn't one boy in a thousand who could complete the course necessary to get to basic school and not have the ability to finish basic training. The only question in my mind was whether I would have the patience to concentrate on the slow students and keep them fairly well up with the rest, since all students had to finish in a certain time. Many of the instructors who had been at San Angelo a long time were infused with the old system of profuse eliminations: if you had two students who were average and one who was below average, you eliminated the weak one before he got a chance to solo. This practice was supposed to keep the level of proficiency of graduate pilots high. I believed flying to be so basically simple that by the time a group of students got out of the advanced school there was not much difference in their flying ability. I set to work to prove my confidence justified.

After my first class was sent on to advanced school I got a break. My name came to the top of the roster of pilots to go to California to pick up new planes and ferry them back to San Angelo. Five pilots went out from Goodfellow Field to the Vultee plant near Los Angeles to bring back five new BT-13s. At that time the ferry command was not the extensive organization it later became, and these small jobs of transporting trainer planes fell to the instructors at the fields where they were to be used.

Ferrying trips were much sought after because the Vultee Company paid expenses at the Hollywood Plaza Hotel for all ferry pilots coming in for aircraft. The arrangement grew out of an old crating charge normally tacked on to the price of airplanes. When they were delivered flyaway at the plant the crating charge was saved and the saving was applied to the pilots' expenses.

When we arrived to pick up our airplanes we had to wait a day and a night before they were ready. There was a shortage of test pilots at the Vultee factory and at that time all new ships had to be test-hopped. We were asked if we would volunteer to test our ships. Most of our group declined. Lieutenant Bailey, another beginner pilot, and I volunteered. Bailey was a classmate from San Diego who had been assigned to Goodfellow Field at the same time I had. I had become more and more closely associated with him, being in the same flight for instruction, and better acquaintance made me like him. He was a smiling, slightly rotund fellow with blue eyes that crinkled in the corners when he laughed. He seemed to think as many things had interesting or funny angles as I did.

We seized this opportunity to call ourselves test pilots. It never occurred to me that my airplane might not fly, or that there was any real need to test it to see if it performed any differently from any other basic trainer. So I flew all over greater Los Angeles, never being able to see anything through the fog except a very narrow area immediately underneath me. Forward visibility was practically zero. I lost Bailey and never saw him from the time I took off until after I landed. When I got back I asked one of the other fellows who came out with us why he didn't volunteer to test a new ship. The reply I got was, "Hell, that's not our job. The next time we come out here they'll want us to put in a coupla' hours work on the assembly line."

That same afternoon we took off in our bright new blue and yellow ships. When we arrived over our home air base at Goodfellow Field the next day we put on the customary, long "rat race" before landing. At that time the air base was new enough that people all over town hearing the noise would come out of their houses, look up and say, "The boys are back from California." It was lots of fun to get in a wide lufbery circle and buzz around the field in all sorts of wild-looking maneuvers. We would dive and zoom and climb in high chandelles and do slow rolls in the big circle around the field. A basic trainer makes more noise than many a larger airplane, chiefly because of its two-bladed propeller. We all put our props in low pitch so they would make more noise and created sound effects like a showing of *Hell's Angels* at the Bijou.

When I landed I was met by a cadet who was an old friend from Lexington, Kentucky. He was in the class of cadets ahead of the one I was instructing and he was just graduating from basic. This happened to be the Saturday his class had its farewell dance. He said he had a date for me and a place saved at his table for dinner. I was tired, but easily persuaded. Early that evening I was scanning the dance floor and the crowds in the dining room for someone spectacular. I was seated with my blind date and several others in a lounge adjoining the ballroom when I felt an exceedingly strong impression that there across the room was a startlingly beautiful girl. I asked and was told that her name was Anne Tweedy; she lived with her widowed mother on a ranch at nearby Knickerbocker.

She was small—about five feet four. She had long, dark hair falling about her shoulders, and she wore a beautiful long, green dress that looked like it might have been Mainbocher. She had features so perfect that it seemed almost the face of a cameo. She wore a little circular gold pin at the neck of her dress. Otherwise her costume was of Grecian simplicity. I managed to get introduced to her and spent the rest of the evening competing for her attention with her many other admirers.

The next morning was Sunday. I didn't feel good, but I woke early. I couldn't remember the name of the lovely girl I'd met, though I could remember everything else about her. The more I tried to think of the name the more it annoyed me. Finally I got out of bed and went downstairs to the telephone. I took the book off the hook and went back to bed with it. There I started with the A's and slowly proceeded to read right through. I knew if I came to the name I would remember it. It was a big telephone book for a town the size of San Angelo. I got almost to the end of the book without seeing a name that rang a single bell. Then a page or two from the very end I came to the name, "Tweedy, Mrs. J. L., Knickerbocker Ranch, Knickerbocker." That was it! It was still pretty early, and I knew she wouldn't remember me, but at least I should have a chance to talk uninterrupted.

I got the Knickerbocker Ranch and asked for "Miss Anne." Yes, she was there, wait a moment. When she answered in her husky voice and eastern finishing school accent, I could almost see her as she was on the dance floor: green and gold and gorgeous. Were there any movies she would like to see? She didn't think there were any particularly good movies showing. What should we do? I was a little surprised and pleased when she consented to go to a drive-in for a beer. The president was making a radio talk I had wanted to hear, but I had more or less given it up. Certainly, I thought, Anne wouldn't be the sort who would be interested in hearing the president. As a matter of fact she was. We had a beer and listened.

After the speech we drove out to Goodfellow Field. As yet Anne had not discovered the fact that I was an officer. She thought I was a cadet. She managed to cover her surprise when we went into the officers' club. We had a nice radio-phonograph, and I knew just the record for this occasion. It was Xavier Cugat's "Night Must Fall." Anne was good at rhumbas. I tried to behave like an Arthur Murray honor student, and I had a marvelous time.

From then on I saw her as often as I could. I was pleased with everything I learned about her: from the fact that she was smart as well as beautiful to the fact that, like me, she enjoyed listening to the radio fireside chats of FDR.

In those summer days of 1941 I found life quite exciting—attributable largely to my interest in Anne, but also to great thrills in flying. The Germans that June reversed themselves and declared war on Russia. Most Americans were delighted but no less confused by that declaration than by the non-aggression pact it violated. As for me, I had definitely given over the idea of being a great geopolitician in favor of becoming an average pilot.

My flying with students was a lark. Yet I didn't get enough flying with them during the week to quench my thirst for it, and several of us went each Saturday to take airplanes up for our own amusement. My friend Alan Bailey and I flew nearly every Saturday afternoon. We would rat-race with each other by the hour, rolling and diving in and out of the white, billowy cumulus clouds doing everything we knew. It was a sort of follow-the-leader with each trying to outdo the other. This flying was great training for us; it helped to pile up hours in our log books and afforded us much pleasurable relaxation.

Another assigned duty I had shortly after my arrival was that of defense counsel on both of the courts-martial of our base. Soon I was made an instructor in military law in the ground school, and this, too, went along with my work in the military courts and my full quota of students at the flying line. I had the time for it all, but I found military law a little stagnant compared to the dynamic branches of law in the civilian world.

I finished instructing my second class of cadets and the season was wearing into early fall when I got my first long-awaited opportunity to go home. I had said goodbye to my father about twelve months before, and the longing I felt to see him and my mother had grown stronger every day. I had thought a thousand times of mother and how I hadn't even been able to say goodbye to her. I wanted to take the car to her and apologize for the way I had gone off to the Air Corps practically without warning. The car was not exactly new now, but when I had it washed and polished it looked very fine, all black and chromium and glisteny with the best of gadgets. Auto knickknacks are so characteristic of America I almost feel a sort of patriotism about them. I was homesick for the sight of Saturday night on Main Street in Paris, Kentucky, and the numerous beat-up cars with as many as four or five radio aerials, fox tails flying from all of them.

I said goodbye to my cadets and, of course, to Anne, set forth early one morning, drove all night, and got in about noon of the next day without making a single stop of more than fifteen minutes. I well remember my joy when I rolled up the gravel drive to the big white house and mother and dad came out to meet me.

I gave mother the car, scoffs of my friends to the contrary. She was charmed with it, and I think the more so because of a few scratches, the stickers on the windshield, and other faint mementos of Lincoln, Randolph, Kelly, and San Angelo.

Mother had a pretty good Oldsmobile which she gave to me. It had a good many miles on it and would have to be traded in shortly, so I decided to take the Olds and see if I could trade it right away to avoid driving it back to Texas. At that time I had about five hundred dollars in the bank and that was all. I looked all over Paris and all the nearby towns for a possible trade-in. On Main Street in Lexington I saw a shiny new Plymouth station wagon in the window of a garage, and learned the price was $1100. The next day dad and I went to the Lexington garage with the old car. The salesman offered me the station wagon for my car and $500. Clearly it was too much and I couldn't have the station wagon. When I reported to dad he said, "What's the matter? I think you ought to take this car—how much does he want?"

"At least a hundred dollars more than I can pay him now. Let's go home."

Dad reached in his pocket and pulled out five new twenties. "Here," he said, "I would not have it any other way. This is a present from me which I insist you accept." The little red wagon looked three shades brighter than it had the moment before.

The next morning I loaded my luggage into the station wagon and set forth to Texas. Saying goodbye to mother and dad, I was at last feeling settled and comfortable about being a pilot in the Air Corps because they seemed completely reconciled to it. I drove away from Lexington relaxed.

At that time on the verge of the autumn of 1941 the storm clouds were so ominous that even the most shortsighted could see them. Soon the storm would break, and then soon after it would all be over and I would come back to Kentucky unharmed. I was sure of that. The white fences and rock walls spun by for a while, and then were gone as the Bluegrass was behind me.

One Saturday afternoon shortly after my return I looked for my good friend Alan Bailey to go down to the Gunter Music Shop to listen to some new records. Bailey and I both loved music, and we spent an hour or two a week in the music shop playing all the new records that had arrived since our last trip. We were commissioned to buy for the officers' club. Also, I had a radio-phonograph, and we would buy many things to play on my machine which we liked but which might not be generally popular. When I walked into the officers' club I was told that Bailey had just been looking for me to go flying with him but, being unable to locate me, had taken an Infantry lieutenant for an afternoon hop. In town I bought a set of records of the "Scheherezade Suite." I knew Bailey would enjoy them as much as I, and as I returned to my room I inquired whether he had come in from his flight. No one had seen him. I went to my room to play the records. After about half an hour Ben, the old Negro janitor, came to my door. He had trouble on his face.

"Did you hear 'bout Mr. Bailey?" he asked.

I looked at Ben and without asking, I knew what he meant. I could see that he was sorry to tell me because he knew how much I thought of Alan.

"What happened?"

"Don't know, sir. But they said he came down near a ranch house somewheres south of here. Both him'n the other officer killed."

The ship had crashed and burned, leaving little that was recognizable as an airplane with two occupants. Two days later I escorted Bailey's flag-draped coffin home to his parents in San Diego.

After Bailey's death a lot of fun went out of my flying. If my joy in it was less, my attention to it was more intense, and my determination just as great to see my students become pilots. I had one of the toughest problems yet to confront me in the person of a big, beefy fellow named Dean Foster. Dean was delightful, but one of the most inept fliers I ever saw. The first day we met he told me he had just barely squeaked through primary training and had been the champion ground looper of his class. I felt in him something of a kindred spirit. During the early phase of his training I saw clearly what I might expect. On his landings Dean was inclined to let the ship get away from him because he failed to make quick corrections. He was not alert enough on the rudder to keep the nose pointed absolutely straight ahead until the ship stopped rolling. He set the plane down without getting the wings perfectly level, he failed to correct for drift, and he made many other mistakes the avoidance of which should have become second nature to him at primary school.

When Dean was given a check ride by the squadron CO the report was a suggested washout for him, but I didn't put him up for the fatal ride with the stage commander, the necessary preliminary to elimination. I kept plugging along with him and by the time his next check ride came along he passed. Dean finished as a solid flyer. I kept check on him after he left our school and I found he went through advanced school in great style. I think after his graduation he became the first of my students to check out as first pilot of a four-engine bomber. He could fly one a long time before I could. I continued to hear from him and I was pleased with his success.

Sometimes after four continuous hours of flying with students I would get out of the airplane unnerved. It was a nervousness that came from correcting again and again the same mistakes made by four different students in four successive hours. After the day's last flight I would go immediately to the instructors' room, change clothes, and make out the grade slips. Then if I had calmed down sufficiently to be helpful to them, I would meet the boys in the outside flight office and talk with each student, pointing out his mistakes of the day. Sometimes, however, I would wave my way out the door saying, "See you guys tomorrow." On such occasions I would meet them when I was fresh before the first flight the next day, and go over all the points I might have covered the day before. I tried not to talk to them unless I could be sensible and calm instead of irritable and upsetting.

I knew several instructors who used the verbal abuse technique of instruction. They seemed to believe it brought results. I didn't. I felt the boys knew when they had done poorly and that knowledge was punishment enough. The result of my tolerance was that as the need for pilots grew, I frequently found myself with someone else's problem cadet on my hands. In the earlier days when an instructor put a cadet up for his elimination ride, events from there on out were cut and dried. There were practically no instances of cadets being given another chance. But from the fall of 1941 to the end of my work at basic school it was not unusual for a cadet on such a washout ride to "beat the stage" and be given a try with another instructor. During each of my last three classes I was handed one or more of these lagging gadgets. I liked helping them, except for the fact that it made me fly my pants off to give enough instruction to keep my own students going and pull the extras out of the lurch.

In spite of my efforts to be gentle and understanding, toward the beginning of winter in 1941 I had a spell of very bad instructing. Sometimes I flew an hour or so without quite knowing what I was doing. I would sit in the back seat of the airplane gazing away at the billowing cloudbanks around me in a daydream. Clearly, I was in love. I knew I wasn't the marrying kind and that, I suppose, was what made it tough. I had never lost my determination to get out of instructing and to get into a tactical flying command. I still preferred service in a fighter squadron. I had a war to fight, and every day that passed made it clearer that the war was upon us. I had come close to marrying once, and that was another thing that made me shy away from the subject. I guess it was a little peculiar for anyone as girl-conscious as I had always been to get to be almost thirty years old and remain a bachelor.

But I knew I would be no good as a husband now. If I lived through the war then marriage would be just the thing for me. Now I must get set to fight. That decision was final. It was so final that each day when I went out to fly I would not notice what was happening in the plane until suddenly I would find we were on the ground. I would get out and tell the student that I would see him in the flight room, and then like as not I would forget and leave the flying line without exchanging another word with him. But this thing grew and grew, until it was having a very marked effect on my sleep and my digestion, as well as

giving me an air of complete preoccupation about my work. I
had heard about such things before and not believed them.

One night I telephoned Anne. We had arranged to go to a
movie together, and I told her I was coming early to take her
to dinner. I went to the big old house on Twohig Street where
she used to stay when she came to town. She answered the door-
bell and together we walked in an unusual silence down the
steps to the curb where the little red truck was parked.

She got in and I walked around and slipped under the wheel
beside her. I felt for a moment as if I were pulling out hard from
a screaming dive and about to black out. Then in an instant of
horrifying anxiety and a voice that sounded like no one I had
ever heard before, I said: "Anne, will you marry me? You've got
to. Don't answer now. We will have dinner and talk about it."

Anne replied with a calmness I would have given anything
to equal: "I don't know, but I don't believe I will."

The next morning when I saw Anne I was confident things
would be all right. I gained confidence from her manner, but
I still seemed to be acting like a man with a high fever and in
somewhat of a delirium. That day at the ranch I received the
final approval. My excitement blew its top. I had a long and delightful talk with Anne's mother, in which I assured her that I
had practically not a cent in the world, but only a devotion to
her daughter that was the most unbounded impulse I had ever
sensed. She laughed at me. She was a sentimentalist. I think I
must have convinced her I was passable when we first met and
yapped at each other all afternoon about politics. From the time
of the engagement, at her suggestion, I have called her Eva.

Anne's brother Joe had a cadet visiting him who had been
his classmate at Yale. His name was Jake Doar. I liked Jake immediately. Before lunch that day when the members of the family, guests, cousins, and all were assembled in the living room
of the ranch house, Eva opened the bar and called on Jake to
give a fitting toast. He gave one I had never heard before, but
have heard many times since: *"Amor y pesetas y tiempo para
gastarlas"*—"Love and money and time to spend (waste) them."

That weekend was in the middle of November. Anne and I
decided to try to have the wedding early in December so that

it would come at the finish of my current class of cadets. I would be able to get leave and we could go to Kentucky. Events followed each other in such rapid succession that I was completely lost in a maze of detail until Saturday, December 6, the day set for the wedding. What had me up in the air were strings of parties, wires of congratulations from friends, wedding gifts, and many other things that gave me a stark conviction I was really going to get married. They half scared me to death.

Anne got wire after wire from her friends in the East, all of which said: "We wonder if your fiancé knows how lucky he really is?" I remember only one wire of congratulation I got. It was from Edward F. Prichard, Jr. of Paris, Kentucky, a friend of mine since childhood, then working as secretary to the attorney general in Washington. In a newspaper announcement of the engagement he had read that Anne's grandfather was one of the founders of the American Tobacco Company, and he joined that point with an antitrust suit the government was then leveling at all the big cigarette manufacturers. Prich said in his wire only this: "Best wishes stop Don't count on the American Tobacco Company."

In the midst of such incidentals I found myself hard upon the day of solemn pronouncements. I stood whitefaced with parched throat in the vestry room of the Emmanuel Episcopal Church looking out into the rows of pews through a crack in the door. Ninety percent of the guests were friends of Anne's family —ranchers, business people, and generally civilians. I knew only a few of them, but on the front row and staring directly into the crack in the door from whence I peered were four fine-looking young men, resplendent in the blue uniforms of aviation cadets. Their names were Nichols, Nowak, O'Sullivan, and Poole. They caught a glimpse of me through the crack, and I could see broad smiles spread over their faces. I must have looked more like a wraith than their instructor. All I wanted was to get the spectacle over, grab up my pretty bride, and get both of us out alive if possible.

That was done in a manner which is now very hazy in my recollection. I do remember as I walked up the aisle with my gorgeous Mrs. Ardery that we saw a row of Mexicans in the back of the church and more just outside the door. They were some of the good people who had known Anne since her birth and had loved her to the extent that they were completely unreconciled to her leaving the ranch with a transient like me. They wept copious tears that their Anita should meet such a fate.

We drove back to the ranch house for the reception and at each of the three gates on the ranch road was a mounted Mexican boy with a big hat and a look of utter desolation on his face. We got changed, got the bags in the truck, and started for Kentucky. In the ranch house the reception was going strong as we left. Late that Saturday afternoon, December 6, 1941, war was a far cry from our thoughts.

The first evening we spent in Dallas. The next day, Sunday, December 7, we drove on. Not far from Little Rock, Arkansas, we stopped for gas at a filling station. The proprietor was a talkative man, and while filling up the tank he said, "What do you think about those Japs?"

"What about them?" I asked.

"They just bombed Pearl Harbor, didn't you know? Must have done a hell of a lot of damage. All Army men ordered back into uniform immediately and all Army leaves canceled, radio says."

Anne had heard the conversation. She sat in the car and said nothing. As I got in and drove off I said, "Well, I suppose we better stop in Little Rock. I'll call the field and see if I have to return. If I do we won't leave until tomorrow morning."

In the lobby of our hotel there was a fever of excitement. By telling the operator it was a matter of military urgency I managed to get a call through in about two hours. I talked to the director of operations, who said, "Go on, if we need you we'll wire you in Kentucky, but I think you should be able to get the leave that's coming to you." Two minutes after I hung up Anne and I were as happy as before we got the war news, and much more excited.

The next day we drove on. As we drove Anne sang a song I have always associated with that trip. She had a sweet, husky voice, and sang it over and over again. It was "Room with a View." We stopped about noon and bought a paper. As I drove along Anne read it to me. It was full of stories about the attack written in the same vein as the president's speech to Congress. The attack was pictured as shocking, a "stab in the back." I felt we could scarcely expect a nation so much weaker than we to present a signed and sealed formal document giving ample warning before the attack. My feeling was that the attack was an act of war and as such was as fair as acts of war may be expected to be.

I imagine that everyone who was in uniform at the time felt very keenly the confusion that existed on all sides. As I had guessed, when I returned to Goodfellow Field things were in such an uproar that I wasn't even noticed as being present for a week or ten days. The new class of cadets I was to instruct had not come in and there would be nothing for me to do until they did. In the stress of wartime emergency that was regrettable, but true. Finally the storm began to subside and the policy emerged of a gradual speedup of the same procedures we had been following. We had been on the right track and the beginning of the war required no great change, except that everyone had to work harder.

As the beginning of 1942 came and passed I fell ill with one of the worst maladies that can beset an Army officer. I found myself sweating out my promotion. I had been promoted to the rank of first lieutenant, Infantry Reserve, more than four years before, but now I was a second lieutenant, Air Corps. I wasn't allowed to take my pilot training "in grade" and had to consent to "reallocation" of my commission from first to second lieutenant to get my rating as a pilot. Officers of the regular Army of other branches than the Air Corps were permitted to go through pilot training in grade, but this privilege didn't at that time extend to reserve officers. That was at length rectified. One day the bulletin board carried a memorandum from the War Department saying that all reserve officers who had previously held higher rank in another branch, but who had surrendered rank to take a rating, would be promoted back to rank previously held. And so in early March I was made a first lieutenant Air Corps. A first lieutenant Air Corps, especially a pilot, was a rather splendid figure in those days.

At about this time the first of my flying instructor colleagues were being sent out to train for tactical flying. They were sent to four-engine schools for the most part, to learn to fly heavy bombers. I was among those who had volunteered for such service, and finally in June I was told that my name would be on the next list of orders that came in. I was delighted, and yet I felt a glimmer of uncertainty and a hope that I was not making a mistake because life in San Angelo with Anne had become more enjoyable than ever. I met many people there whom I liked and whom I never would have met except for Anne. I was exchanging this life for one unknown and beyond a doubt much harder.

Sebring, Florida, where I was to spend six weeks in four-engine training, seemed the hottest place on earth during July and August, 1942. And for a fellow with 1100 flying hours in a basic trainer it was a long hop to get checked out as the first pilot of a Flying Fortress and at the same time learn the things a tactical flier in heavy bombardment has to know. Learning to work with a crew of ten men, learning to fly a proper bombing run, learning a new type of formation flying, getting used to high altitude flying using oxygen, all were new to me.

The chief purpose of the school at Sebring was not to teach tactics in flying operational unit numbers of B-17s. It was to teach pilots how to handle their individual airplanes. We got a little of the tactics of formation flying, and to some degree of bombing. But in the main we received crews, and we worked with those crews to learn the use of a single heavy bomber. Our crews consisted of four officers—pilot, copilot, bombardier, navigator—and six enlisted men—engineer, assistant engineer, radio operator, assistant radio operator, tail gunner, belly gunner. The assistant engineer and assistant radio operator doubled as gunners in the waist gun positions when not needed up front.

Sebring was an indispensable part of my training. I was glad to learn to fly a Fortress, though I had always longed to be a fighter pilot. Perhaps I had seen too many movies about World War I. I rationalized that in this war the bombers perform the magnificent role of the offense. Fighters are merely the defense, and I would rather be one who carries the ball than one who runs interference. As a generalization at that time that was fair.

But later the fighter boys changed this concept a lot. They protected the bombers, true, but they also went out on sweeps on which they bombed and strafed and threw rockets into enemy installations.

The best thing about Sebring was the fact that the time passed quickly. I got on well with my flying in spite of the personality clash I had with the instructor, and suddenly I was graduated. Although nearly all of the students in my class had expected to go into combat, we were told that many of us were now too valuable to go. Many of us would become instructors. And though most of us were given no definite idea what to expect, we must realize the need for instructors.

A few boys went out with their crews to operational units; most of them were sent to Caribbean and South American bases. The rest of us were directed through Salt Lake City, which was the redistribution center of the Second Air Force. There we were to receive orders to other stations. I was listed to go to Salt Lake. I sent Anne to Kentucky to wait until I found what to expect from the assignment at Salt Lake. The morning I arrived in Salt Lake I went to the redistribution center and checked in and checked out almost in the same motion. Our group from Sebring was split four ways to four different stations, some going on in B-17s and others going to schools where they were to be put into B-24 Liberators. I was on the list to go to Tucson, Arizona, to fly B-24s.

At Tucson we were simply told that here cadres were being made up that would eventually land overseas, and some of us would go more or less directly out on such a cadre. Others would go out after some other intermediate duty. I didn't care particularly, except that I wanted overseas service, and I thought Tucson would be as nice a place for Anne and me as any I could think of to spend the remaining days together. With that in mind I wired Anne to join me.

The business of getting checked out in B-24s was easy because they were not too different from B-17s. The crews of the two airplanes were the same size and the B-24s seemed only slightly "hotter"—that is, they landed a little faster and were slightly more difficult to handle. But they were bigger, they had longer range, and were faster at their altitude than the Fortresses I had been flying.

I had been at Tucson a little less than a month when the major, who was my CO, told me I was not to be sent out on a cadre headed for combat, but was to be retained as an instructor. I was quite angry that my path seemed endlessly beset with obstacles. I went through the whole rigmarole with him about not being able to do well what I disliked. The major heard me out and then said: "Of course you'll do this whether you like it or not. But I'll tell you what I'll do: If you'll work hard in this job until New Year's, I promise I'll send you out with your own cadre. If you left now with your experience in four-engine flying you would be a flight commander. I promise you will get a better job than the one you would have if you went out now." I stayed, of course, and liked it.

By far the best news for me about that time was that Anne was pregnant. Lesser good news was that I got a house. It was only very little bigger than the motel hut we had become used to, but it had a homier look about it. Our lives in that delightful spot were more enjoyable each day.

My only important duty at Tucson was to fly with students. They were, of course, student officers, not cadets. When a new group of officers came in we would check them out very quickly for daytime operation of the ships. Thereafter we instructors would fly almost entirely at night. I didn't mind night flying because when I flew at night I usually stayed home all day. I used to fly every week night, usually for four or eight hours between midnight and dawn. Some thought that a rough schedule, and I think the operations officer kept me on it as a penalty for not hanging around the flight office more in the daytime. When I understood the situation I began to spend a few hours a day around the flight line, though there was little or nothing to do.

I piled up hours in Liberators. I flew one hundred of the several hundred hours I got at Tucson with only twelve hours of logged daytime flight. I would sit in the right-hand copilot's seat and gaze into the star-punctured desert night, enjoying the thoughts those enjoy who are alone. The student pilot would be working with rapt attention to the flight instruments as he flew his radio beam orientation problem. My eyes would flit automatically over the dully lit engine instruments without disturbing my train of thought. Cylinder head gauges, okay; oil temperatures, normal; vacuum up; gas pressure a little low but sufficient; oil pressure good, and steady except on number 2 engine. That one fluctuated slightly, but I knew the ship well enough to know it was nothing to worry about. The manifold pressure and tachometers rode at a good easy power setting so as to give a slow cruising speed and low gas consumption.

I remember the view from the northwest leg of the beam coming into Tucson. I could see the lights of the city down there and off in the distance ahead curtained behind by just a faint moon-streaked outline of the Catalina foothills. I would think about getting my share of the war over as soon as possible and plan that Anne and I would go back to Kentucky and start out together in some small town like Frankfort or Paris or maybe Lexington. There I would practice law and try to support the large family I hoped for.

The day after New Year's I moved out to El Paso, Texas, as a squadron commander of a cadre group beginning its training for overseas service. The Germans then were losing their long offensive at Stalingrad, and in two weeks the Russians were to break the siege. Our cadre was a skeleton organization and had a long way to go to become a real command. But my CO at Tucson had made good his promise to get me a better job than the one I might have had by going out earlier, and from now on it was up to me to take the people given me and weld them into a fighting unit. The other three squadron COs who went out with me and were assigned to the same group as I were Captains Paul Burton, Adelbert Cross, and William Yaeger. A squadron of heavy bombardment consists of four flights of three airplanes and crews per flight. Four squadrons make up a group, and usually two or three groups make up a wing. The actual number of aircraft in any unit may vary from time to time because of the need for replacements, the current attrition rate, and a number of other things. But basically four flights of three crews and airplanes each made up a squadron, and four squadrons made a group. Consequently, though my squadron hadn't reached anything like the strength it would attain before going overseas, it would ultimately consist of twelve heavy bombardment crews with all the equipment and administrative support that go with them.

The first day I reported to the field I met the group commander, David Lancaster, then a major. He was a North Carolinian who had flown many of the transoceanic hops for General Olds in the early days of the Ferry Command. He had won a Distinguished Flying Cross (DFC) for his pioneering flights, and in those days a pilot with a DFC was quite a man. I had respect for his experience and liked his simplicity of manner and solicitude for his men. He felt the best way to develop the command was to give the commanders under him leeway to use their own initiative. In the case of our group it was a successful training policy.

Almost immediately I found myself engaged in a race of intense competition with the other squadron commanders. I was determined to make my squadron the best. I believe Captain Yaeger had about the same competitive spirit as I, but Captains Burton and Cross had less of it. Sometimes Del Cross seemed almost indifferent to comparisons between the squadrons. Paul Burton was not, but his ideas differed so from Yaeger's and mine that I never felt an adversary spirit with him like I did with Yaeger.

Somewhat in between the squadron commander and our group commander was Captain John A. Brooks III, West Pointer, and now the group operations officer. John was a tireless, imaginative fellow whose position put him in line to catch such flak as flew off the squadron COs. About this time Brooks had commented that he didn't think Del Cross was of a serious enough turn of mind to have command of a squadron. His comment found its way home to Del and almost overnight the feeling rose to a pitch somewhere close to civil war. Major Lancaster had always felt his squadron commanders should rank the group operations officer, and so he was not very happy about Brooks's comment. He indicated his dissatisfaction to Yaeger, the senior squadron CO. I liked all the other squadron COs, but I also liked Brooks. I felt John had a tendency to usurp power not properly delegated to him by military regulation, but I admired his energy. He was a tireless worker, and his energies seemed bent in the direction of general betterment of the group.

In the midst of the heat of the quarrel, Yaeger called a squadron commanders' meeting. He stated the case against Brooks and suggested we go together to Major Lancaster and ask for a replacement for him. I put in a plea against precipitate action. I made no apology for Brooks because I knew such an apology would meet with no approval. I merely said we should not be hasty. We were about to do something very injurious and therefore should give Brooks the benefit of every doubt before taking such action. After I had talked a while Del remarked that he thought I was right. That was quite a generous attitude for him to have, and I began to realize what a good-hearted spirit Del really was. Paul Burton declared he also thought we should not ask for Brooks's removal at this time. The case against John collapsed, though I believe from the way it started it might have easily gone the other way. For a time after that meeting the feeling continued to run high. The presence of factionalism was felt by all, but I think all of us hated it so that it soon was put down to a level below notice.

My new combat crews were coming in and I flew with them a lot. My operations officer, Don Buck, was as good a person as I ever met, but I would get upset with him for not working harder, not flying more, and not being more zealous to have the best operations in the group. He didn't feel so keenly as I the competitive aspects of our squadron's progress in the group. My assistant operations officer was a ball of fire by the name of Ed Fowble, from Hobart, Indiana. He was a very young fellow with a childish way about him, but he was the most ardent flier in the squadron and perhaps in the group. Ed would fly twenty-four hours a day if permitted. Once he did fly eighteen in one day, and I got a call from the flight surgeon about it, threatening to ground him if I didn't slow him down.

Ed felt as I did that it was a good thing for any young flier who wanted to live a long time to spend some time each day planning how to meet emergencies in the air in the type of ship he expects to fly in combat. We agreed on the wisdom of landing a B-24 from a very steep glide using as little power on the approach as possible. Then, we reasoned, when we got in combat and were coming home with a couple of engines knocked out, we would know how to bring the ship in without much power. You can fly okay on two engines. Sometimes you can keep aloft for a while on one. But once you put your landing gear and flaps down and start an approach for a landing the airplane is coming down. With an engine or two out you can't afford to miss the first approach because it is likely to be the last, and you can't drag into a field from five miles back. Time after time I've seen Ed land a Liberator without using any power at all from the time he turned off his base leg onto his final approach. He would pull his throttles completely off and leave them off. This is what is known as making a "dead stick" landing, and it isn't easy to do. I've never seen another pilot with Ed's ability and zest for flying. He was never too tired to learn more or to fly more or to talk more about flying. Thus he acquired a great deal of experience in a short time.

All the squadrons had what was known as a "model crew." The pilot of my model crew was a tall, dark, good-looking fellow named Ben Walsh. Walsh was a very serious, unsmiling, hardheaded young man. I may have thought him hardheaded because he disagreed with me fundamentally about the way a B-24 should be flown. Though I was his squadron commander, in his eyes it gave me no right to suggest to him anything about the conduct of his flying. At times a good deal of heat was generated by our difference of views. Ben loved to make low approaches. He would get his ship right down on the treetops and pull it in from about a mile back from the field with a lot of power on all engines. I would watch him from the flying line and shudder.

In spite of the differences in the squadron it was evident the combination of types was good. I tried to be a bit of a public relations man with my organization. I was obviously not supermilitary like Yaeger, and I rarely resorted to pulling my rank or issuing orders because I believed the success of a command of Americans largely depended on something more solid than rank. My men responded well and gave me reason to be proud of them.

The group that trained ahead of us at Biggs Field lost a number of planes and some crews during their training, partly because of their getting some poorly rebuilt engines. When the engines were put in their airplanes many of them failed in flight. The pilots were green and unused to the emergency procedures in case of engine failure. Soon after our arrival they lost a few airplanes because of mistakes made by pilots after engines failed. The result was to create an inordinate fear of engine failure in some of the other pilots. The effect of the combination of mechanical and personnel error sometimes produced near panic among pilots.

Some of the difficulties of that group aided us, I know. I was constantly going over emergency procedure with my pilots and trying to convince them that our ships were rugged and safe in such emergencies as engine failure. The only thing that had to be watched was that the pilot not make some mistake to add to his difficulty. I had two pilots who were continually complaining about the airplanes. I made a point of taking them up and feathering both props on one wing. That is, I shut off two engines on the same side and used the feathering mechanism so that the props of both engines stopped windmilling. I demonstrated how nicely the airplane would fly with two good engines on one side and two dead ones on the other. This calmed these pilots and thereafter they did better.

All our new pilots practiced three-engined operation and three-engined landings with competent instructors supervising. In the beginning I did much of the instructing myself. New men saw that three-engined flying took only application of common principles and calmness. They learned how to set the trim to make a ship fly straight and level when it had an engine out. And they learned that when a ship is so trimmed it must be untrimmed carefully as the power is reduced on the glide into the runway for landing. If it isn't carefully untrimmed, since the airplane was set to keep itself flying level with three good engines and one dead one exerting only drag, the trim would take over. This would pull the plane to one side and off the runway as the power was reduced.

The group that preceded us had several pilots come in with

an engine feathered and miss the runway. On several occasions the pilots had tried to go around on three engines to make another landing. In each such case the ship had crashed, not having been able to clear the field on three engines with landing gear and flaps fully down. And so that group had a rule that under no circumstances would a pilot attempt to go around for a second approach if his airplane had one engine out. Once the pilot committed his plane to a landing he would make it even if he was off the runway.

One day just after Fowble's arrival, when he was still a little green in B-24s, I was flying with him when the principles of three-engine landings were well demonstrated to us. Ed and I had been to the bombing range northeast of the field and had lost an engine. With absolute calm Ed went through the procedure of feathering the prop on the dead engine. He trimmed his ship properly to fly on the three remaining engines and increased the power on those engines to give a safe cruising speed. Then we started back to Biggs. Ed made a good traffic pattern and a good turn from his base leg into the final approach to land. He set his glide perfectly and then with his landing gear fully down and locked and his flaps fully down, he started to pull off power to slow up the glide for landing. As he pulled off power the trim started to take over. It pulled the ship into the good engines. Our engines are numbered from left to right and the number four engine, that is the right outboard engine, was the dead one. The ship had been given a lot of left trim against the good engines and when Fowble pulled the throttles back the ship started turning to the left. The power of the trim was too much for him to correct on the rudders and the wheel. Obviously the only thing for him to do was to take off some of the left trim.

I started to coach him or take over but I decided not to. I thought he was far enough along to handle it himself, and I didn't want to show lack of confidence in him. As his glide continued he got farther off to the left of the runway. Just as it was apparent he might not be able to get back on the runway without making a low steep turn to the right into his dead engine, I said: "You've failed to untrim the ship properly and you've let the trim take over. Give her the power now and go around."

Captain Brooks was in the tower, having come there when he heard that a ship in trouble was about to make an emergency landing. He was frantically calling instructions to us over the tower radio. He didn't know I was in the airplane, or I think he would have given fewer instructions. Faking complete calm I answered him: "We missed our approach and are going around."

At that moment I gave full rpm on three good engines and full throttle. I locked the throttles wide open and set the superchargers to give fifty-two inches of manifold pressure—the most they would give—pushing them hard up against the stops. I pulled the flap lever into the up position little by little, drawing the flaps up to halfway position, and then locked them. Then I jerked the landing gear lever forward to bring the wheels up. We were just wavering over the fence at the end of the field. The ship was lumbering and struggling with everything the three engines had. Ahead of us was a desert expanse of rolling sand dunes covered with scrub growth. I had seen what happened to a B-17 that piled into those hills two nights before. The only one of the crew who lived was the pilot and he was seriously injured.

For what seemed hours we flopped along, only half flying. Ed started to gain altitude, but I had my nose almost against the air speed indicator and seeing it only register 120 to 125 miles per hour, I held forward on the wheel to keep the nose down. We were too close to stalling speed to try pulling the nose up. We were turning a little to the right because of the force of our good engines under full power, but we let it turn a little. It seemed an eternity that those wheels took coming up. All the while I heard Brooks calling loudly over the radio, "Don't stall it! Don't stall it! Pancake it in if you have to."

For a distinct moment I thought we really were going to have to pancake it in. We must have gone two miles past the boundary of the field before the wheels came fully up and we gained enough speed and altitude to start making a turn.

Finally when we had about six hundred feet under us we started a wide sweeping turn to the left and made another approach. This time when Ed pulled off the power, I untrimmed the ship. We hit the runway squarely and stayed on it. We taxied up to the line and cut the engines. I said nothing but got out of the ship and walked away. The men in the crew knew I was scared and mad. I didn't feel I ought to say anything, for I knew Ed wouldn't forget that lesson, nor would I.

It would have helped had it happened that day, but it happened the next that as I was taxiing in to the line I saw my adjutant, waiting in my parking space waving a piece of paper at me with a big smile on his face. I guessed what it was. It was my captaincy! With it I felt much more the part of a squadron commander.

Several weeks before we were to complete our training in El Paso, upon the advice of the group surgeon, I had Anne go home. Her mother came from San Angelo to drive her back and I moved to the field to live in the bachelor officers' quarters for the remainder of training at Biggs.

Time went by in which Major Lancaster became a lieutenant colonel, and Yaeger, then Cross, and then Burton became majors. Colonel Lancaster twice recommended me for promotion to major, but both times the recommendation was returned owing to my not having enough "time in grade" as a captain. That was really a fair enough reason for my promotion not going through.

We took on maturity as an organization. When we arrived at Biggs Field we were only the skeleton of a heavy bomber group. Gradually sinew and muscle grew on the skeleton. It became a unit with as much individuality as a person has, and was as different from other organizations of like size and designated purpose as one human being is different from another. As our spirit grew, we found ourselves harping on our points of superiority and minimizing our weaknesses in contrast with other organizations.

During those last days at El Paso I felt increasing anxiety about Anne. I knew the doctor had predicted the great day would fall on April 2, but I felt he did that just to be kind. What he really meant was April 1, but he didn't want to say we would have an April Fool's baby, so he put it back a day. My thoughts about the day the baby would arrive seemed prophetic when about noon of April 1 I got a long-distance phone call from Anne's mother. She said quietly, "If you can I think you'd better come now. Anne has been in the hospital since early this morning and the doctor says he believes the baby will come sometime today."

I rushed over to Colonel Lancaster's room. He was in bed with a cold but I burst in on him: "Can I take a ship and fly to San Angelo?"

"Sure, Phil, go ahead. Hope it's a girl. Boys are more trouble than they're worth."

All my flyable aircraft were flying. I went to Yaeger's operations and found a ship they would let me have. I got a crew together, rushed across the ramp, jumped in, and started the engines. Despite a slightly vibrating engine, I took off and headed east. I was pulling more power than I was supposed to, but I didn't have too far to go and I knew the ship would take it. I slid through the Guadalupe Pass and across the flat plain toward San Angelo faster than my anxious mind would admit, and soon I looked down on the familiar sight of Goodfellow Field. The air was swarming with basic trainers. I had to look out for them. They were flown by a bunch of wild gadgets who knew little and cared less about my having the right of way. I called the tower and requested transportation to town. When we taxied up to the line I jumped out without much more than a goodbye to my crew and ran to the car that was waiting.

It was a long afternoon and evening and about two in the morning of April 2, a nurse came out of the room and said: "That boy'll be here in a few minutes." In a little while they wheeled Anne back to her room. She was groggy but all right, and we had ourselves a fine baby boy. The day after he was born the nurses let me hold him up and hug him. We named him Peter Brooks.

A persistent rumor going the rounds of the group for some weeks was soon confirmed—we were to leave Biggs Field to complete our last phase of training for combat at Lowry Field in Denver. And one morning we began to load our Liberators to fly north to Lowry with as many men and as much equipment as they would carry. We made several shuttle trips and transported all the crews and air support people, plus a good deal of extra baggage. The ground troops followed by rail.

At Lowry Field the battle of housing facilities started all over again. But there the natural layout was more conducive to equal division. My squadron got as good a break on its headquarters as any of the other squadrons had, and on the flying line a little better one. My men had the only building available out there for their engineering and technical supply shack. The fact that we had it was simply due to my luck at drawing straws. Training continued pretty much as it had been: the missions were a little longer and more intricate as the level of crew proficiency rose. The men saw Denver as a warm-hearted hospitable town, with lots to do and many places for a soldier to spend his money and not be gouged.

Flying at Denver was certainly nothing like what I feared it might be. Usually the sky was clear as quartz and the backdrop of mountains to the west gave the optical illusion of being right up against the field. Their snowy, majestic tops were typical of many natural beauties which are real hazards to the flier.

Much of the work of my squadron's operations during those days was characterized by the very imaginative and ingenious efforts of two smart young officers, Bill Goodykoontz and Fred Willis. They were continually coming up with some novel idea to interest the boys and add pep to the organization. They bought a little cocker spaniel and sold "dog shares" to pay for him. They had a voting contest to name him, and the popular will dictated his name to be Propwash. They finagled around a rule that no one would be allowed to sell Coca-Cola but the PX and managed to have it for sale in our intelligence section. This not only drew personnel of our squadron but also of the other three squadrons which had no Cokes for sale. They ran a lottery on the Kentucky Derby that was won by a shy PFC truck driver who had been nicknamed Lovebug. The revenue of these enterprises went to purchase a Speed-Graphic camera for the squadron. We had not been able to draw a government issue camera and we needed one for keeping the squadron history. In the midst of all these antics, Goodykoontz and Willis put out the news of the day, taught aircraft identification, and performed in a superior manner all the normal functions of a squadron intelligence section.

One day when we were almost ready to leave Denver we got the bad news that Colonel Dave Lancaster was considered temporarily physically incapacitated for overseas service. He had been in the hospital a good many days. It was a distressing blow to him, and we hated to lose the good friend and commander who had taken us through such a successful period of training. He asked me to fly him to his home near Daytona Beach, Florida. I was glad to accept, not only to be with him, but also because I hoped on the way back that I might be able to stop by Kentucky to say goodbye to my parents. A few days later I left Denver at ten o'clock one night and landed in Daytona Beach about eight the following morning. There I said goodbye to Colonel Lancaster and, with his permission, routed my return trip via Kentucky. After some delay in servicing I arrived over the land of the bluegrass and the white fences about three in the afternoon the same day. The Lexington airport was incomplete, but its runways were finished and I had clearance from flight control for a ten-minute stop there. I had brought an extra pilot to take over the ship and fly it to Bowman Field, Louisville.

To hit my runway I had to circle over a pasture which was part of Warren Wright's Calumet Farm. As I cut throttles and glided down to the end of the runway, I looked under me and saw a half-dozen broodmares madly racing around the pasture. I was sorry to scare the great ladies like that, but I was bent on a matter of real importance to me. By the time I landed several cars were there that had not been there a moment before. I'm sure this was the first four-engined aircraft ever to land at Bluegrass Field.

I caught a ride into Lexington and called mother and dad. It was good to see them again and assure them I was ready for combat. I had every reason to believe I would come through without serious harm. My feeling of confidence helped allay their worries.

Returning to Denver I found the new CO, Colonel Jack Wood. He was an extremely good-looking man with wavy, iron-gray hair. If he is up to his looks, I thought, he will be a wonder. In a matter of days after my return, brand new B-24s began coming in. We were to shake them down and then take them to the staging area. There they would be given the final checkup for the flight across. Up until a very short time before we left we were virtually certain we were headed west to fight the Japs. Now we found we were going to England—at least we were headed east, and we supposed that meant England.

Some of our old ships had to be delivered to San Antonio. I managed to fly one down as far as San Angelo and drop off there for two days. I got the chance I needed to see Anne again and catch a final glimpse of Peter, now two months old and still a good bit of a squirming infant, but considerably changed from the time we'd met on his birthday in the hospital. Anne and I both realized we were living in a time when issues were being decided which cosmically transcended personal considerations. Even if I don't come back, I thought, we are lucky. I had loved Anne and Peter and that is much more than many ever have.

A day or two after I returned to Denver we were on our way to the staging area. There we sat around the officers' club, talked about our wives, called them long-distance, and played the slot machines to while away the time as the ships were being checked.

In those last few days at the staging area I had plenty of time to reflect on the events since that day in the late summer of 1940 when I had said goodbye to my law practice in Kentucky and set forth to become a pilot. In less than three years I had logged 1800 flying hours—close to 1000 hours in the heaviest four-engined aircraft the Army used—and I was entrusted with what was then estimated at $10,000,000 worth of equipment. But the greater change was in my point of view. Bacon, I remembered, said, "He who hath a wife and children hath given hostages to fortune." I had arrived in the Air Corps filled with an attitude which would forbid giving hostages to fortune. Now I had given hostages of the dearest kind, and I was sincerely glad.

3

Ted's
Flying Circus

The crews of my squadron came into the staging area the last of the group. This was in accord with the way the movement out of Denver was ordered. I was determined not to get left behind, and so when I got into staging I did everything I could to rush up the departure. As a result I managed to get ahead of them all, and my ship was the first one in the group to leave for overseas.

I picked an excellent crew with the ship I was flying, that of Second Lieutenant Lloyd H. Hughes of Corpus Christi, Texas. Hughes was a laughing, youngish, handsome lad and a much-better-than-average pilot. I had taken Fowble out of his assistant operations job and made him a flight commander of C Flight. This flight consisted of his own crew, Hughes's crew, and the crew of Lieutenant Robert Lee Wright of Austin, Texas. As a patriotic Kentuckian I was a little jealous of the ascendancy of Texans, but I had to admit that next to Kentuckians they were about the toughest competitors of all.

I felt that perhaps Hughes somewhat resented my taking over as pilot of his ship for the long hop across the ocean. He probably was a better pilot than I, since administrative duties had recently kept me from flying as much as he did. But I wanted to sit in the pilot's seat and "fly my own ship" across, although it was really Hughes's ship. He took it with good nature.

From the staging area, by a couple of hops, we soon reached our jumping off point in Newfoundland, where we stopped momentarily. The weather was reasonably good over the Atlantic, with a prospect of soon getting worse. And so we were almost immediately briefed for an early night takeoff. As the sun was sinking low on the horizon in the subarctic night we took off. It was June 11, 1943. At that time of year and in the latitudes we flew, we didn't see much darkness on our way across, except where we met heavy cloud cover. As we cruised along, the sun dipped a little lower than it was at takeoff; then it seemed to ride along on the rim of the horizon for a long time. Finally it dropped into the sea for about half an hour at midnight and then popped up again. There was always a red glow in the northern sky, and beneath us we could see the cold black water, sometimes with great snowy icebergs floating in mock peacefulness.

I set the autopilot on course and sat placidly in the pilot's seat watching the indicator lights on the automatic control panel flash lazily as the impulses of the servos were transmitted to the controls. The wheel in my lap moved slightly back, slightly forward, a little to left and then right in a jerky, mechanical way. It reminded me of the wheel of the car in the old Topper movies when the invisible hero was driving. Here we were, a bomber load of people who had never seen the other side of the ocean, flying our own airplane over to join the war. Beyond a doubt within the next few months the greatest and perhaps even the last adventures of our lives would be taking place.

From time to time I checked my position and heading with Lieutenant Sidney Pear, the navigator. Pear was a New Jerseyite from Weehawken and a navigator whose skill was exceptional. He knew how to use his sextant, and he was as busy as a pack rat facing a hard winter. I could see him up in the astrodome taking starshot after starshot. Then he would make his calculations and call me on interphone and give me the word on our course and, as expected, his readings continually placed us within a few miles of where we should have been.

The engineer every half hour would stick his head in from

the flight deck and report on fuel consumption. When we were half way across we were pulling along at thirty inches of manifold pressure and 2,000 RPM, indicating a good 165 miles per hour airspeed. When these readings were corrected for altitude and winds, I knew we had a true speed considerably higher. Our gas was spending according to expectation; we had passed the point of last return and the boys in the back waist compartment were dozing. They never gave a single call over the interphone.

After the sun got a good start into the sky again from its shallow dip at midnight, we managed to pick up the beacon from the other side on our radio compass. The needle pointed the direction to the station hundreds of miles ahead, and showed we were exactly on course on the heading we had been steering. We passed through a moderate stretch of cloud with a slight bit of rime ice in it, but nothing to worry about.

We cruised on into the morning and finally I got a somewhat stern but proud announcement from Lieutenant Pear that we should see the coast of Ireland in about half an hour. The weather was thicker now. The clouds were heavy in some places, though occasionally there was a hole and we could see the ocean, cold and green, below us. On the very dot of the time Pear gave us, we were lucky enough to find a break in the clouds and there beneath us lay the surf-crested coast of Ireland. We were thrilled. We had come from one world into another that none of us had ever seen before, and as we caught other glimpses of the shore and later the patchwork of perfectly kept, tiny fields bounded by stone walls, we noted the accuracy in the name the Emerald Isle. The isle had been washed by a June rain that morning and it glittered like no emerald ever has except, of course, those gems of the great Emerald City of Oz.

Through patchy rain and cloud we crossed Ireland and approached Scotland. The weather was warmer over the land, but patches of cloud were thicker and steamier. We came in to our designated field at Prestwick, Scotland, in a heavy downpour of rain, but by the time we had taxied to the place where the tower operator directed us, it had cleared considerably. One of our first vivid impressions that we were far from home came from our headsets and the theatrical voice of the tower operator. His replies to our queries about where to park were packed with such words as "aihcrahft," "roight chew ahh," and "straight away, cawn't miss it."

After we parked we walked to a building where it appeared we were supposed to check in. Before we reached it there were a half-dozen pink-cheeked children who surrounded us. "Ya ga ahnie goom, Yahnk? Ahnie Ameddican kahndie?" We had goom and kahndie, but we didn't have it long.

For our quarters we had a beautiful old brick house, large, ivied, and rambling, which looked almost like a converted castle. Rhododendron bloomed in profusion in clumps scattered over the well-kept lawn. The place was lovely, the meals were terrible, the beer like brackish water, and the people most cordial and kind.

That night McLaughlin, bombardier of the crew, who was Scotsman enough to effect a great burr, held the limelight uncontested with a matchless set of stories. Mac had knocked around New York City most of his life in a variety of jobs, among them bartending in Greenwich Village for a year or so, and he really knew the underside of big city life. The enlisted men of my crew, Sergeants Dalton, Hoff, Kase, Mix, Smith, and Wilson, were on a par with the officers. It was an extremely competent and compact unit trained in a style prescribed by the soft-voiced, good-looking Texas Pete Hughes.

The next morning we reported to operations to find that we were leaving immediately for our new base. There were a few other airplanes, B-17s, which had come in destined for other stations in England near ours. They would join in a formation with us and we would be led by a navigator of the Air Transport Command to our permanently assigned bases. In England, it was said, navigation was difficult until one became accustomed to it. There were so many airdromes it was very confusing, and there were cases of crews getting lost within a few miles of home base. There is such a sameness to the country that the checkpoints generally used for navigation have little individuality. Each might look a lot like any one of a hundred others scattered all over England. Under you there may have been a town with three railroads leading in from the north and only two rail lines going out to the south. The map might show five towns which looked like that. We heard that when the crews were properly trained on navigation in England, the various radio aids to navigation would make it a cinch in any kind of weather. Naturally it would take some time for training before we would know how to use these aids properly.

We flew down the west coast for a while and then headed straight across the island and in a very short time reached our base. That was the first of many surprises I got about the size of England. I never got used to its being a little island so small that we could fly over all of it in an afternoon—at least, nearly all of it. It looked like a broad expanse of beautiful country, much of it quite similar to the horse country of Kentucky. There were seemingly hundreds of airdromes, some cleverly camouflaged so that we were right over them before we saw there was anything under us but open country.

The CO and a few members of the group staff had preceded us traveling by Air Transport Command, so we expected to be met by at least one or two familiar faces at our new base. When we flew over the airport that was to be our home, the lead navigator called us on the radio and told us that was it. We peeled out of formation and circled the drome to get a look at it. It was a clear, beautiful day, and to the north we could see the town of Norwich squatting underneath a lazy flock of barrage balloons. In our headsets we could hear the squeakers of the balloons—radio transmitters sending out warning signals that in one's headphones sounded very much like air raid sirens signaling an alert. I imagined the noise could be terrifying to one lost in bad weather. What might it be like to listen to the screaming of these things when you couldn't see but a few hundred yards ahead? I hoped that the proximity of our field to the town would not result in our ships plowing through the wall of cables in bad weather.

We called the tower and a British voice gave us permission to land. Hard to understand those people over the radio! And they never seemed to be able to hear us properly, so that it frequently bogged down into a process of each asking the other to repeat his last message. As our plane rolled to a stop at the end of the runway there was a jeep to lead us to the place where I could park. I taxied out some distance to a dispersal area, turned the ship around on a concrete circular emplacement which we called a hard stand, faced it back towards the taxi strip, and cut the engines. Just as the four props slowed to a stop, another jeep pulled up. Captain John Brooks was in it. He had come ahead with Colonel Wood to help in preparing things for our arrival, and I welcomed him.

"Where are the rest of them?" he shouted.

"Back in Maine," I replied. "I'll bet you don't see the next one in here for at least two days."

I was right. It was three days before the next ship came in. It happened that those behind us hit bad weather, which delayed them. While we were waiting for the rest of the crews, I enjoyed relaxing and looking around. I managed to draw a bicycle from the supply office. The base was so spread out it was difficult to get around without a jeep or a bike. The English summer was at its height, though it never really got warm enough according to my idea of summer. The air was fresh and cool, like a day of spring at home, and the woods which were scattered all over our airdrome were beautiful. Through the woods small lanes were cut leading to the various living sites. I found in those first days in England many of the acquaintances of my early years: there were rooks and jackdaws flying overhead, and grouse, plover, and pheasants in great numbers just off the runways.

The second afternoon I was in England I rode my bike into the small village of Wymondham (pronounced Windum) near the field and was impressed by its picturesqueness. The lane leading into the village was narrow and winding, with hedgerows on either side and well-kept fields over the hedgerows. There were haystacks in the fields that were so perfectly formed they looked like loaves of gingerbread.

On the edge of the village was a little pond with ducks on it. Farther on the streets were narrow with brick buildings almost to the edge of the pavement; they seemed particularly incongruous when an occasional tremendous American Army truck lumbered through. At the far end of the town was a very old

church that looked like it might have been started as a Stone-
henge in pagan times, and continued having parts added down
through successive ages of Christianity. The whole scene had
a kind of beauty strange to me.

When I returned to the base in the late evening I went to
the bar of what would be our officers' club. Our base had been
an RAF station, and there were several officers of His Majesty's
service still lingering around. They were there with a few American airmen of a veteran group waiting to give our fellows some
combat instructions and had grouped themselves congenially
around the bar. With mugs of incredibly insipid English beer
in their hands, they proceeded to make the rafters shake. They
seemed to know only one song:

> Oh, they say there's a troop ship just leaving Bombay
> Bound for Old Blighty's shore
> Heavily laden with time-expired men,
> Bound for the land they adore.
> And there's many an airman just finished his tour,
> And many a twirp signing on—
> There'll be no promotions this side of the ocean
> So cheer up my lads, bless 'em all!
>
> Bless 'em all. Bless 'em all. The long and the short and
>   the tall.
> There'll be no promotions this side of the ocean,
> So cheer up my lads, bless 'em all.

On and on it went, till when it stopped nobody knew. This, I
thought, is just as it should be—sort of Hell's Angels setting
modernized for the latest war.

In the twilight of that evening almost at midnight we heard
a low throb begin in the sky above and grow to a mighty cre-
scendo. In the bar when the sound began the song stopped a
moment. We listened and someone said, "The RAF's out again.
God bless 'em." I walked outside to see, but against the darkening sky the big black airplanes, Halifaxes and Lancasters, scarcely showed up at all. They were evidently going over at medium
altitude, and they flew in a peculiar manner not at all like our

formations. Still it was a discernible pattern with distances of about half a mile between airplanes. Sometimes I could pick out a ship, but not many. I felt intense gratitude to these hardy lads going out just as we were having a final beer before going to bed. They were fighting a tough war and had been for a long time. Theirs was a beautiful country and one could understand their determination to defend it. Just at dawn the next morning when I heard the first squawk out of our loudspeaker system to wake me up, I heard the RAF boys coming back, some with engines sputtering. A few of them, I discovered later in the day, landed at our base. They had been unable to make it to their bases farther inland. Our Air Force was in its infancy in England at that time, and I couldn't help wondering how it would stack up against the RAF when it had had a chance to grow a little.

Several days later I got word that we might expect five or six ships in from Scotland, and suddenly in the sky we saw a formation. Sure enough it was headed our way. I got on my bike and pedaled the road from the operations building to the central control tower in the middle of the field. Several of the ships were not of my squadron. But my men Fowble and Blackis had brought in their planes and crews. Blackie was a keen little Greek from New Kensington, Pennsylvania. He was in my A Flight commanded by Lieutenant Ben Walsh. I was awfully glad to see him and Fowble and as soon as I was sure who it was I biked over to the supply office to get bicycles for them. There weren't many bicycles, and with the ships coming in I knew soon they would all be gone. I didn't want my boys to be walking while the men of other squadrons rode. It was a real holiday when the ships came in. I enjoyed taking the men to their living sites and doing what I could to see that they got such comforts as were to be had. There was much talk on these reunions of narrow escapes, weather flying, major and minor incidents built up into great escapades, and Fowble and Blackie certainly had their share.

On successive days after that, the crews arrived by threes and fours. Gradually the "Ardery Squadron," as censorship designated my unit, rounded itself out. A Flight was complete with Ben Walsh, Blackie, and McLaughlin. B Flight, headed by Captain Frank Ellis, came along with Duane Lighter, and shy red-headed Smitty. Smitty, another Texan from Fort Worth, had paid me the rare compliment of asking me to be the best man at his wedding and I would not forget that. And of course there was the famous C Flight, Ed Fowble, Pete Hughes, and Bob Wright. We were again a fighting unit and as great a squadron as could be without combat experience.

Combat school consisted of lectures by pilots who had completed combat tours in the theater and were about to be sent home. There were a couple of pilots among our instructors who had been in the combat zone a long time but had quit flying combat. One of these fellows I picked as a coward by a lot of the boastful, outrageous things he said. I questioned some of his colleagues and found my supposition to be true. I felt it would have been better to let the school go without lectures than to have these grounded pilots making such comments. Eventually our group commander, Colonel Wood, heard about the cases and had the instructors withdrawn and we heard no more of them. The remainder of the pilots who were instructing us did a great job. They had been in one of the first two B-24 groups to hit the European theater and were a part of the famous Ted's Flying Circus. That name was applied to a group of heavy bombers which, with another Eighth Air Force Lib group, had been temporarily detached from the Eighth Air Force to fight the Battle of Africa with the Ninth Bomber Command. The long range and weight-carrying capacity of Liberators at slightly lower altitudes made them the answer to the needs of the Africa campaign. These groups did great service in Africa after El Alamein in the late summer of 1942, when the British were driving Rommel back to his final stand. That was just about a year before our arrival in the combat zone.

Later on these Liberator groups were brought back to England. There they had had a tough time bucking the vastly superior numbers of B-17s. Plans for all the missions were more or less based on the Fortress—an inevitable factor as a result of the small number of Liberators compared to the Forts. The different flight characteristics of the airplanes frequently were disadvantageous to the Libs, so that Fortress men were heard to say they didn't care whether they had friendly fighter support on missions as long as the B-24s went along. If the B-24s went they would draw all the Nazi fighter attacks, and the protection to the Forts would be as good as if they had fighter cover. Of course, such comments were pure propaganda, and we knew it. The main difference of superiority between airplanes was one of numbers, but wherever there are Americans in such circumstances there must be intense rivalry.

During this time Don Buck and I were busy setting up a squadron operations office. The rest of the guys helped out here and there to make up for the fact that our ground echelon had not arrived. They were coming by boat and were expected to land soon. The ground training of the combat school lasted only a few days and after that we immediately started flying training. During those days we heard thousands of rumors. The main one was that we weren't going to stay in England. One puzzling part of the training was that we were practicing flying formation at extremely low altitude. No one ever flew low altitude formation in heavy bombers in daylight over Europe. What could this mean?

I flew nearly all the practice missions, but one day when my administrative duties kept me on the ground, the boys were out flying and I noticed a lone bomber circling the field. It made a long, careful approach as though something were the matter. I wheeled my bike over to the tower as fast as I could and arrived just in time to catch a glimpse of the big ship slowing up its roll at the end of the runway as it turned off on a taxi strip. The tail section swayed peculiarly, and there painted on the tail I could see the large letter *I* for Item—Ed Fowble's ship. It was taxiing in the direction of the subdepot shops and I followed.

When it finally came to a stop, I came alongside. A huge hole had been torn in the main tail section, leaving one vertical stabilizer hanging by a shred of metal. The whole tail of the ship wobbled even as it stopped, for it was almost cut through. The bomb doors opened and out stepped Fowble and his engineer, Sergeant Le Jeune; both were livid.

"What happened?" I asked.

Ed's lips worked a couple of times without saying anything.

Then he said: "We were flying a very tight formation watching our lead ship when all of a sudden another ship in the low left element pulled up under us without any warning whatever. Some of the fellows in the back of our plane had reported his weaving in and out. Evidently he was trying to fly closer than he comfortably could and when he pulled up, his number four prop got our left vertical stabilizer and cut almost all the way through. Maybe both his right hand props hit us because after the collision he nosed down and pulled off to the left and I could see his number three and four props fly off and go spinning down. He evidently tried to pick the first place he could to set the ship down. It went in near the edge of an airdrome in fairly flat ground, but it was a combination of a crash landing and a flat crackup." His lips trembled as he spoke, but his voice was steady. It turned out there was luckily only a skeleton crew aboard the other airplane. The pilot received only bruises; one officer was killed and another very seriously injured with compound fractures and other complications. The rest got out with only minor injuries.

In a way I was sorry about Ed. This episode probably calmed him down to the point where he lived longer in combat than he would have otherwise. But after that he never again showed the puppy-like enthusiasm so characteristic of him in the beginning. He had always been one to plague Murph, our engineering officer, in order to get new gadgets fitted to his airplane. Ed had had more stuff put on his ship than anyone else in the squadron, chiefly because he had taken a more personal interest in it. Now it was apparent the question was whether the ship would be worth repairing.

The next day or two brought forth the decision that *I* for Item would not be repaired. Her wounds were mortal, and immediately began the process of stripping her of badly needed parts. Our technical supply was almost empty of spare parts in those days and a wrecked ship was likely to be picked clean of everything salvageable within a matter of a few hours after it cracked up. Every time a nose wheel tire, or a wing light, or a flight indicator was removed from his ship it cut Ed's heart out. I hurt for him! An old battle-weary Liberator with the name

Eager Beaver painted on its nose came in and was assigned to Fowble's crew to replace *I* for Item. It had to have lots of work done on it. In the waist section of the *Beaver* you could see light through hundreds of small holes where bits of flak had let the sun in. Ed tried hard to be satisfied but in his heart, as in mine, there was a definite feeling that it was a turkey.

Quite suddenly we received news that the group was going out to Africa. We would be going along with the two more experienced Liberator groups, which had been there before. This time it would be a larger and much better equipped Ted's Flying Circus which would go ripping at the Axis's soft underbelly. I was pleased to be included in the Flying Circus. Colonel Ted Timberlake, for whom this small air task force was named, had been a group commander, but now he was in command of this wing composed of the first three groups of Libs to be sent to the Eighth Air Force. Ours was the third group.

I had got in a new crew to be assigned to my squadron. The pilot was Lieutenant Andy Opsata. I planned to fly to Africa with him because I had had no chance to look over his crew carefully and I thought this the logical opportunity to become acquainted. Fowble's *Eager Beaver* was the only ship of my squadron left behind, but we expected it to follow as soon as it was put in shape. Andy Opsata was a quiet, blond fellow who looked more like an altar boy than a heavy bomber pilot. I could see at once he was a very good man and I was glad to get him. I committed the same indignity with him as I had with Pete Hughes: I took over the first pilot's seat for the flight to Africa.

We left about midday of the day after we were told to pack, and we landed late that afternoon at a field near Newquay on the coast of Cornwall in southwest England. Most of the ships of our group came in just before dark in a fast-dropping fog. A good many ships of the group had dropped behind for numerous reasons. Some had not arrived in England, and some like Fowble's were back at base undergoing repairs. I think in having left only the one crew behind I was missing fewer crews than any other squadron CO.

When I landed in Cornwall late that afternoon in the summer of 1943 I was elated. We were a part of a fighting outfit on the way to adventures my imagination wildly exaggerated. I was thinking about those adventures as I parked the ship and got out to watch the others come in. The fog, which had been bad when I landed, was worse now and some of the pilots of Yaeger's squadron were having quite a tough time of it. They could see the field when they were right over it, but not when they got back to make an approach to the end of the strip. As a result they made approaches not properly lined up with the runway. Each time some of the ships would go around for another try and one or two would hit it right and come on in to a landing. Others nearly made it aided by the traffic controller in the tower, who fired red flares directing them to go around and signaling that he thought an attempted landing on that approach would be too hazardous. One ship that had a particularly rough time carried Major Yaeger. After half a dozen attempts he did come in. He was off to the right of the runway, but he made a violently steep turn very low to the ground. He straightened the ship out at last over the runway, cut the throttles, and tried to set it down. The ship lost flying speed about fifteen feet high over the runway and practically fell in from there. Several of the bulkheads were buckled in the landing. No one was injured, but it would take quite a long time to repair the plane.

That night we were briefed for a takeoff to Africa and early next morning we took off. We were going in a rush and were to fly through the Straits of Gibraltar to Oran, on the African coast of the Mediterranean. We were briefed to expect a front and some rather poor weather just about the time we hit the Straits. The mission started in clear skies. My squadron was in the lead except for a ship carrying group personnel, including Colonel Wood and the newly promoted Major Brooks, which was slightly ahead of us. We maintained contact with them for a number of hours out. As the trip wore on the skies darkened and visibility lowered. According to our plan, we were laying no great emphasis on maintaining formation and so the formations, such as they were, began to split up.

I was still flying *H* for Harry, Opsata's ship. I had Bob Wright on my left wing and Smitty on my right. As we turned east to go through the Straits of Gibraltar the weather got much worse.

Rain fell in patches, and the visibility was reduced to less than a mile, with some spots where we could scarcely see our wingtips. I let down to less than fifty feet over the water to enable Wright to stay with me if he wanted to. He apparently was going along flying close formation even though there were times when I was strictly on instruments for as much as a minute or two. I could catch occasional glimpses of the water when I went on instruments, which was enough to assure me that, though I was flying very low, I wouldn't fly into the sea. How Bob Wright could see me well enough to fly close formation during those moments when I could scarcely see my own wingtips, bothered me, but apparently not Bob.

Our navigator announced that as well as he could figure we should be passing through the Straits, and at that moment I noticed a black smudge on a cloud of rain in front of us. Then there was another off our right wing, and one a little above and one on the left at the same time. The thought must have occurred simultaneously to all of us that we were being fired upon. Andy was in the copilot's seat, and Sergeant Quinlan, the engineer, was standing between the seats looking out with us. Evidently we had come a little too close to the shore of Spanish Morocco and some of Franco's Falangists had opened fire in the hope that they might prevent us from ever becoming operational.

Very quickly I pulled up to get in the cloud close above us, just as Sergeant Quinlan said: "My God, they're firin' on us."

I wasn't frightened at all. Those little puffs looked harmless, there weren't many of them, and I hadn't seen enough of the effects of flak to cure my casual attitude about it.

"That stuff couldn't hurt you," I laughed.

"Not until it starts bustin' under my fanny," said Quinlan. "Tell that man don't shoot, I'll marry."

We flew on in the rain on instruments for a while and let down gingerly a little way. Then we could see the water under us, though we were a few hundred feet above it. We had passed the front and the weather was improving. Soon we saw Wright again, about a mile off our left wing; he saw us and soon we were merrily on our way again in formation. After a while the sky over us broke. We could see a speck or two in the distance here and there. They were ships of our group headed toward Oran. We picked up two of them, which increased our two ships to what looked like the beginning of a formation. We compared notes on navigation, using radio communication in a way not to violate radio security, and found we were just about on course and on time.

When we touched the north coast of Africa well inside the Mediterranean, one pilot put on power and nosed down, pulling away and ahead of the rest of us. He was evidently trying to beat us to the field at Oran. I wanted to be the first in, but I knew it was wise to conserve fuel, even though we did appear to be coming along with plenty to spare. The ship ahead was not of my squadron, and so I made no effort to restrain the pilot. We were told by the navigator to expect arrival at La Sénia airport, Oran, within the next ten minutes. We hit it as he called it, and let down there in the middle of the desert feeling a bit the swashbuckling heroes. After all, we had come from America only a week or so ago. We were the vanguard of Ted's Flying Circus on its way back to Africa to pummel the hell out of the Axis.

When I got out of the airplane I didn't even think to look it over. But Sergeant Quinlan took me by the arm and led me back to the tail of the ship, where he pointed out a jagged hole in the rudder. It wasn't very big, but if it had been in a vital spot it might have been quite dangerous.

"You don't mind the flak?" he said.

I laughed and jumped into a truck waiting to take us to our quarters.

The fort at La Sénia was a typical, desolate French fortress. It appeared to be malaria ridden. The barracks were depressing piles of red brick which rose out of the desert as symbols of past French colonial power. To the west of the fort and on the shore of the Mediterranean was a tall mountain with a castle on its very pinnacle that could be seen clearly from my barracks window. The road leading up to it looked extremely precipitous and tortuous. The castle was the castle of Monte Cristo, and I felt it added measurably to the romance of the setting. Little romance was lent by the fact that our barracks stank. They stank in just the way I imagined they would. Del Cross observed that the odor of the barracks was like the odor of the part of a zoo where the lions are kept. At least, I thought, barracks like these would be good for giving someone a viking's funeral.

That night we sat around the bar and sipped a native version of cognac, a concoction only an imaginative vintner could call cognac and sell to an American. But the effect was about the same as cognac, so that the officers' bar was a convivial place. There was something about just getting one's money changed into that worthless-looking, dirty French paper that gave me the feeling that this was a long way from home. The food was horrible, and the only choice the menu offered was between quinine and Atabrine. The water was heavily chlorinated not only to kill the germs, but to chlorinate one's stomach. They said it made it safe to eat the food.

That night we found that the ship which carried Major Brooks and Colonel Wood had put in at Gibraltar because of a shortage of fuel. There was a small field on the rock where we had been briefed we might land in case of necessity. So without stretching it too far, I still had a chance to be the first at our new base.

Early next morning we took off. We were about three hours out when we got to that part of the North Africa coast where the army of Rommel had beat its last withdrawal. So far as the eye could reach the coast was littered with burnt-out tanks and half-tracks, shot-down aircraft, and all sorts of material wrecked by the advancing Allied armies. Time and time again we flew over airdromes where numerous German aircraft were parked, some of which looked almost intact but all of which were obviously damaged by Allied bombing beyond the point of ever flying again. Many months later when we were dropping fragmentation bombs I learned that our "frags" or "daisy cutters," as they were called, had a way of making a parked plane look at close range like a Swiss cheese facsimile, while at a distance it might look perfectly all right. I muttered something about getting my line chief to rebuild for me a good Focke-Wulf 190 out of the numerous ones I saw lying around. I might even fly home in it.

As we flew down the coast of the Mediterranean, the land

looked like a lot of desert country in the southwestern part of the States except for occasional camel trains and villages of rambling Arab tents. Finally we made our destination, which was supposed to be secret. We were based just outside the city of Bengasi, which, at that time, was one of the most bombed and shelled cities in the world. Bengasi is in what the British called Libya, and what the Italians called Cyrenaica. There were numerous airdromes in the area and by flying over and calling the radio tower of each, we finally surmised which one must be our new home. There was no radio at the field where we decided to land, but it fit the description and so we put down. Two ships of our group had beat me into the field, which dealt another faint blow to my pride.

There was a runway leveled out of the desert and that was about all. It didn't have a hard surface, but it obviously didn't need one for this season of the year. It was dusty but plenty hard to sustain the ship. We landed and taxied off the end of the runway pulling the heavy plane over some rough ground to a spot which seemed safe from incoming aircraft and traffic in the immediate vicinity. Looking out of the side window I could see an Arab tent, some goats, and a camel a few hundred yards from where the ship was parked. That was all that broke the expanse of the desert. Picturesque, but what about security?

Soon a truck appeared to take us to the living site. We left one member of the crew to guard the ship and took off, riding about a mile and a half to what appeared to be the beginning of a tent city. A service unit had been sent in only a few days before and had put up a tent for us to use as a mess hall, and that was about all. There were other tents available which we could draw and pitch for ourselves. We learned all over again what I had known from my old Infantry days: that good soldiers, no matter where they are, and with no matter how little, will immediately begin to better their living conditions. If given long enough they will even manage a degree of luxury—anywhere.

The officers of highest rank and the enlisted men of lowest alike began to pitch tents and put up cots and in the process found a few snakes and a great many scorpions. Across the desert there was nothing but flat, arid country shimmering in the clear, dry air. You could see for miles. It was July and this was the Middle East, Cyrenaica, Libya, Bengasi—take your choice. And aside from the really objectionable snakes and scorpions there were literally a million huge locusts—grasshoppers to me. While we pitched our tents they lit on our necks, flew down our backs, hit us in the face, and got in anything left lying around. They were nasty things, but after a while we got tolerably used to them.

Shortly after we landed we were given a desert snack of grimy sandwiches and synthetic lemonade. After we pitched our tents and worked on them for an hour or so our regular dinner, which consisted of powdered eggs with a good deal of dust scrambled in them, bread, and canned sausage, was served. There was a little apple butter which soon ran out, as did the sausage. However, the excitement of being here was enough to keep us from worrying about the food. We were sure it would improve after our whole group arrived and our normal supply channels began to function. And there was one aspect of this location we liked—the Mediterranean beach was only a short distance away. Tomorrow we might go and have a swim to ease the pain of the desert. We felt, in time, we could make our new home a fit place to live. I thought about it all that night as I lay in my tent too tired and too excited to sleep.

The darkness kept coming long after I thought it had all arrived, until it was several times darker than any night I had ever known. Just finding one's way from one tent to another only a few yards distant was a real accomplishment. As I finally fell asleep in my tent, I remember dark figures stumbling by the door. They were men looking for their own tents, and as they went by some would call out, "Hello darky, hello darky, gimme a QDM." That had been our procedure flying in England. When a pilot got lost in the fog he would fly around giving that call to get directional information from the British radio locator stations.

The next morning I was up early to have breakfast, which consisted of poor coffee sprinkled with dust, bread without butter, and powdered eggs. Since it would be several hours before we might expect any more planes, we did a little work on our tents in the morning; then wangled a jeep and went swimming.

We drove into the outskirts of Bengasi before going to the beach. What we saw of the town gave us our first idea of what war does to cities. There were only two buildings in the whole town that maintained any semblance of their original form. One was a very large and beautiful Catholic church. The other was a building out towards our airdrome some distance from the main section of town. It was used as headquarters of the Ninth Bomber Command. The city had changed hands several times, and apparently each side by sparing this building had given forethought to the headquarters housing problem.

In the harbor we saw hulks of ships as thick as schools of fish. There were over a hundred ships sunk in the immediate harbor area. Before coming into the downtown area we turned off to go to the beach. The living area of another of the groups of heavy bombers operating under the Ninth Bomber Command was only a short distance and was right on the beach. It was a beautiful spot with waving palms and soft clean sand in place of the dust we had at our camp. The Mediterranean was navy blue, with white fringes on some of the delicious-looking waves. In the heat of the desert sun the water looked too beautiful to be anything but a mirage. We drove the jeep through the tent area and down to within a hundred feet of the water to find a sandy beach as broad and clean as any I ever saw. It was covered with bathers —all male and in their birthday suits.

Every few minutes a Liberator would come barreling down the beach only about ten or fifteen feet above the sand, buzzing the bathers. Where we had come from not long ago such action would mean a very stern and quick court martial for pilot and copilot. Maybe this was just the natural thing in the combat zone.

After a swim as we were getting dressed we saw a couple of formations of Libs coming back across the Mediterranean. They were in pretty good shape except for three straggling bombers with feathered props following the main formation. They obviously had engines knocked out by flak or enemy fighters but were making it back to home base.

While I was looking around on the beach I found a fellow whom I knew from back in my training days at Randolph Field.

He mentioned several guys I knew who were stationed there. One of these was dear old Sully, my prize Irish cadet, O'Sullivan from Boston. Another was a little fellow named Antonio who had been the navigator on my B-17 crew at Sebring, Florida. He lived in the most glamorous tent I ever saw; it had a marble floor obviously removed from some bomb-wrecked building in Bengasi. The floor was lowered about two feet below ground level and sand was piled against the sides of the tent in revetments, an arrangement that made it much cooler inside. Tony was more than half way through his combat tour of missions. How I envied him his experience; I felt a surge of impatience at the delay in my getting into combat.

Those first days at Bengasi were intensely interesting. I got in to see the town several times. I visited the NAAFI, a British officers' club. I tried chatting with the natives without much success. I worked on my tent, but with little heart. There was too much to be seen and in our spot there was little incentive to beautification. We were in the bottom of a dust bowl. Every time the tent was made neat inside, a wave of hot wind would carry a quarter inch of silt in and spread it over everything. Sometimes I wondered how the airplane engines ran in such blinding dust. Of course it was damaging, but we found that they gave far better service than we had any right to expect. The longer we flew with those Pratt & Whitneys, the more we stood in awe of them. The name given the Arab or Egyptian natives was Wogs. And so Pratt and Whitney engines rebuilt at the local desert depot were accordingly called Pratt & Wogs. If you had a ship powered by Pratt & Wogs you must be satisfied if it flew at all. Remarkably enough, however, some of these rebuilt engines kept grinding out missions with little trouble.

Day after day more planes arrived. After the first four or five days we had something of a strike force assembled and started flying practice missions. There were stragglers of our command scattered all the way back to our base in England, but such was the story for every long movement. We could do without them until at length they caught up.

We had been in Africa only a few days when John Brooks told me he had permission of the group commander of the outfit stationed down on the seashore for two or three of our command and staff personnel to go with them on a mission. We were yet to have our first raid and this flight would give some of us an idea of what to expect. He asked me and one or two others if we wanted to go. I wanted to very much. I felt it quite an advantage to be able to get the experience to carry with me on the first raid when I would be leading my squadron. I was set up to fly with a young first lieutenant who had recently become a squadron commander.

As soon as I was introduced to the crew I was to fly with, I began to feel myself undesired baggage, though I tried to be as helpful as I could. After all, I had a lot of hours flying these tubs; I might be useful. We were going to Gerbini Airdrome. It was one of the network of fields in the vicinity at Catania, Sicily. Half an hour before takeoff we were parked in a line of aircraft off the end of the main runway. Each ship was headed so that it might run up its engines without blinding any other with the dust storm set up by the props. As we were running our engines up the lieutenant in the pilot's seat said, "This thing's an awful klunk. If it gets there and back we'll be lucky. The number four prop has been acting up, but we haven't got enough prop governors to put new ones on every time one acts up. We're lucky enough to replace those which go completely out. Well, here goes."

One by one he advanced the throttles of the engines as I turned the magneto switch on the engine being run up to right mag, to left mag, and back to both, watching the tachometer for a drop off of RPM. It was a borderline Lib, I could see from the ground runup; but if it would get airborne I figured we could get it there and back somehow.

Finally the ships started taking off. We were leading the low left squadron. As we straightened out on the end of the runway and the pilot pushed the four throttles open, I bent forward in my seat to give full attention to the engine instruments. I noticed the number four prop speeding up faster than the others. It hit 2700, its proper top limit, and kept advancing. Quickly I reached to the toggle switch that controls the prop governor and pulled it back to reduce the prop speed. The prop came back to 2700 and the four engines hummed the roar of synchronized power pilots love to hear. The big ship lifted its load of men, bombs, and fuel off the ground, and we were away.

We circled to pick up the ships of our squadron and to join the squadron leading the group. Occasionally the number four tachometer would oscillate and the ship would yaw noticeably. The prop was acting up, and then began a process of the prop gradually increasing RPM. The pilot looked very glum. "I guess if the damn thing runs away there'll be nothing to do but feather it and land. I hate to miss this mission, but we can't start off with an engine out."

I happened to know that there are times when a failing propeller governor may be compensated for by the propeller feathering mechanism. I asked the pilot if he had heard of stopping a runaway prop with the feather button.

"Not except if you want to feather the prop," he said.

"You don't have to feather it all the way," I said. "All you have to do is push the button. Then don't leave it in till the prop completely feathers and the button pops out. Keep hold of the button and watch the tachometer. When the RPM drops to the point you want it, pull the button out. It works for a while and then the prop starts gaining again and you can do it all over again."

"Try it if you want to," said the pilot. "I don't give a damn, if we can get this klunk over the target and back."

I did try it. I had never tried it before, but a representative of the Consolidated Aircraft Company had told me about it when I was instructing in B-24s at Tucson. It worked like a charm. The pilot and I were delighted.

At length, we had our squadron fairly well formed and headed out over the Mediterranean sliding in on the group lead. I was amazed at the delicacy and smoothness with which this pilot led his squadron. The pilot leading the group was evidently a fairly rough leader because he didn't fly with a constant power setting. I had heard some comment about that, with grumbling, before takeoff. My pilot was trying his best now to make up for it in the way he led his wingmen and his second element of three ships. When the group leader began to slow up a little he would gently S his squadron underneath. That is, our low squadron numbering six airplanes for this mission that normally was on the left would slide over slightly to the right and back then to its original position and then back again. All the time my pilot would be swearing.

"Just look at that bastard now. I'll bet in a minute he'll throw on a couple more inches of manifold pressure and if we don't watch he'll run off and leave all of us. Why do they let such a guy lead a group?"

I admired the procedure, for it seemed on the whole very well executed. The group formation for the most part was good. It wasn't always just like a diagram of a perfect formation, but all of the ships were in good mutual supporting distance of other ships. They maintained good integrity in the whole units.

Soon we saw the shore of Sicily, breaking a beautiful line in the constant blue of the Mediterranean. We flew up toward the straits of Messina and could see Italy on the right and Sicily on the left. Then the group leader turned left. There in front of us was what I at once recognized, thanks to the guns that welcomed us through Gibraltar, as flak—and heavy flak at that. Obviously the famous German 88 mm. guns were throwing up bursts a good deal larger than those I had seen before. The formation didn't seem to hang together very well in the flak.

Then we were over Sicily and very near our target. In a minute we dropped our bombs, getting scattered hits on the airfield. We turned left again and headed back towards the Mediterranean. At that moment I saw my first German fighters—not many of them. About four fighters made passes at the high right squadron of our group formation. One poor guy had allowed himself to get behind on the outside of the turn and was way out to the right of our group now. Most of the Jerries concentrated on him. He didn't go down, but he must have been hard hit. It looked like a couple of his engines were out as he started violent evasive maneuvers and headed off in the direction of Malta, the haven of many crippled aircraft of our bomber command. Malta was much closer to the targets in the Italy-Sicily area than any of the home airdromes on the south side of the Mediterranean.

Then we found ourselves over the sea again winging home and in pretty good shape, though a little strung out. We were letting down from our bombing altitude. The pilot sighed as he took off his oxygen mask. "Another one behind me," he said. Then looking at the engine instruments he sounded a little uneasy: "Say! What about that oil pressure in number three?"

"I think it's okay," I said. "I've been watching that oscillation of pressure and I think it's just something in the instrument. But number four prop is acting up worse than ever. When we get a little farther out I think we'd better feather it."

"Okay."

With number four feathered and the last red streaks dying away in the horizon off our right wing, we sighted the Libyan coast. There were the flares signaling our field, and in a few minutes I felt the wheels touch the runway.

Our group had really not had a great deal of practice formation flying at high altitude at the time we got to Africa. We learned we might be allowed only one practice workout before our first combat mission, and we wished we had flown more formation at altitude to get everyone used to doing his job while on oxygen. Ben Walsh, flight commander of my A Flight was the man I picked to be the lead pilot of the squadron. I was going to fly in the lead ship of the squadron as command pilot. Fowble had not yet arrived from England or I would have had him as the lead pilot. Ben was a good boy, but he didn't fly the way I thought he should. My other alternative was to let Frank Ellis, B Flight Commander, lead. Frank was a tall, angular, handsome Kentuckian whom I liked very much but who hadn't as much flying time in B-24s as some of my other pilots and needed a little more time to polish up his technique. At that time Frank was a poor formation flier and I didn't believe the squadron could stay with him.

And so Ben led our first real practice mission in Africa, and I was seated beside him. From the time of our takeoff he was out of formation and in and out again. He would get far back and put on a lot of power and then overrun. He didn't anticipate power changes far enough in advance to maintain his position properly and make it easy on the other fellows flying on him.

And then we got in each other's hair. I was trying to tell Ben how to handle power settings, and he was going to the opposite extreme just to let me know he was the pilot. When I got on the ground I said to him, "Ben, I don't think the squadron can stay with you on a combat mission if you fly like that. For that reason I am going to pilot the lead ship myself on the first mission. You can sit in the copilot's seat and see how I want it done if you wish. After that you will doubtless get what I mean. If you don't want to go under those circumstances you may let your copilot go with me. But I don't want to take a chance on shaking a lot of my boys out of formation in the midst of enemy fighter attacks."

Ben was livid. He was the only man in the squadron as pigheaded as I, and his retorts to me were not much in keeping with the canons of military courtesy between inferior and superior officers, but I took it and made no comment. I had several hundred hours more flying time in B-24s than Ben, and many more hundred in general flying experience. But it was clear he thought he was the best pilot in the squadron and it enraged him to have anyone, including the squadron commander, imply otherwise. I had been told by the group commander and Major Brooks that normally it would be the policy of the group for squadron commanders to ride as command pilots leading their squadrons. As such they must occupy the copilot's seat in order to be free of the duty of piloting to monitor their formations properly and make command decisions affecting the whole formation. However, it was explicitly stated that on occasions we might like to do our own piloting and on such occasions we would be permitted to do so.

From pieces of the story that came to me later, it was evident that the insulted Ben went straight to Major Brooks and told him I had directed him to fly in the copilot's seat, substituting myself in his place as the lead pilot. I suppose without thinking of the impropriety of Ben's having skipped the chain of command as he had in going over my head, Brooks went immediately to Colonel Wood. Colonel Wood allowed his operations officer a good deal of latitude in formulating group policy, and apparently at Brooks's behest the colonel sent word that I would not fly as first pilot. I must occupy the job of command pilot and the copilot's seat, though, of course I could pick the ship I would fly in. In very short order I learned of this decision.

This blow hit me pretty hard because I felt it reflected strongly upon my authority as a squadron commander. I had been told I might fly as pilot and had relied on that. I felt if I were to be overruled it should not affect a decision already made, but only similar ones in the future. This was simply allowing a flight commander to overrule the squadron commander, which is no good for the maintenance of command authority. I'm sure Colonel Wood didn't think the matter nearly as important as I did. All of my pilots knew of my criticism of Walsh's formation flying and were wondering how it would come out. I was the obvious loser.

And so I decided to ride in the "tail-end-charlie" ship of the formation on the group's first combat mission. Brooks wanted Walsh to lead my squadron. Then, let him lead! Since my squadron was "tail-end-charlie" in the group, I would fly in the corner end ship of the whole unit. I would be riding for no particular purpose other than to ride. Smitty had been designated to take the generally unwanted tail ship position on this first mission, so I would fly with Smitty.

The night before the mission we were briefed. We were to hit Maleme Airdrome on Crete. It was supposed to be an easy break-in raid. We were told by Colonel Wood that he had asked to be given a few more days for training. Brigadier General U. E. Ent, commanding the Ninth Bomber Command, had said he was sorry, but the need was so urgent we must consider ourselves sufficiently trained to go. We were told there were only a half dozen to a dozen German fighters based on the field we were hitting and we might expect enemy opposition to be light. But it had been several days since the intelligence report on enemy strength in Crete, and during that period there had been a British commando landing. It was possible the German forces had been strengthened, but it was believed unlikely.

There was a little Britisher named Barwell, a flight lieutenant, who wanted to go in the ship with Smitty and me. He was a gunnery officer assigned to the Ninth Bomber Command to teach German fighter tactics and gunnery. He had numerous kills to his credit, and always picked the most vulnerable spot in a formation to ride. He felt he had the best chance of getting some shots from the position most open to attack. For this mission he had picked the "tail-end-charlie" ship of a brand new group—Smitty's ship and my ship. As Barwell and I walked up and down in front of the plane while the ground crew put in a last minute's checkup prior to takeoff, he confided in me. "You know," he said, "I don't know how others feel about this bloody business. But when I see the bomb doors open and I hear the bombardier call 'bombs away' over the intercom, I get a thrill that's almost sexual in its intensity." Barwell is a great gunner, I thought, but maybe he has had just a little too much of it.

At length everything was ready and, upon a flare signal from our small, improvised tower, the first ship took off. We were flying number two ship of the last element, or flight, of three bombers. That is, we flew right wing on the last leader of three ships. Leading the element was Captain Frank Ellis, a very sterling character, but at that time a very poor formation pilot and element leader. The ship on the left wing of Captain Ellis had to turn back because of engine trouble. This left us an element of two airplanes. Nearly all the way out Ellis was a good half mile to a mile from the formation with my ship flying as close a right wing position as we could possibly maintain. There was the group formation, and here were our two ships stuck way out like a decoy to enemy fighters. I worried a good deal on the way out, but I knew our job was to stay with Ellis no matter how much we longed to leave him and join the group. If we were to get the right spirit into the squadron and into the flights, we must stay with the element leader no matter where he led.

We crossed the Mediterranean without mishap and saw the shore of the beautiful island of Crete ahead of us. At last Ellis made a great effort to tack on to his position in the group formation. It was a difficult one for him to hold, but he was doing a little better, thank goodness. We were over the island and we turned right to come in on our bombing run when suddenly we saw enemy fighters, dozens of them. Not according to briefing, thought I. We began to get into some light flak. Our altitude put us pretty much out of range of the guns firing on us, though there were occasional bursts near an airplane.

We saw the bombs falling from the lead ship. All others immediately let go, and as I heard the famous call Barwell loved so well—"Bombs away"—I saw the indicator lights on the instrument panel showing bombs dropping. We were coming out of the meager flak, but there were the fighters and they were coming in for head-on attacks. Most of them were ME-109s and FW-190s, with one or two sleek Italian Macci 202s. Those fighter pilots were awfully good. One flew right between Ellis's ship and our own at about five hundred miles an hour, his guns blazing. I wondered where his shots were hitting. Our turret guns were chattering and I could hear Barwell's top turret firing until his guns jammed and the firing stopped.

"Got one! Got one!" I heard the tail gunner shouting over the interphone. "The bastard blew up—went all to pieces." Several more passes were made at us but from a distance. It happened that the tail gunner, when all the smoke cleared away, had got one sure kill and one probable, the latter having been seen to catch on fire. The belly turret gunner got credit for one sure kill. So our ship counted two kills and a probable, and we later received official credit for them. Barwell later reported over the interphone that he knew we had done a lot of damage to several others with likely chances of other kills which of course we could not claim. He made no claim for himself and cursed his luck at getting a stoppage of his guns just at the time the fighting was at its height.

Our bombs had been scattered all over the place, with only a few of them in the airdrome area. As soon as bombs were away it was apparent that Captain Caldwell, piloting the lead ship in which Colonel Wood was riding, had thrown on a lot of power and left the target area like a scalded cat. That, we learned, is just what the enemy fighters hope for. It leaves stragglers aplenty because the guys on the end can't catch up and the whole formation comes apart.

One airplane in Cross's squadron caught fire from a volume of German 20 mm. shells poured into it and went down in flames.

Several chutes blossomed out of it and then it blew up. Quite
a tragically colorful sight for the first group mission, and how
surprisingly like the movies present it. We really were amazed
that an airplane blowing up in midair looks exactly like the Hollywood directors picture it. I didn't know whose ship it was at
the time, but I found later it was piloted by a fine young fellow
named Scates.

I particularly noticed how suddenly an enemy fighter attack
materializes. Usually with practically no warning, you look out
to see a bunch of 20 mm. cannons blazing at you. Then there
will be a moment or two when all hell breaks loose. Attack after
attack can come within a matter of seconds, and the whole thing
can easily take an unwary crew completely by surprise. Then as
a rule the show is over. If your ship is flyable, you are lucky. But
if you have really been taken by surprise, there isn't much chance
that it is flyable. It is more likely to be on fire, and by the time
a few more seconds pass it may be in bits floating casually
through the four miles of air between where the bomber was
and where the earth is.

Our ship was holed pretty badly. We happened to have no
apparent hits in vital spots and we felt pretty sure of our chances
to get home once the main fighter attack was over. As soon as we
could we caught up with the lead ship of the formation and
stacked in close formation. In our ship we had no wounded. We
had drawn blood from the enemy fighters, even though perhaps
we had done little damage to our assigned target. We had seen
one crew of our good comrades lost and we felt this experience
enough of the real thing to let us know we were now a combat
organization, fighting a rough, mean war.

After this first raid, missions came thick and fast for a while.
Our next target for two missions on two successive days was
Reggio di Calabria, just across the Messina straits from Messina,
Sicily. Reggio was on the toe of the boot of Italy.

The second of these Reggio missions was run July 12, 1943.
On it we had a rather bad piece of luck in finding a cloud layer
over the target just at the altitude we had planned to bomb. We
had to drop under it, and by so doing gave our altitude away to
the flak gunners. The town was loaded with heavy guns, and, as

always, the altitude of these clouds was already plotted. When we came in just under the cloud, we made the gunners' job simple. Everywhere there were planes shells were bursting. Hank Yaeger had an 88 mm. shell go right through his bomb bay. These shells were supposed to be fused two ways: to go off at a certain altitude or to go off on contact with anything. Well, lucky for Hank the contact fuse failed, and all that 88 mm. shell did was to tear a clean hole right through the center section of his ship. But other shells knocked out an engine for him, and he limped off in the direction of Malta as the rest of the formation turned south to return to base on the other side of the Mediterranean.

I was flying with Frank Ellis that day. I remember just after bombs were away I was leaning forward in my seat trying to see some shipping in the harbor when a piece of flak smashed through the side window and flew right across my shoulder and into the back of the ship. Splinters of the Plexiglas window tore into my flight jacket and left a small cut in my right cheek, which bled a little. But I had suffered little more than a severe case of fright.

The most remarkable thing on that raid happened to the slow, easygoing Robert Lee Wright of my C Flight. Bob had his numbers three and four engines knocked out by flak, and after dropping his bombs with the group he turned the nose of his Lib toward Malta. He ordered the boys to jettison as much equipment as they could and when he figured they were comparatively safe from enemy fighters he had them throw their fifty caliber guns over with all their ammunition. Bob had a toilet seat in the back of his plane. All of our airplanes had come equipped with these conveniences, but most of them had been taken out before the planes reached the combat zone. Bob called his waist gunners to check to be sure they had thrown out all the stuff they could, and one big gunner let his eye light on the can. The gunner reached over, put both arms around it, ripped it from the floor of the airplane, bolts and all, then tossed the whole business out the window.

After Bob and crew had passed the coast of Sicily and were heading across the expanse of water toward Malta, the number one engine sputtered and quit. They feathered it and with one engine in a ship which had been said to be unable to fly on two, Bob coolly and deliberately decided to set the airplane down on Sicily. The coast was still in sight to the rear, so he turned back. His ship was losing altitude pretty fast, but he had conserved a lot of altitude for just such an emergency. He had had it drilled into him to save the plane if possible. Of course it would be easy to abandon it, but not for Bob. There was a lot of emergency equipment in that airplane that would have to be lost if the crew hit the silk. He had also had it drilled into him in such cases to conserve altitude.

He picked a field, a little field, clearing up from the beach and ending abruptly in an olive orchard. It was the best to be had, and so that was it. He still had time to put his landing gear down, and with his emergency hydraulic pump on he got first his wheels down and then his flaps. The number two engine was chugging along, but the ship was in its last glide now and coming down fast. Bob made the kind of steep approach with practically no power that he and Fowble and I used to practice back at Biggs Field, Texas. The plane skimmed low over the waves. The wheels hovered over the beach and then touched with an exactness which was unbelievable on the very edge of the open field. A B-24 is not made to operate in such fields. Neither, as a rule, will it operate on an airdrome unless the ground is unusually hard or unless it has hard surface runways. I have seen B-24s break up concrete when it is not thick enough. But Bob landed his Lib in that field, and didn't do it any damage except to blow a nose wheel tire. It rolled up almost into the edge of the olive orchard and stopped.

Anyone who has ever flown a B-24 will admit this is the story of a near miracle. But that wasn't all. It just happened, and completely unknown to any of us on that raid, that that was the day of the landing on Sicily. As luck would have it Bob had come down on a narrow stretch of beach which had just been taken by Canadian forces. As he and the crew got out of the plane, he saw the Canadians running toward him. The bomber crew gleefully joined the ground forces and went up to the front. When Wright's crew finally got back to Bengasi about two weeks later, they were laden with every conceivable item of Italian gear and arms. They had taken some Italian prisoners, and from them had recovered these mementos of their great adventure.

Before I started combat the most important question in my mind was how I would take it. I knew I had no more courage than the average American, but I had studiously followed the methods suggested by psychologists to overcome fear. Early in my flying career I discovered that when you have an airplane in your hands and you feel yourself getting scared, the first thing you must do is force yourself to relax. That sounds paradoxical, but that is just what you do. You can fly an airplane with a lot of things wrong if you relax. If you become tense you completely lose that all-important feel of the controls that gives advance warning of what the ship is likely to do. You know what kind of glide to set for landing. You know whether you have enough speed to clear the tree ahead of you, or you know if you try to clear it, you will stall out at a critically low altitude. Then you must plan to point the nose of your ship down and let the tree take a wing off to break the forward motion as the plane pancakes it. I have prayed for a greater capacity to keep cool in pinches, because I know that panic may be the equivalent of suicide. If I maintain calm, I think there is a good chance I can land an airplane in any sort of terrain without injuring myself.

My first few missions hit me just about the way I thought they would. Sometimes I was scared, but on the easier runs I didn't feel much more than a pleasant exhilaration. Still, when the flak started breaking right against my airplane, or when I saw the enemy fighters practically flying through our waist windows, I could feel my pulse rise. Particularly, if I saw one of our ships filled with friends of mine sprout flames for a few seconds and then blow up—which wasn't uncommon—the icy fingers which I hated would reach right around my heart. I would shut my eyes for a brief instant, pray for a little more nerve, and then say to myself, r-e-l-a-x, you jerk! My temples would pound, but I would keep my hands flexible and easy of motion and feel. I've heard lots of pilots tell of narrow escapes and say, "Things happened so fast I didn't have time to get scared." I found no matter how fast things happened I always had time to get scared.

A few of those raids from Bengasi were comparatively easy, though nearly every time we went out we lost one or two ships and crews. A number of the raids were rough enough to keep some of the boys from sleeping at night for sweating out the next one. But there again I was lucky. When I got my feet on the ground after one mission I rarely had trouble sleeping because of the next one. The raids went quickly. That, too, was another factor to help. We didn't have too much time to sit around and think about the next mission. Another thing that helped was that we suffered absolutely no limitations of weather. Sometimes the haze was very heavy over the Mediterranean; but the sky was always clear at our base, and we never had to cancel a mission because of cloud over the target.

My old reliable Ed Fowble arrived after our group had run its third raid. He was ready and eager to catch up with us in combat experience and feel himself as mature a combat man as the rest. Ed had been able to pick up a brand new airplane in England at last, after proving that *Eager Beaver* was in no condition for a long trip to Africa. He had had the letter *I* painted on the tail, loaded up, and set forth. When he joined the group he was proud to hear about the record Bob Wright had established in his one-engined landing on Sicily. Ed justly deserved some of the credit for that landing because of the way he had trained his flight.

Suddenly we heard we were going to Messina, where we would meet what was by reputation the roughest flak in the theater. I decided to ride with Fowble, since it was his first trip in combat. The flak was all it was supposed to be. Our group lead ship, carrying Captain Frank Ellis and Colonel Wood, was shot right out of the lead position a few seconds away from the bomb release line. Frank did an excellent job and got his crippled ship in to Malta after three of his crew members had bailed out. I tried to take over the lead, but we were too close to the bomb release line for our bombardier to do a very good job. Our formation scattered bombs all over the general area of the point selected for bombing, and Fowble and I flew home in a ship leaking air through many holes it hadn't had on its way out.

Ed and his crew performed well. They got a rough view of this business on their first raid, and I could see the effect of the mission pile upon the effect of their harrowing midair collision in England. I've heard it said of many men after a little combat, and it may seem trite, that they change. I noticed more change in Ed than in almost any other pilot I had. He was just as good a pilot, even better, but the sight of death seemed to have cost him some of his enjoyment of living.

On every one of the first seven missions I made, the ship in which I was riding was shot up. Sometimes the damage was light and sometimes pretty serious, but at least I seemed to be something of a Jonah. McLaughlin, our plump and jovial Irishman from Syracuse, seemed to be my luckiest pilot. I took turns riding with all my pilots, and when I rode with Mac I told him I was glad to be assured of my luck on that mission. His ship was named *Ole Irish* and had a big green shamrock painted on it. It was officially called *B* for Baker. Mac was angry with me afterwards because his plane picked up its first holes on that mission.

Part of my reaction to my luck and general combat experience was to sense a resurgence of religion. Fellows who hadn't attended services in years found themselves going to Sunday services. My religion didn't take me to these services with regularity, but I went occasionally, not only for myself but to let the men in my squadron know I didn't consider attendance a sign of weakness. I felt if they saw me there it might help some of them to go who wanted to but were kept from going out of embarrassment.

In my case religion made me say short prayers before going to sleep at night, and sometimes during a fleeting instant at the height of combat. I think this undoubtedly made me a better combat officer. It comforted me so that I could sleep before missions, even though I had been briefed for the next mission and knew the assignment of the morning might be my last. It helped me say to myself with complete calm: "You can't live forever. You have had a great deal in your life-span already, much more than many people ever have. You would not shirk the duty of tomorrow if you could. Go into it calmly; don't try too hard to live. Don't ever give up hope; never let the fear of death strike panic in your mind and paralyze your reason. Death will find you sometime, if not tomorrow. Give yourself a chance." And then I would remember that very appropriate sentence of Shakespeare: "Cowards die many times before their deaths; the valiant never taste of death but once."

In Bengasi we had no regular Protestant chaplain. One assigned to the Ninth Bomber Command used to come out for Sunday service. He was overworked by having about a dozen other services to perform each Sunday. Because I am a Protestant I tried to support this overworked man as best I could. Our Catholic boys were more fortunate because there was a Catholic chaplain assigned to our group. His name was Beck, and to my last day I shall never forget him. He had a shock of almost white-gray hair. He had twinkling blue eyes, and he was withal one of the most charming men I have ever met. He was unorthodox in his mode of religion. If there were no rabbi to perform the rites, Father Beck would preach a Jewish funeral service with as perfect form and dignity as any Catholic priest ever did. He would give all possible aid and comfort to the Protestant boys when no Protestant chaplain was available, and in giving he didn't push his religion upon them. But Father Beck played those Catholic boys like a great artist plays an organ. I know one of the uppermost thoughts in his mind was to make his men better, braver soldiers.

Father Beck flew on combat missions with us time after time until at length the group commander gave him a direct order to stop going. He slept in various tents with the enlisted men, and later when we had barracks he slept in their barracks. They would carry his cot and bedding from one sleeping place to the next, each group anxiously awaiting his time to visit them. The superstition was that a crew would not be shot down as long as he was sleeping in their quarters. He had a very worldly side that caused some comment. He loved to gamble on cards or dice. He gave his winnings away, but he was nearly always a heavy winner. I saw him make six straight passes with the dice one night, and the game broke up—not because he had all the money, but because no one in the game had nerve enough to fade him.

Being ordered to do so by Colonel Wood, the squadron commanders, Yaeger, Burton, Cross, and I, moved into a tent just behind the movie screen of our open-air theater. The theater was a sheet stretched out on poles in front of a number of rows of empty oil drums. And there in the theater all religious services were held on Sunday mornings. I had the experience several times of lying on my cot in the tent and listening to Father Beck talk to his men. Once when we were facing a very tough mission I heard him say, "You fellows know tomorrow or the next day you're going to have a very hard mission. I want to urge you all to do what you can now to prepare yourselves for the eventualities of this dangerous task. If allowed to I'll be flying with you. One thing I will particularly ask you to do is to go to confession sometime before takeoff. If you find a good priest, let me know and I'll go with you." Lying on my bed I could imagine his blue eyes twinkling as he said this. He played the sense of humor of the men with great dexterity. In times of tense emotions, as he knew, a laugh can make the difference.

Those days when the squadron commanders lived together in one tent did a lot for me. My almost vicious sense of competition between my squadron and the others softened a lot. I still did my best to make my squadron a topnotch fighting unit, but my softening was also noticeable in my dealings with my own men. I think I learned a little about putting first things first. I wanted my men to do a good job of fighting and next to that I wanted them to be comfortable and happy. I had cultivated an intense dislike for Hank Yaeger without much cause. It largely stemmed from the fact that he had managed a bit better with Colonel Lancaster, our first commanding officer, than I had. Now, on knowing him better, I found Hank quite an amiable person.

Then there was Paul Burton. Paul was the handsomest of us all by a good margin. He was from Arkansas and came of a family of very good people of modest means. Paul had started out like a boy who would never amount to anything, and then suddenly pulled out of it as a very responsible squadron commander in the Air Corps. Early in life he had run away from home intending never to return. He never did go back for help, but later, when he became completely independent, he went home to make peace with his family. He was then a civilian pilot who applied and was rejected by the USAAF. Ultimately his efforts got him into the RCAF. He had become a highly rated flight lieutenant in Canada when our country started calling for the American pilots who had enlisted across the border. In the squadron commanders' tent Del Cross, too, was quite a figure. Del was a native of Springfield, Massachusetts, and had a naive way about him which endeared him to us all. I felt in him a friend of unquestioning loyalty, and tried to respond to some degree in kind.

Frequently in the afternoons when we weren't flying, the four of us would get a jeep and go swimming. We found a little strip of beach, not much used, which we claimed as our own. Del would take a mattress cover, wet it, and tie the ends. That way it would hold air and float with great buoyancy. He would splash around in the water with the thing while the rest of us kidded him about his childishness, or while Paul and I engaged in some solemn political argument.

We would hunt relics together by the hour. There were piles of expended and unexpended German ammunition lying around. We took 88 mm. shells back to our tent and cut the tops off them to make ash trays. We tore the ends out of shells and set fire to the powder. We stacked up 20 mm. shells and shot at them with a .22 rifle to set them off. Once while we were enjoying this latter pastime Hank got slightly wounded. Paul, Del, and I were crouching behind our jeep while we shot at a pile of 20 mm. shells. Hank sat in the jeep haughtily denying that they would go off. When the explosion did occur it was something more than we expected. Though we had thought ourselves at a safe distance, a bit of shell whizzed by and cut Hank's leg. It was nothing serious—just another laugh.

4

Ploesti
and the Circus Ends

When we left England for Africa we heard rumors about a great raid we were to run. The stories hinted at a maximum-range mission to be flown at low altitude. The first one I heard, which was typically weird for the Air Corps, was that we were going on a raid which could almost be characterized as a suicide mission. As the tale went, anyone who participated could be sure he would get at least the Silver Star. It was funny how great the percentage of truth in that one turned out to be.

After the group had run five raids, all of which I had made, plus the one I went on before our group started combat, we began strenuous practice in keeping with the rumors. By this time we were sure we were really going to make a long, low-level raid on the oil fields of Ploesti, Romania. We hadn't been told officially, but the strength of the rumors made the matter almost incontrovertible.

We practiced low-altitude formation until we almost got vertigo when we found ourselves flying above five hundred feet. It was usual to see a three-ship flight or a six-ship squadron of big Libs scudding over the flat desert land actually four or five feet from the ground. Of course the lowest ships of those formations were about four or five feet above the ground, and the highest were not over fifteen feet. I have seen three-ship flights approach our field so low they would have to pull up to get over a parked aircraft. Arab tents were knocked down in what some thought great sport. Two of the ships practicing for the mission actually hit the ground and got into the air again. They didn't make the raid because of buckled bulkheads and other damage they sustained from the collisions, but they got home okay.

This was the type of flying every hot pilot had dreamed of all his life, but it was the sort that had cost many hundreds of pilots' lives in the States—pilots who were on their cross-country flights home and couldn't resist giving the home folks a show. Now it was legal and, of course, as such it wasn't quite as much fun; but it was still a thrill, because when you fly that low you get a sense of speed which you lose at a few hundred feet altitude. When you go 200 miles per hour at an altitude of eight feet, you really know you're going 200 miles per hour.

I heard that Colonel Ted Timberlake had spent months working our big mission down to the minutest detail. His ideas were joined with those of General Ent and many other bigwigs in on the general planning of it. Evidently, and from the piece-meal bits of information we got, it was going to be the most ornately planned thing of its kind ever done.

After we had practiced low-altitude formation for a long time in small three- and six-ship formations, we began to practice shifting from a group formation of thirty ships or more to break up into sixes and later into flights of three, so as to pass over a given point in a matter of seconds. We would get considerable altitude and at a given signal would pull off a lot of power and start getting down as quickly as possible, still maintaining a sort of formation and yet splitting up into these smaller units. After going over the designated point we would practice reassembly in the quickest manner possible.

Finally, in the last stages a series of squares were drawn in the sand of the flat desert. They were of the exact shape and dimensions in width and length of the targets we were to hit. We practiced coming in one flight after another, the first flight making a run straight over, the second coming in from the left, the third straight over, the fourth in from the right, the fifth straight over, and so on. It was a precise pattern and required precise flying. We tried to clip as many seconds as possible from the lapse of time between the bomb run of the first flight and the runs of the flights succeeding. We wanted to take only enough time to insure each flight unobstructed bombing. Towards the end of our training our ships were equipped with a new type of bombsight. Sighting for this kind of low-altitude bombing was extremely simple. We were not planning to carry our complicated Norden sights, which were primarily high-altitude instruments. Furthermore, a major came in to demonstrate what could be done with this low-altitude sight.

We erected a target consisting of a wooden frame standing vertically about twenty feet square. From the top of it we hung strips of cloth, and across the bottom we placed empty gasoline cans. These were to give better reference as to where the bomb went. We set up a two-way radio at the target to control the approach of aircraft and give us two-way communication with bombers on the target. The major would fly his ship over loaded with hundred pound practice bombs, and call out to us: "This time I'll put one right through the middle." He would fly at an altitude which would permit clearance of the wooden frame by about five feet, and he would do exactly what he said. He would put his bomb right through the middle of the target. The next time he would announce that the bomb would drop twenty feet short and skip through the target. Sure enough, the bomb would hit twenty or twenty-five feet short and skip right through the center of the frame. The third time he went over he said he would knock out one of the middle gasoline cans standing in the row across the bottom of the frame. This, too, he did, and thus we were completely sold on the accuracy of this new method.

We worked hard perfecting the technique. And then about four or five days before the great day, the officers were called in. We were told officially for the first time that we were going on a long, low-level attack on the Romanian oil fields and were given to understand that this raid was considered of greatest strategic import to the future conduct of the war. It was said we must expect extremely heavy losses, but if we were successful we might take consolation from the fact that our losses would be given in a great cause. If we should fail, many thousands might die who otherwise would live. However, if we were successful we would cripple Germany's oil production sufficiently to require a general rearrangement of the Nazi plan of war.

We knew no matter how successful we were we could not destroy the oil fields. But we believed if we did a good job we could cut down the output of the refineries 50 or 75 percent. Our aim would be to knock out the refineries as effectively as possible, realizing if we did it right it would be a matter of months before they got going again. By that time, who knows? We might be able to hit them from bases much closer with much greater tonnages and at high altitude. That would mean lighter losses that could be sustained in repeated raids.

A day or two after the first, sketchy information came out we were all called in for a more extensive briefing. This time the briefing included everyone who would participate. We were shown movies of how our run into the target would look. There were a couple of British Intelligence men who were authorities on the oil fields to answer questions. One had lived in the Ploesti region a good part of his life. He brought a relief miniature of the town near our target and the Steaua Romana refinery, which was to be the aiming point of our group. The model was so perfect that he could even point out to us a house where he used to live.

Very soon the eve of the big raid was upon us. Special services were held, Protestant, Catholic, and Jewish. Father Beck gathered his flock of Catholics to give them the comfort our Protestant chaplain was giving us, and a rabbi gave his.

Paul Burton was the only squadron commander who was not flying the mission. Instead Colonel Wood would ride with Captain Caldwell, Paul's prize first pilot, and John Brooks. It was decided to carry as little extra ballast as possible, and unless an officer had a definite mission to fulfill he was not supposed to go. Del Cross planned to lead his squadron, Hank Yaeger was going to lead his, and, of course, I would lead mine.

Before I went to bed that night I took a piece of masking tape and secured a hacksaw blade to the bottom of my right foot. The tape was just about skin color. I felt if I were shot down I might be carefully searched. My clothes would probably be gone over, but one way or another I could so divert the attention of my captors that the hacksaw blade would escape notice.

I had decided that if captured I would try to escape and make my way across the mountains to the west of the oil fields, across the Danube and into Yugoslavia. I had instructed some Yugoslavs in Tucson, Arizona, in flying B-24s. I had picked up a few words of the language and I also remembered some of their names. I thought that with luck I could make Yugoslavia, where I would join Tito's forces and continue to fight with the guerrillas. I packed a musette bag with many things, including two clean suits of underwear, chewing gum, cigarettes, and many other odds and ends. I didn't smoke, but I thought the cigarettes might be good for bartering.

Hank Yaeger packed his Air Corps type B-4 bag—a large affair that would carry enough stuff to keep him well furnished for a month or so. He and Del and I had talked the situation over many times and had agreed that if we were so badly shot up we couldn't get home we would not parachute out of our airplanes. We would try to crash land them in some isolated spot where we would be unlikely to be found for a few hours. This would enable the crew to take many items to assist an escape. It was a common comment in the group afterwards that all the combat crew members had so many compasses concealed on them "the only way they could walk was north."

On that night before the raid I was certain the next night would see parts of Romania overrun by American fliers. I had commented that if enough of us were shot down all we would have to do would be to call a general election, vote the old government out, vote ourselves in, make a quick peace with the Allies, and the war would be over in Romania. At any rate, I had the feeling that there was more than a fifty-fifty chance I would be shot down. That feeling was parent to what might be called a sense of exhilaration about how I was going to make my escape. I had spent weeks planning it. I had conditioned my mind completely to the trials of such an eventuality, and I had confidence in my ability to come through it.

That night before I retired I wrote a long letter to Anne. I went to bed not as early as I would have liked to, but as early as I could in view of all my packing and preparations. Hank was outside the tent sitting in the dark in a jeep talking with Paul. Del was asleep. While it was still dark the racket of all the alarms going off woke us. Men in jeeps tore around from tent to tent blowing horns. "Get up, get up, you guys! This is the day. Get up! Roll out of those sacks!"

This was it. My stomach felt a little sinky and shaky, possibly because I hadn't had a chance to put any coffee in it. We ate hurriedly, though quietly, then walked to the briefing room for last-minute instructions. Weather might be a little bad, we were told; but we would go anyway, and we would get there, and we would destroy our target. Nothing was said about getting home. When the general briefing was over I told all the boys of my squadron I wanted to see them outside. I saw my men gathering in a little knot by the briefing room door. There was Fowble, pale as a ghost. He had been in the hospital with dysentery and had been let out a day early at his own insistence so he could go on the raid. Others had been ill, but not a man would sell his chance to make this mission for anything.

"Fellows," I said, "today is the great day. If our hearts are in this war, this is the time to pay off. Last night I said a prayer for myself and in it I included a word for all of you, my good men and great friends. I would like to be able to tell you all how deeply my feelings will be tied up today in the welfare of each of you. I can't. Good luck. Let us say we'll see each other here tonight."

We went to our ships and fired up engines. Flames blasted from exhaust stacks and dust flew in clouds around our propellers as the first rays of dawn crept over the edge of the desert. And soon we were winging our way across the Mediterranean. Just off the coast of Greece, over the Adriatic, I saw a smoking oil fire in the sea. Obviously a plane had gone down burning. We learned later it was the lead aircraft of one of the groups ahead.

We took pictures, commented, and flew on. Across Yugoslavia we went, and on to the wide, blue Danube River. There we saw a tremendous amount of river traffic. Barges were lined up side by side six deep in some places. Some of the boys reported seeing a nude bathing beauty in the Danube.

As we went farther and farther on I felt it necessary to go to the flight deck, the little room just behind the pilot-copilot compartment, to use the relief tube. Good old Ed Fowble had warned me that the thing wasn't working right. Sometimes it caused a smear to come over the glass of the tail gunner's turret. The outlet was somewhere near the tail of the ship. I decided circumstances demanded that I give it a try. As soon as I started Ed, who was standing by on interphone, broke out in a laugh. "You'll have to hold up. Tail gunner wants to know who the louse is smearing up his turret. He's swearing like a trooper." I held up only long enough to discover a stack of Dixie cups on the radio operator's table. With the lever in the bomb bay I cracked open the bomb bay doors a little way and sat on the floor of the flight deck dropping out several full Dixie cups and chuckling to myself about the tail gunner.

I got back in the copilot's seat as we went on across Romania. The weather was getting worse. We couldn't maintain our formation at the altitude we were flying because of increased amounts of cloud, and so we began to let down under it. Until we struck the darkening skies over Romania we had been able to keep in sight of two of the other groups. When we got under the stuff we appeared to be completely alone. On we flew over rough terrain, trying as well as we could to follow out our flight plan.

Finally we turned down a valley between two steep ridges of mountains. We were supposed to make a run down a valley to the little town of Campina, north of the town of Ploesti. Steaua Romana, the most modern refinery in all Romania, lay on the edge of Campina in the Ploesti region. As soon as we turned down the valley I got a call from Lieutenant Solomon, the navigator. Sollie's voice was the voice of calm as he said over the interphone, "They've turned too soon. We are not in the right valley." He was an excellent navigator and his calmness on that harrowing day is something I'll not forget.

Sure enough, after we had flown about twenty minutes on the wrong heading we got a call from the lead ship indicating they had located their error and were turning north again to resume the proper course. One of the factors that we were briefed on as a most hopeful aspect of the mission was that we might take the enemy defenses of the oil fields by surprise. Now we realized that asset was spent. We must have been picked up by enemy radar, and we knew that after all this milling around we would meet enemy defenses fully alerted to our presence.

We turned south again. This time we were going down the right valley. My squadron was to be the second over the target. Ahead of the lead element of my squadron—that is, the three ships in my immediate formation—were six airplanes. We saw them spacing themselves the way they had been briefed. We slowed up. The first three ships headed straight down the valley, letting down fast to hit the deck as quickly as possible. The second element of three turned to the left for a few seconds and then turned back to the right to come in from the briefed angle. We spaced ourselves for a straight-in run over the same course as the first three ships. The bombs we carried were fused to allow sufficient delay so that all our ships could get over the target before the first bombs began blowing up. They were also fused so that if any rescue crews tried to enter the refinery after they were dropped and remove the fuses, they would blow up at once. This would, of course, prevent successful rescue work.

We were very close behind the second flight of three ships. As their bombs were dropping we were on our run in. There in the center of the target was the big boiler house, just as in the pictures we had seen. As the first ships approached the target we could see them flying through a mass of ground fire. It was mostly coming from ground-placed 20 mm. automatic weapons, and it was as thick as hail. The first ships dropped their bombs squarely on the boiler house and immediately a series of explosions took place. They weren't the explosions of thousand pound bombs, but of boilers blowing up and fires of split-open firebanks touching off the volatile gases of the cracking plant. Bits of the roof of the house blew up, lifting to a level above the height of the chimneys, and the flames leaped high after the debris. The second three ships went over coming in from the left, and dropped partly on the boiler house and partly on the cracking plant beyond. More explosions and higher flames. Already the fires were leaping higher than the level of our approach. We had gauged ourselves to clear the tallest chimney in the plant by a few feet. Now there was a mass of flame and black smoke reaching much higher, and there were intermittent explosions lighting up the black pall.

Phifer, the bombardier, said over the interphone, "Those damn bombs are going off. They ain't supposed to do that."

"That ain't the bombs," I answered, "that's the gas they're cookin' with."

We found ourselves at that moment running a gauntlet of tracers and cannon fire of all types that made me despair of ever covering those last few hundred yards to the point where we could let the bombs go. The antiaircraft defenses were literally throwing up a curtain of steel. From the target grew the column of flames, smoke, and explosions, and we were headed straight into it.

Suddenly Sergeant Wells, our small, childlike radio operator who was in the waist compartment for the moment with a camera, called out, "Lieutenant Hughes's ship is leaking gas. He's been hit hard in his left wing fuel section."

I had noticed it just about that moment. I was tired of looking out the front at those German guns firing at us. I looked out to the right for a moment and saw a sheet of raw gasoline trailing Pete's left wing. He stuck right in formation with us. He must have known he was hard hit because the gas was coming out in such volume that it blinded the waist gunners in his ship from our view. Poor Pete! Fine religious, conscientious boy with a young wife waiting for him back in Texas. He was holding his ship in formation to drop his bombs on the target, knowing if he didn't pull up he would have to fly through a solid room of fire with a tremendous stream of gasoline gushing from his ship. I flicked the switch intermittently to fire the remote-control, fixed fifty caliber machine guns specially installed for my use. I watched my tracers dig the ground. Poor Pete. How I wished he'd pull up a few hundred feet and drop from a higher altitude.

As we were going into the furnace, I said a quick prayer. During those moments I didn't think that I could possibly come out alive, and I knew Pete couldn't. Bombs were away. Everything was black for a few seconds. We must have cleared the chimneys by inches. We must have, for we kept flying—and as we passed over the boiler house another explosion kicked our tail high and our nose down. Fowble pulled back on the wheel and the Lib leveled out, almost clipping the tops off houses. We were through the impenetrable wall, but what of Pete? I looked out right. Still he was there in close formation, but he was on fire all around his left wing where it joined the fuselage.

I could feel tears come into my eyes and my throat clog up. Then I saw Pete pull up and out of formation. His bombs were laid squarely on the target along with ours. With his mission accomplished, he was making a valiant attempt to kill his excess speed and set the ship down in a little river valley south of the town before the whole business blew up. He was going about 210 miles per hour and had to slow up to about 110 to get the ship down. He was gliding without power, as it seemed, slowing up and pulling off to the right in the direction of a moderately flat valley. Pete was fighting now to save himself and his men. He was too low for any of them to jump and there was not time for the airplane to climb to a sufficient altitude to permit a chute to open. The lives of the crew were in their pilot's hands, and he gave it everything he had.

Wells, in our waist gun compartment, was taking pictures of the gruesome spectacle. Slowly the ship on our right lost speed and began to settle in a glide that looked like it might come to a reasonably good crash-landing. But flames were spreading furiously all over the left side of the ship. I could see it plainly, as it was on my side. Now it would touch down—but just before it did, the left wing came off. The flames had been too much and had literally burnt the wing off. The heavy ship cartwheeled and a great flower of flame and smoke appeared just ahead of the point where last we had seen a bomber. Pete had given his life and the lives of his crew to carry out his assigned task. To the very end he gave the battle every ounce he had.

My attention was drawn back to the task of self-preservation. We flew over part of the town of Campina after bombing. We could feel the heat inside the ship that resulted from flying over that furnace-like target with bomb bays open. The engineer in the top turret said he saw flames blown up into the bomb bay by the explosion that occurred as we went over, but we were not on fire. At that time there was no visible evidence of damage to our ship at all. Bob Wright held his position on our left wing as we skipped over the tops of trees and tension lines, keeping at almost zero altitude to reduce the effect of ground defenses.

After we left the little town we passed over grain fields. The top of a big straw stack in front of us slid back and two Nazi gunners appeared there firing 20 mm. machine guns at us. I switched on my remote control guns and watched their tracers spray out. The boys in the nose were firing their flexible guns, too, but I could see my fire going over the target. "Shove the nose down a little, Ed," I shouted. Just at that moment he saw what I was yelling about. He pushed forward on the wheel and kicked a little rudder back and forth and we saw a mass of tracers of all our forward firing guns splitting into the gun emplacement. The Jerries stopped firing and fell beside their guns. Maybe they were dead; I hoped so. That was the nearest I ever got to killing men I could see. The brutality of heavy bombardment is highly impersonal. I was used to carrying out my mission four miles above the point of impact. It is difficult under those circumstances to get any feeling of injuring the enemy at all. But here I got the satisfying sensation of thinking I had stopped at least two of the maggots corrupting the body of Europe.

Then I looked out to the left and discovered that Bob Wright was gone from his position. I looked around but couldn't find him anywhere. We were in no perceptible formation at all at this moment. Our ships flying south were meeting other Liberators flying north that had attacked targets in the region south of ours. The sky was a bedlam of bombers flying in all directions, some actually on fire, many with smoking engines, some with great gaping holes in them or huge chunks of wing or rudder gone. Many were so riddled it was obvious their insides must have presented starkly tragic pictures of dead and dying, of men grievously wounded who would bleed to death before they could be brought any aid; pilots facing the horrible decision about what to do—whether to make a quick sacrifice of the unhurt in order to save the life of a dying man, or to fly a ship home and let some crew member pay with his life for the freedom of the rest.

By this time, with my mission accomplished, I had at last come to the point of being frightened for my own safety. Earlier I had reconciled myself to the probability that I would not return, and I was willing to stick by that decision. Funny, but when it seemed to me there was slight hope of my returning from a mission—as there had been in the beginning of this one—I didn't worry much. But when it appeared I had passed the point of greatest danger and thereafter stood a good chance to make it, I began to sweat it out in earnest.

Soon we appeared to be out of danger of the ground fire emplacements protecting the immediate target area. We had a semblance of a formation now, though I could count only five ships that had regrouped out of an original formation of thirty-two. Some of these were damaged, others showed no damage on quick observation. I caught sight again of Bob Wright who seemed to be all right, and I heaved a sigh of relief.

We were still very low. We flew over farmers in the fields. It was a Sunday afternoon. I recall going over a railroad station peculiarly situated out in the country miles from any town. A train was coming in, and a crowd of gaily dressed people on the platform waiting for the train watched us with what seemed every kind of reaction. Some waved, some shook their fists, some jumped up and down gleefully, some ran, and some just stood and looked. As we swept on I saw a man run around the side of a farm house, grab up a little girl in his arms and dash through the door of the house. Then I saw a shepherd tending his flock in a field. He had a long rifle and I wondered if he would fire it at us. He just leaned on it and looked as we roared a hundred feet over his head.

Romania is a pretty country. I got to see a good deal of it

from rather close range that day. My general impression was that the initial effect of our raid on the people was to give them real gratification. Most of them who were sufficiently off to one side of our flight path to feel tolerably safe, waved to us what looked like a friendly welcome. Our crews might have fired at a good many things they shouldn't have, but it was certainly not in the plan. We were briefed not to, and we started the mission with the expectation that we might find the people generally favorable to the attack.*

As we headed west for the mountains and home, to our backs the sky was black with smoke. The oil fires of the refineries were tremendous and darkened the whole sky. Our tail gunner gave us a running commentary except during those moments when we had to shut him up to get other messages out over the interphone. The turret gunners had had great fun shooting incendiaries into the great storage tanks of gas and oil in the vicinity of the refineries. They had been targets not considered worth the expenditure of bombs. But the gunners did a big job on the tanks with their 50 caliber guns.

Late that evening a great gaggle of battle-scarred Liberators struggled to get over the mountains separating them from home. Many had only three functioning engines and some only two. Most were short of fuel and many suffered cut hydraulic lines and punctured fuel tanks. The sun was settling in the west as our own little formation, now seven aircraft, cleared the mountains and flew on toward the Adriatic Sea. Our radio was jammed with tragic calls, announcing, "fighters everywhere," "all the ships we were with are gone now but us—don't see how we can last through these attacks"; followed so frequently by the call, "bailing out, ship on fire." We saw some enemy fighters but had only a few halfhearted attacks on our formation. Why should they attack us? We had a pretty good defensive unit. The sky was full of dying airplanes that were severely crippled by ground fire and could be knocked down with little danger of strong de-

---

*A fine example of the attitude of Romanians was Princess Caterina Caradja, who protected a number of American airmen on her estate near Ploesti until their liberation by friendly forces.

fensive action. We got by simply because there were many easier targets.

Our ship touched down at Bengasi just as it was getting completely dark. It was thirteen and a half hours since takeoff. A hurried inspection proved we were hit many times, but again we were lucky enough to have the hits where we could take them. We went directly to group operations to await the summing up of information about all the planes. At the time we got there eight other ships of our group of thirty-two had landed.

Through that whole long night story piled upon story of a heroic struggle. One pilot had come in with his control cables completely shot away. He had flown most of the way back on the automatic pilot and had even managed to land his airplane on that instrument. Thank God, the autopilot didn't depend on control cables but on servos mounted directly on the controls. He had to come home to bring two wounded men and the body of a third. His landing was done with such calm and perfect execution that the ship suffered no additional damage in landing, but it was so wrecked from battle damage that it was towed off the end of the runway and left to be stripped of its remaining serviceable parts. Many others had flown for hundreds of miles on three, or even two, engines. Many crews had put out fires, had done amazing jobs of first aid with the seriously wounded, and had shown in hundreds of ways examples of the highest type of battle stamina.

After a while listening to these accounts, I bade goodnight to Ed at operations, and stumbled through the dark to bed. I lay on my back with my eyes open in the dark, my senses stunned beyond ability to receive any further impression. Hank Yaeger was a Catholic and about 2:30 A.M. Father Beck came in looking for him. He had not and would not return. The padre had wound up all the work he could do that night among the men and remains at the field hospital.

The code words for the attack were *Tidal Wave*. Official figures for the entire mission had it that 178 B-24s took off, of which 53 were lost, and 446 airmen were killed or missing.

For a week or so after the big raid life itself continued to seem anticlimactic. Then things were slowly lifted out of limbo and gradually reestablished in their proper place. If I didn't fear death, then why should I allow such a thing as a mission, from which I returned unharmed, to paralyze my senses? Suppose I could look at the figures and discover that logically there was no reason why I should have returned when so many others didn't? The fact was that I had returned, and I would be remiss in my duty to myself and the Power that helped me if I permitted the shock of the experience to make me a zombie.

There was only one string left that I wanted to tie up. Then I would put the whole raid behind me until such time as I could think about it without recurrence of shock. That remaining string had to do with Pete Hughes. We had had many heroes living and dead and many who were prisoners, but from it all the example of Hughes stood out in my mind as a case of most conspicuous merit. Others might have been as great, but there was not quite the tangible evidence to support their cases. We even had pictures of Pete trying to land that flaming Liberator. I went to Colonel Wood and told him I had written a citation on Pete for the Congressional Medal of Honor. I asked him if he would approve it. I felt also that all the other members of that crew should have the Distinguished Service Cross. Colonel Wood turned me down. Perhaps he felt it impossible that such a recommendation would clear higher headquarters, but I was upset about it until I was approached one day shortly after the raid by an Office of War Information representative from Cairo. He had seen the pictures of Pete's ship and came to me for the story. I showed him the citation I had prepared to send through and told him the story according to the way I saw it. Three days later Colonel Wood sent for me and told me General Ent had heard of the case and said he would be glad to approve a recommendation for the Congressional Medal on Lieutenant Hughes.

Months later, after more than one award of the Congressional Medal had been announced by the War Department from this raid, orders came out announcing the posthumous award of that great honor to Lieutenant Hughes. I had a big poster made bearing Pete's picture in a design of the Air Corps wings, and carrying under the picture the citation. This I displayed in squadron operations to impress upon the minds of all what a great tradition of fearless, selfless patriotism and honor Pete Hughes had left with our command. It was something which made its impression on every newcomer as soon as he arrived, and it was something which gave us what every squadron should have if it is to be a high-spirited fighting organization.

We had thought upon completion of our oil fields raid that we would go directly back to England. But not so. We stayed around and about two weeks later found ourselves facing another mission that would be almost as long, though no one believed it would be as hazardous. We were going for the first time to Wiener Neustadt, just south of Vienna, Austria, to bomb a factory producing frames for German fighter planes. It was a great production center and an extremely important target. The raid was to be run in conjunction with a shuttle England-to-Africa raid of Eighth Air Force Fortresses based in England. We would take off at our home station and land in Tunis. We would fly back down the coast of North Africa to Bengasi the next day. Colonel Wood had planned to lead the raid, but he was stricken with "gippy tummy," more scientifically known as dysentery. He tried to stay on his feet, but he looked like a walking ghost and was not able to make the raid.

Just before takeoff I was standing outside the group operations hut and noticed a full colonel standing there. I had never seen him before. He was blond and stocky with high color in his extremely strong face. He was wearing a broad grin, which seemed a frequent expression of his, as he chatted with Colonel Wood. Standing off to one side was the famous polo-playing Major Mike Phipps. Mike was our wing intelligence officer and a very good guy. "Who's the colonel, Mike?" I asked.

"Gee, don't you know? That's Colonel Timberlake. He came out to lead the mission when he heard Colonel Wood was sick."

So this was the famous Ted of Ted's Flying Circus. Well, he certainly looked the part. He also looked a good deal like a typical all-American quarterback.

Our trip to Wiener Neustadt was long, tiresome, and uneventful. We ran into a little flak at a small town on the Adriatic coast, and that was virtually all the opposition we had. Other formations behind us encountered some fighter attacks, but on the whole the opposition was light. Over the target there was no heavy flak, and the light stuff we did encounter broke ineffectively beneath us. We landed in Tunis on schedule with no losses and next day flew back to Bengasi.

This was my eighth raid, and the first one I returned from with no battle damage to my aircraft. I had planned to go on all of them as long as I lasted or until I finished a tour. If I got through a combat tour of operations of course I wanted to go home. But we were told that squadron commanders should not expect as prompt a return to the States as individual crew members might. The story was that higher-ranking officers would be more subject to other demands and the general needs of the combat Air Force at the time their tours were complete. I felt if I did get a tour finished and had to stay on I would want to go on missions occasionally, but I wouldn't want to go on them all. A squadron commander or anybody else in the combat zone for that matter, can't hold much prestige if he is qualified for combat and doesn't sally forth occasionally, tour or no tour. A combat tour in heavy bombardment in the European Theater at that time was twenty-five missions. The fighter boys flew fifty, but the actual combat hours were approximately the same.

The news I received when I got back to Bengasi from Tunis was very annoying. Major Brooks told me that Colonel Wood and he had decided that henceforth squadron commanders would not go on every raid. They would be told what ones they might go on if they wished. Apparently it would be left somewhat to the squadron CO himself to volunteer to go. But his offer to lead a raid for his squadron or for the group would not always be accepted. I knew John had felt the squadron COs hadn't been functioning as they should. I thought some of his criticisms were justified, and some purely the result of envy. I felt particularly irked about John's attitude because I knew he had carried severe criticisms of the squadron COs to Colonel Timberlake. The latter hadn't the personal acquaintance with our abilities that someone in the group would naturally have. And so it was logical Colonel Timberlake would rely on John for some comment.

One day when I had had several reports of the program going on to discredit squadron commanders, I went up to the group operations hut and asked John if he would come to my tent with me. John came into the tent with apparent innocence. I told him I knew about some of the comments he had made to Colonel Timberlake concerning the efficiency of squadron commanders. I informed him also of all the details of the meeting of squadron COs that had been held back in El Paso resulting from comments he had made about Cross. "You probably don't know it," I said, "but had it not been for Paul Burton and me on that occasion you would have been thrown out. We went to bat for you and persuaded Colonel Lancaster to give you another chance. Your successor had already been chosen."

I mentioned that we all had heard rumors that Colonel Wood was shortly moving on to another job. I told John I had no ambition in the Army other than to do my share of fighting and then go back to Kentucky, that I'd as soon see him be group CO as anyone else if we could only get along, and that I certainly would not obstruct his military ambitions, but would like to keep the job I had.

I could see John was taken aback. He assured me I was mistaken. He criticized the other squadron COs but said he had always held me in high regard. He said a few other things I thought markedly inconsequential, and with that our discussion ended. I tried to leave him with the feeling I was intending still to make a sincere effort to get along with him, and generally just to get along in the work of running my squadron. I hoped no action would be taken regarding me or my command until the wing CO knew the picture well enough to judge fairly for himself about my capabilities. I felt that would be as good a break as anyone in my position would deserve.

With that off my mind and in compliance with the new group order against squadron COs flying every mission, I took a few days off and went to Alexandria. It was the first time I'd had off since leaving the States. Alexandria was a good change of scene for me. Dan Minnick, and one of our group intelligence officers, handle-bar mustachioed Major Marshall Exnicios, and I went together. We enjoyed sitting around the Union Bar paying a native "Gillie-Gillie-Man" to perform tricks for us. He did all his tricks of black magic while keeping up a running chant of "Gillie-Gillie-Gillie." He was superb. His chief artistry lay in the fact that, though he worked at such close range to his audience, usually just across the table, he still kept his trick well concealed. He had a bunch of white mice that he would pull from parts of an onlooker's clothing. The names of the mice were Sidi Barrani, Bengasi, and Alec Thompson.

A typical personality of Alexandria, as the place where currents of humanity meet, was a telephone operator in the Cecil Hotel. She whipped back and forth in seven different languages, handling all of them perfectly and saying usually little more than a word or two in one before switching to the next. I stood in the lobby and listened in stunned amazement to her performance. I always wanted to be polylingual.

After three days in Alexandria we returned to Bengasi. We ran right into a Hollywood performance scheduled for showing at our base. It was starring Jack Benny, Winni Shaw, Anna Lee, Larry Adler, and others. The show was terrific, particularly Jack Benny. It afforded us diversion for days mulling over the gags. I have heard much discussion since that time about Hollywood celebrities taking the line of least resistance in entertaining troops in the field. These certainly didn't. Their performance was superb in spite of the fact that they all looked worn out from their travels, dysentery, and the usual miseries of the Middle East.

After we bombed Wiener Neustadt everyone in the group was impatient to go back to England. A lot of the guys were sick. Nearly everyone but me had had dysentery at least once, and a rough case of dysentery leaves the stomach and intestines in a very delicate state for a very long time. All of us had lost weight and seemed to have less resistance than when we arrived. I think I fared as well as I did physically because towards the last of our stay in the desert my meals consisted of practically nothing but white bread and water. It wasn't that I liked bread but it was about the only clean thing we had to eat, and the rest of the stuff was certainly no more palatable than bread. Bread seemed to agree with me better than the average diet did the others, and so I crammed myself with it.

The last of my combat flying in the Middle East occurred when I led the group on a mission to one of the Italian airfields at Foggia. One day shortly after, the long-awaited order to move came in. We packed with great haste and departed for Marrakesh in French Morocco, where we spent part of the night. About midnight we took off for England. We were supposed to be flying a rather loose formation until it got light enough to see well; then if we had kept together well enough we planned to stack into a close formation flight the rest of the way. There was one hitch—the existence of a front off the Spanish coast that was accompanied by some pretty rough weather.

We took off on schedule and followed the plan almost exactly during the early part of the flight. We met the bad weather sometime after daylight, just as we were briefed to expect. I had the Lincolnesque Frank Ellis flying the right wing position on the ship that Fowble and I were in, and he was flying so close that I was a little nervous. I had had much to criticize about Ellis's formation flying and had taken him out of leading flights and set him to flying wing position on combat missions in spite of the fact that he was a flight commander, a captain, and in many ways an extremely capable officer. He was angry about it, but in a short time he became quite proficient in flying wing position. Now he was flying too close. After all, we had many hours to fly and he certainly didn't want to work himself to death on this trip. Then we began to hit weather.

It thickened and thickened. We hit patches of rain. Most of the clouds seemed to be low, and so we began to climb. We couldn't go on oxygen because we had more men aboard than there were oxygen masks. There was little we could do except go on instruments and fly through the stuff. I was in the pilot seat and Ed Fowble, for a change, was riding copilot. My friend Sollie down in the nose compartment kept shouting at me to hold a better heading. I wouldn't answer him over the interphone, for I think he thought Ed was flying. I would get four or five degrees off course and take my time about coming back to the proper heading. That made Sollie extremely angry. Sollie was from Brooklyn, and Ed and I got a lot of laughs out of hearing him shout and swear over the interphone in Brooklynese. I

finally settled down to doing a good job of instrument flying such
as he was used to.

After a few hours of flight through the weather in which I
was on instruments about half the time, except for some clearing
spots, we broke out on the other side. We looked around to find
only one airplane with us. It was the indomitable Frank Ellis.
After a short flight through clear weather we landed at one of
the fields near Newquay in Cornwall. We waited several hours
for the other ships to come in and then realized there were some
that failed to make it through the front. They were, I thought,
doubtless in Lisbon. We were told in case of emergency we
might go in there, but if we did we would be interned. One of
the ships, that of Lieutenant Lighter of my A Flight, we heard
giving calls indicating engine trouble and heading for Portugal.
That was the last we ever heard of that crew.

How wonderful England looked to us that day. From the first
glimpse I got of the spray-washed coast of Cornwall coming in,
to the last of the countryside I saw flying across England to our
base next day, it was lovely England. And though the dust of
the Middle Eastern desert was in our ships and would be for
some time, the effect of the desert was quickly out of mind. I
hated everything about Bengasi except for the swims in the
Mediterranean, and I cheerfully welcomed a theater of operations where the living was a little easier, even if the missions
were generally tougher. The airplanes were all given a complete
bath inside and out. Dead grasshoppers by the thousands were
washed out along with a few dozen scorpions in a current of
Middle Eastern mud, now to be mixed with the soil that "is
forever England."

We found our base little changed from the way it was when
we left it. The ground echelon of the squadrons had come in,
and the servicing of our unit was much better than it had been
before our departure. Almost overnight we were one again with
those who hadn't been to Africa. For some time the boys who
were left behind got pretty tired of hearing about all we had
done in the desert. I know my engineering section showed the
effect of it. My prized engineering officer Murph told me one
time that he hoped his crew chiefs wouldn't have to hear too

much more about what we were able to do in the line of maintenance in Africa with our extremely abbreviated maintenance section. Murph was a wise man. I took the hint and put out the word to the pilots to calm down in dealing with their newly reacquired ground crews. These men had been left in England to do nothing but be on KP and cleanup details while we were off to Africa being glamorized. There wasn't one of them who wouldn't have given a lot to be with us and endure all the hardships, to be able to crew his own airplane. I had a deep feeling of gratitude toward the ground crewmen of my squadron, as I'm sure most squadron COs had. For them there was little but bitter, rugged work—not glamorous, but indispensable.

When I arrived in England I heard rumors that my recommendation for promotion to the rank of major had gone in again. There were indications that this time it would go through. And sure enough about a week after I arrived at the old base it did come through. I had been the "junior squadron commander" for a long time—too long! Now I was no longer the junior. Captain Conroy, who succeeded Hank Yaeger, was the new junior.

From captain to major seemed quite a jump to me. Most civilians don't see the distinctions between the grades with the clear perspective that the military sees them. Officers up to and including the rank of captain are called "company grade" and are generally classed as "junior officers." From major to include full colonel they are "field grade" and "senior officers." The distinction applies frequently at officers' messes. It also applied frequently when orders came through requiring an officer to take a certain important assignment—so often the directive would say the officer selected must be "of field grade." I had held down a job for a long time that authorized me to be of field grade, and there had been times when the fact that I was not pained me. Indeed I thought I had bridged quite a military gap in this advancement and I also appreciated the increase in pay. There was an addition of about a hundred dollars a month that Anne and my son Peter could well use.

My pride in the squadron swelled mightily. I had come back to England with a much more sympathetic and tolerant attitude than I had when I left. I discovered it was only important that we fly the way we were supposed to and put our bombs on the target in order to bring about the greatest damage to the enemy. Discipline is a large part of this and smart appearance may have a little to do with it. But if a heavy bomber squadron is to reach anything like its humanly possible maximum in bombing efficiency, it must shortcut a lot of niceties. And when men are tired from continued physical exertion and mental strain, a CO must be able to gauge accurately the limits obtainable from them in matters of secondary importance. I felt in my men a strong response to those changes in me. Their response was a spirit of loyalty that made me happier than anything I had experienced in my military life.

The ability of my lead crews was being increasingly recognized in group headquarters. The way we bombed, with all ships dropping bombs on the leader, required special emphasis on training and proficiency of lead crews. Fowble's crew was recognized as one of the very best in the group. Ellis had started out slowly but was coming along fast now, as was Wright. I did everything I could to sell these crews in group headquarters so as to give my squadron more opportunities to lead the group. In the beginning of our operational work my squadron was low in its number of leads. Now it was at the top by a wide margin.

For the first few weeks after we got back to England we got little experience in operational work over Europe. I made one uneventful raid on an airfield in France. We came back just as it got dark and got jumped by fighters as we left the enemy coast. Their attacks didn't seem very determined, though it was a wonder they didn't follow us right back to our bases in the darkening afternoon and hit us while we were in the traffic pattern. That did happen once later, and it showed us what damage could be done at that particularly vulnerable moment.

It was then the second week in September of 1943 and General Mark Clark had made his landing at Salerno. He was hard put to hold his beachhead and every available bit of air power was called to assist him. It was not much of a surprise to us that Ted's Flying Circus, famous for its ability to move into a new position efficiently and quickly, would have to meet this call. I hadn't got used to being back in England in these two weeks or so we had been there and I didn't want to go to Africa again, but here was an assigned task and that was all there was to it. We were supposed to be going down to operate for a period of from two weeks to a month to bolster the Fifteenth Air Force. How long we would actually be gone was a matter we knew we had better not count on. This time we would go to Tunis. The new destination was far west of our old base at Bengasi. Bengasi had been termed Middle East and this was called North Africa. We remembered Tunis from our landing there after our long raid on Wiener Neustadt.

Anticlimax of anticlimaxes, but it was back to Africa! One of the things I hate worst in the world is an anticlimax, and war is full of them. It just wasn't won in the time I had planned it. This was a war where newspapers and magazines showed the enemy lines continually being split a dozen ways by great spearheads. How could the enemy withstand the spearheads we had pointed so ominously at them from all directions in Italy? How could the enemy stand it elsewhere? The newspapers showed maps with spearheads pointing in huge arcs. Every great slash was a partial encirclement. Then, as so many times after I read of "flanking attacks" "threatening to cut off" so many thousands of the enemy; strong units "pocketed," "trapped," or in any one of a dozen ways rendered hopeless in their efforts to avoid their inevitable fate. Didn't the enemy know what was going on? What was the sense in their trying to sustain such weak defenses, when all one had to do was to look at a paper to see how our great spearheads were smashing them to bits? I hated the pictorial representations of the progress of the war and I especially hated those maps with spearheads on them. I was going back to Africa just because the enemy had managed once more to blunt all our journalistic spearheads and break away to attack again. I made a mental note never to look at another war map.

How we got back to Africa, I don't remember. I remember being there, but I don't remember flying there. We found ourselves plunked into the lap of another group operating from a small, inadequate base at Tunis. We were as welcome as the visiting in-laws. The theory was that with a minimum of effort on the part of everyone, each squadron of our group could be processed and serviced by a squadron of the group permanently stationed there. I was lucky to be stationed with a squadron that had an incompetent major commanding. Without ever saying it, I convinced him I ranked him by a long time. Actually, he had received his promotion to major about two months prior to our arrival, and I had received mine about two weeks before that date. I did have a much lower serial number than his and that convinced him. I never "pulled my rank" on him, but I left in his mind a strong suspicion that I might if I didn't get what I wanted. I have always hated the sort of officer who resorts to pulling rank, but I had to veer a little bit here to keep my men from suffering. And the result of this bluff was that my boys ate better, had more transportation, were better housed and cared for than they might have been. But in spite of it all, we didn't fare so well.

Africa was turning from a furnace to a quagmire. We had such quaint occurrences as cloudbursts. Our tent was on the side of a hill that kept water from standing in the floor, but during the rain there was little we could do but pull up the sides of the tent and lie in our cots while the water ran through in a solid sheet. After an hour or so, if we were lucky, we could walk to the mess hall without completely bogging down in the muck.

As the days passed Murph, my engineering officer and tent-mate, made living a little easier for us, for he turned up with some eggs, which were a special treat. I discovered he had located the family of a French farmer nearby and had taken the jeep I had talked out of our host, the other squadron commander, and visited them. He carried some candy he had bought at an American PX to "le petit enfant de la Famille." Though he had a vocabulary of about twenty words, when he said the ones he knew with gestures you'd think he was glib at it. But his pronunciation was superb, and, given a month to practice the language, he would have it down pat, both grammar and idiom. For the moment it was good enough to produce fresh eggs.

In spite of rains and mud we did operate. The worst part of the trip by far was the fact that, though we had come post haste, we really served no great purpose when we arrived. The crisis had passed with General Clark's army. That might have been foreseen, but no risk could be taken that it might have gone otherwise. We had come to be available if needed and I could understand that. Those ground soldiers must have had some bitter times on that beachhead. And I wished that since we were there, the order sending us might have come sooner, so that we could have helped more. As it was, most of our operations were against several rail junctions in northern Italy and the port town of Bastia in northern Corsica. Though these raids were of some benefit to the armies in Italy, they were, for the most part, considered "milk runs" by our crews.

After running two or three missions that seemed only moderately important, we heard a rumor that we might bomb Wiener Neustadt again. It hadn't been bombed since that day back in August when we hit it from Bengasi. From Tunis the raid wouldn't be as long as the first one was, which was one real advantage. When we first heard that we might be going back many thought that it would be a long but easy mission. The idea behind that was that we'd been there before and met only meager opposition, and so we should find it easy to go there again. I disagreed. I knew from the intelligence reports that we had on the importance of the installations there that the Nazis must have bolstered their defenses a great deal. I felt it would be the same old story told about many heavy bomber units hitting an important target the second time. The second time you usually get your pants shot off.

Then too, I had heard stories about flak guns—that only brand new flak guns are extremely accurate. After firing even a comparatively few rounds the carriages loosen up, so that the guns are much less accurate firing on a formation flying at twenty-three or twenty-four thousand feet. When we were over Wiener Neustadt before there was no heavy flak. Whatever guns they had there now, I reasoned, would probably be new ones, since they certainly wouldn't bring in used guns to a place as important as that. In addition to my reasoned ideas, I had a host of unexplainable suspicions that the second raid on Wiener Neustadt, if run now by us, would be a very rough raid.

After a few days of rumors I got word that we really would run the raid. There was no particular pressure on me to go. In any case, I wouldn't be allowed to lead the group or even be deputy leader. Thus if I went it would be merely to lead my squadron. But one thing entered the picture to make it a little different. That was that General Jimmie Hodges, our division commander, would be in the lead ship of our group and with us he would be leading the three groups flying that day. When the general rode, the bars were down for other subordinate unit commanders. That is, though I might generally be limited to fly on those missions where I might be group leader or deputy group leader, if the general flew I could fly in any capacity I could fit into. At that time I didn't know General Hodges except as one of the big names far up the line. He was older than many of the young generals of the Air Corps. In the latter class would fall our wing commander, the newly promoted Brigadier-General Ted Timberlake. But General Hodges by this and other similar indications was giving us to understand that he considered himself a combat man. He not only considered himself one, but I came to find out he really was one.

I had known if there was another trip to this Austrian airplane factory I would be on it. I set up Ed Fowble to lead my squadron of six ships flying the low left position on the group lead. Ed and I had seen some rough ones together. We rode over Messina together in the old days before the Sicilian invasion began and saw the best flak the Jerries had to offer in Sicily; we ran the gauntlet at Ploesti together, and we'd damn well take a second look at Wiener Neustadt together.

The raid was held up a day or two after the first briefing because the runway, which had no hard surface, was too muddy to bear our loaded airplanes. It is a bad thing to hold up a mission after it has been briefed. Somehow we felt that it was evident there were leaks in our security, and we were continually afraid the enemy intelligence knew in advance where we were going. After a couple of days of weather without rain we got up just before dawn one morning to hear that this was the day. We got another hurried briefing chiefly on the weather, ate one meal and took another in the form of K rations with us to the ships.

We took off and assembled our group over the field and headed out on the long course. We were going across the Italian peninsula, then up the Adriatic Sea to the hip of the boot and on into Austria. We would turn left when abreast of our target and make a bombing run from east to west. After leaving the target we would let down a thousand feet or so to facilitate regrouping of the formation, turn left again, and come home.

The mission went about as planned. One surprise was that over Italy on the way in we flew over a town where we got a good deal of unexpected flak. We swore at our intelligence for not warning us about the guns there. There had been absolutely nothing said about them at briefing. But then the Germans were withdrawing in Italy, and it was likely the guns had just been moved in from a point farther south. It was a good excuse, but little consolation to us. We were a long way from the target to be running any risk of flak damage. We felt bursts all around our ship, but we suffered no apparent damage, and on we went.

We turned up the Adriatic and progressed on into Austria. We made our turn and started from the IP—the initial point— into the target. A few minutes later we were on the bombing run. Just as we started, and even when there were long minutes to go before we reached our bomb release line, huge black flak bursts suddenly puffed up all around us. It was a clear day, we were at about fifteen thousand feet, which was a moderately easy range for heavy guns. One thing proved the type of fire being directed at us—there was no cloud of flak ahead of us to fly into. The very first shells that went off broke almost between our engine nacelles. That let us know it was aimed fire, and not a barrage. The guns were brand new—they had to be to shoot like that. They were not the 88 mm. type; they were 105s.

Here I would like to correct a frequent fallacy made by writers describing bombing raids. The noise a bomber pilot hears is awful, but that noise isn't the loud noise of shells bursting. The pilot is encased in many thicknesses of clothing—even his head is almost completely covered. Tightly clamped against his ears are his headphones, built into his helmet. Out of these headphones comes most of the noise he hears. The horrible screaming is the noise of the enemy radio-jamming apparatus. It is like a death cry of the banshees of all the ages. On our missions it usually started faintly in our headphones as we neared the enemy coast and grew louder and louder. A pilot had to keep the volume of his receiver turned up high in order to hear commands over the air through the bedlam of jamming. After a few hours of it I felt that I would go crazy if I didn't turn the volume down. I would turn it down when I was out of the target area, but I knew when I did that I might be missing an important radio order or a call from another ship asking for help or direction in one way or another.

We could hear the firing of our own guns. Chiefly we could hear the top turret. In addition to the noise of the top turret we could hear the nose guns, the waist guns, the ball turret, and finally the tail turret. We really couldn't hear the tail turret, but after we had ridden in our bombers for a while there was a peculiar faint vibration that would run down the skin of the ship and up the seats to let us know little Pete Peterson of Fowble's crew was warming up his guns. When Pete's guns chattered, some Nazi always regretted it. And when I felt the vibrations of his guns coming through the seat of my pants it was like someone scratching a mosquito bite in the middle of my back.

But then about the flak. You could hear it—faintly. When flak was very very near you could see the angry red fire as the shells exploded before the black smoke formed. You could hear the bursts sounding like "wuff, wuff, wuff" under your wings. You could see the nose of the ship plowing through the smoke clouds where the bursts had been. You could hear the sprinkle of slivers of shrapnel go through the sides of the ship if they were hitting close to you. I always said that if you hear the flak —if you get the "wuff, wuff, wuff"—and really hear it over the screaming of the radio and other sounds, then it is deadly close. You don't realize the terror it strikes into some airmen's hearts until you've had your own plane shot to hell a few times. I laughed at Franco's flak coming through Gibraltar. It wasn't much flak, but I wouldn't laugh six months later when I had seen more of it.

And yet with the increasing terror came a greater understanding that there was little a heavy bomber pilot in the midst of a large formation could do about flak. There came a determined calm to contain one's terror. The leader of a large group or a larger combat wing formation knew that attempts at "eva-sive action" simply could not be made anywhere that enemy fighters were active. Usually the worst flak we saw was while we were on or closely approaching the bombing run, when we could not afford to make turns for any reason, except to put the bom-bardier over the target. After the bombs were away, if the for-mation was one of medium or larger size—that is, twenty-four ships or more—the wisdom of turns, except as briefed, was ques-tionable. If fighters were about such turns might loosen the formation. Loosening the formation meant greater vulnerability to fighter attacks. The way we were flying there was really noth-ing you could do when the flak started breaking around your ship but sit and look at it—and pray. If we knew some localities on the route in or out were heavily defended we would try to fly around them. But once in flak, we just had to look at it.

That was certainly the way it was our second trip over Wie-ner Neustadt. The shells broke on all sides of us as we went in. We heard the angry "wuff-wuff-wuff" of the bursts above the maniac's ball of noise coming over the radio. We could see the flare of fire in the bursts of the shells. I was looking out to the right of the ship. The formation was good and tight in spite of the flak, and to the high right of my ship was the lead squadron and the ship in which General Jimmie was flying. Just under his left wing was an airplane flown by a Lieutenant Matson of Paul Burton's squadron. General Hodges's plane was piloted by the indefatigable Captain Ken Caldwell, the group first pilot in whom Colonel Wood and Major Brooks had the greatest con-fidence.

As I looked out on that hell of shellfire I think I felt as much terror as I have ever felt in an airplane. For some reason I think I was more frightened than I had been over Ploesti. I can't ex-plain it unless it had seemed to me this was a raid that would be costly without reasonable results to compensate. Somehow we had no adequate purpose on this raid to bolster up our cour-age. I felt it was just a "big raid" to give bomber command some satisfaction for having sent us to Africa.

As I was looking out watching the group leader and wonder-ing how any of us could get through the fire, I saw a direct burst of a shell center the bomber directly to my right front—Matson's ship. It was in the low left element of the lead squadron, and almost in front of me—a little high and to the right. Matson's Lib was perhaps a little more in line with the ship of Mac McLaughlin than with my own. Mac was flying his beloved *Ole Irish* on my right wing. But the hit Lib was so close in front of both of us that I wondered how we were going to get by. When the shell went off inside the bomber the sides of it seemed to puff out momentarily. It didn't blow to bits, but big chunks of it flew off and tongues of flame licked out of its spread seams in all directions. The stricken plane pulled up right in front of us. We nosed our ship down, and so did Mac. The flaming Lib then pulled up high and out to the left, pieces falling off of it all the way. As we went by and under it we could see it glowing like the inside of a furnace.

The next moment our bombs were away. Then in another moment Sergeant Le Jeune, our Louisiana Cajan flight engineer, was trying to get the bomb bay doors closed. The bombardier hadn't been able to close them from the nose compartment. Communication with our crew stations in the rear was cut off. Flak had evidently cut the interphone lines. It had also cut several of the hydraulic lines in the bomb bay and consequently the bomb doors wouldn't go closed. With the bomb doors open our ship wouldn't fly as fast as the others without use of excessive power. That meant one of two things: either we would drop behind and run the danger of being hit by enemy fighters, or we would stay up with the formation by using added power and run the danger of giving out of gas before we got back across the Mediterranean. It seemed a long way home at that point.

Sergeant Le Jeune went out on the catwalk and hung between the gaping doors, the icy wind blowing through, and the whole inside of the bomb bay including the precarious point of his footing covered with slippery hydraulic fluid. He tried to pull or kick the doors closed. Finally he decided to cut in the last reserve of hydraulic fluid to get the doors closed. The hydraulic lines would be temporarily charged and the doors might close before all the reserve supply of fluid ran out. If so, that would mean that when we got back we would have to use the emergency manual procedures to get the landing gear and the flaps down and we would probably be without brakes. Le Jeune had done his best—even hanging head down in the open bomb bay and pulling at the doors—so this seemed to be the only other thing to do. He crept aft on the catwalk and cut in the reserve supply. Then I moved the lever to the "Close doors" position and the doors slammed shut as the remaining fluid poured out like blood from open veins into the bomb bay.

Later Le Jeune made another checkup inside the bomb bay. He found one serious fuel leak that already had filled the inside of the ship with heavy gas fumes, but he managed to get this patched well enough so that, though the fumes were heavy, the additional loss of fuel was slight. With that job completed, I asked him to go aft again and check particularly to see if the crew members were all right. I had not been able to use the interphone to any of the rear stations, and I thought it likely that someone might have been hit in the midst of that flak storm. Then I took stock of the ship and was happy to see that all the engines were apparently functioning okay. Ed and I could tell quite easily that the cables to the control trim were cut, but with both of us on the main controls we managed to keep the ship steady without too much difficulty.

The formation had loosened during the last minute of the bomb run and now began to close up again. We were clear of the target and at last out of the field of fire of the guns below. We were not at that moment under enemy fighter attack, but we could hear many distress calls over our radio coming from other ships and other formations in the rear not as lucky as ourselves. We held a tight formation and evidently that sufficed to render us at least temporarily immune. On such missions it always became a contest in formation flying. The Jerries jumped the loosest formation and shot it to pieces. It behooved us to fly better formation than some other group in order not to be elected.

In a few minutes Sergeant Le Jeune came forward and reported that all personnel in the rear were okay, though there were holes in the ship by the score, big and small. Our trim tab cables were beyond repair and one of the main aileron cables was partly cut through. It might give way, but there were enough strands holding so that if we handled the ship gingerly we stood a good chance of getting home. I knew it was by the grace of God and nothing else that we could have so much flak damage and yet none of it critical.

We kept our place in the formation and after two endless hours found ourselves a long way out on the way home. We were almost beyond the point where fighter attack was likely. As we passed north of Rome we saw a great flak barrage thrown up, but we flew around it. The flight across the Mediterranean seemed almost interminable. I was wondering all the time about the difficulties we might have in landing our ship. Finally, just about as our navigator Sollie predicted, we saw the misty coast of Africa ahead. The formation, which had loosened up a bit on the flight across the water, tightened up again to get in proper shape for the peel off to land.

There were many other ships that had obviously suffered flak damage, but we seemed to be in worse shape than any of those that had made it back from the target. I called the formation lead plane to say that we would pull out of formation and wait until all the other ships had landed before we came in. We had enough fuel left to risk the wait, and we didn't want to take a chance on blocking a runway when there were others behind still to land. We got acknowledgment of our message and pulled out of the formation in a gentle diving turn to the left. We had had about four and a half hours of anxiety.

The group was lined up in tight formation going over the field in the direction for landing. Now the peel off was beginning and one after another of the big ships banked sharply to the left and swung around the traffic circle, putting landing gear and flaps down to land in rapid succession. We hovered above and waited. Finally the last ship cleared the runway. We called in for our landing and started the arduous process of getting the landing gear down by the manual emergency procedure. Sergeant Le Jeune went through it as though he had to do it every day. Finally he got the big wheels cranked down after cranking the winch back in the bomb bay until his back almost broke. He checked the gear and announced to us in the cockpit, "Gear down and locked."

We turned on the base leg, putting it far back from the field. I started the manual system of working the flaps, broke the safe-tying wire, and began vigorously pumping the hand pump. I was afraid that the pump wouldn't work because I watched the flap indicator for about the first fifty pumps and saw nothing happen. But finally the pressure built up enough so that the flaps started slowly down. I managed to get them down about half way as we were on the final approach to the runway and I left them there. Sergeant Le Jeune had ordered the waist gunners to go as far to the rear as possible so that they would weigh the tail of the plane down. We would probably want to drag the tail on landing, because it was obvious we would have little or no brake pressure. As a rule the accumulators hold brake pressure up pretty well even though the rest of the hydraulic system is gone. But once the brakes are applied, they must be held in the on position. If the central hydraulic system is out when they are let up, the accumulator pressure goes out.

We touched down easily, nose higher than usual. Ed pulled back on the wheel and I helped him on my wheel, so that the nose rose even higher until we could hear the tail skid touch and drag down the rough runway. Dragging might buckle a rear bulkhead, but that would be all right. It would slow us down and prevent going off the end of the runway with a possible landing gear failure on the uneven ground beyond.

The ship slowed down more and more until it became neces-sary to let the nose down. It wouldn't stay up any longer. The nose wheel came down pretty hard and we were wondering if the nose strut would fail, leaving us down by the bow. It held. "Brake her, Ed," I said. "We'll see what we've got." Ed applied the pressure and the brakes took hold. He held his pressure on them until the ship stopped. Then he tried them again, but the pressure gauges showed his last pressure gone. We cut the en-gines and left the hulk that had flown like an airplane to be towed in by tugs. It wasn't safe to taxi without brakes.

The landing and general handling of the ship had been a

tribute to Ed Fowble and his crew. Sergeant Le Jeune and Ed had done everything the way the Consolidated handbook prescribes handling emergencies. The result was that the crew was safe and sound, and the ship had only battle damage. We got out of it and looked it over. Holes were poked through it in every direction. A couple of the members of the crew had been hit by flak, which had failed to puncture their flak suits. We had turned out to be too tough a nut for the Nazi defenses to crack. Besides the myriad of holes in the wings and fuselage we noticed the sad old ship dismally leaked gas out of several of her self-sealing fuel cells, which had been punctured. They were going to have to be replaced, but the self-sealing feature of their construction had worked well enough to slow the fuel leaks so that the amount of fuel lost coming home was not critical. Here was old *I* for Item, the second one Fowble had had, in which he had taken no less pride than the first. She would fly again, but not until a great deal of work had been put in on her. I said a prayer of thanks that we all got home.

I felt this would probably be my last raid in Africa—a happy thought. At least rumors had it that this would be the last. After this we should be ready to go back to England for good. And yet I felt some melancholy mixed with happiness that this was probably the end of Africa. I had seen a good number of our boys go down that day, which was not easy to forget.

When I went to dinner I found the great Murph there. He had prepared for my return by bartering for a bottle of red Tunisian wine and a loaf of good French bread. I drank almost the whole bottle of wine and ate several big chunks of bread and then curled up on the cot and went to sleep.

The next day the squadron commanders were called over to Colonel Wood's headquarters. We were told to bend every effort toward getting our ships ready. The rains would soon set in for good and he wanted to lose no time in getting out. That was the best news I had had in ages.

As I came out of the tent I saw the smiling face of Mac McLaughlin waiting for me. Mac had some pieces of metal in his hand. "Thought you might like some of these," he said.

"What are they?"

"Pieces of Matson's ship. They lodged in my number one engine nacelle. Pieces of that ship hit both of us. I guess I got most of them, though. You might want these and you might not. Anyway, here they are if you do." And, of course, I did.

I went to the area where my ships were parked and told Sergeant Peterson, my line chief, to turn on full steam to get the ships ready. Those boys on the line already had the rumor about leaving and were working like beavers. They got news by some medium that is faster than two-way radio. I've known engineering men on the line to know a mission was scrubbed before it was announced in operations.

I walked from ship to ship noting the damage. Much of it could be repaired in England. Jobs of patching holes in most cases, if they were just holes in the airplane skin, wouldn't be done here. New fuel cells had to be put in several ships because the Wiener Neustadt guns had let too much sun into the old ones. On my tour of inspection I picked up two more pieces of flak which had come out of the airplanes and which I wanted as additional mementos of hell over Austria.

In a very few days we had the first ships ready to go. The rest were just about ready. This time I decided to fly with Wright on the trip back. Sergeant Peterson told me Ed Fowble's ship would probably be ready to go the same day as the rest of them, but for a later takeoff. If not it would be no more than a day late. And so we planned takeoff of the first ships for early one morning about a week after the trip to Austria. We were given a forecast of good weather to Marrakesh. The moment seemed propitious, and with the sharp edge of dawn we were warming up engines. I had said goodbye to Ed and received his unnecessary assurances that he would not be far behind. No one would ever leave Ed far behind. When I got into our ship I didn't even look back at the field where we had been so singularly uncomfortable for the month past. We didn't circle, we just turned on course to Marrakesh and kept going.

Arriving in Marrakesh, I was suffering from a virulent case of dysentery. I had had a touch of it at the time of takeoff, but upon landing my tummy was sending signals one right after the other which were unmistakable. This was my first attack out of two trips to Africa, and it was starting out to make up for my past immunity. My intestines were writhing like a basketful of snakes and occasional flashes of pain made me think of hara-kiri. I reported directly to the infirmary where I found a doctor busying himself with a patient. He looked at me and, without even asking me what the trouble was, he said, "I'll be with you in just a minute; I've got just the stuff to fix you up." He put a bottle of white liquid and some pills in my hand. "Take these according to direction," he said. I must have looked decidedly green to make diagnosis so simple because I hadn't said a word. I took the medicine and tried to eat a little. After that I lay on a cot I found in one of the buildings kept for transient officers until the time for the briefing for the night takeoff.

I must have slept an hour or so before Bob Wright came in to wake me. We walked over to the briefing room together. I was weak but happy and confident that in a few hours I would shake the dust of Africa from my shoes for the last time. Ted's Flying Circus was about to wind up its last road show and go back to the big town for keeps. I sat in the briefing not listening to much that was said. Yes, the weather would be bad part of the way— nothing to worry about—this is the route you follow, etc., etc. Then Lieutenant Colonel Bob Miller, our group air executive, wormed his way through the seated crewmen to my chair. "I want to see you," he said and walked out. I followed him.

Outside he turned and said, "Did you hear about Fowble?"

"What is it?"

"He just crashed. A few miles north of the field. Out of gas. Men in the tower saw his landing lights go on and saw him glide in trying to make a dead stick landing. The ship burned. All of them were killed instantly except Sergeant Mike and Sergeant Le Jeune. They are in a serious condition but have been able to tell a little bit of the story."

Ed had been unable to get properly gassed up at Tunis. He also had a slight fuel leak in addition to the ones that had been discovered and repaired after the ship's last mission. Being given a good weather report, he had taken off with less than a full load of fuel. He would not be left behind, and waiting for more fuel made a difference of enough hours so that his flight would have been delayed until the next day. Bad weather, plus a slight variation from course, plus the slight fuel leak combined to make the plane run out of gas within a mile or two of the field. And now, except for two, they were all dead. I thought of Ed and Byrd, his copilot, and Phifer and Sollie, the bombardier and navigator, and little Pete, the tail gunner, and all the others. I prayed that Sergeants Le Jeune and Mike might live, but the later news was that they lingered only a short while and died.

The news of this incident hit me with soul-shaking impact. "Please tell Wright I'll wait for him in the ship," I said. I left the building where the briefing was going on and wandered through the desert darkness the mile or so out to where our plane was parked. I crawled into it and curled up on the flight deck. I don't think I really went to sleep. I think I sank into a kind of morose stupor.

When next I remembered anything we were winging our way out over the ocean. Someone had thrown an Army blanket over me. I could hear the drone of the engines and the noise of the radio man at my feet pecking out his message to Casablanca radio hundreds of miles to the rear. And I could see a star out the little bit of window visible from where I lay.

5

The Air War
of Western Europe

Once again in England there was much rearrangement work to be done in order to get the group in shape to fly as a proper part of the Eighth Air Force. It was evident that the days of Ted's Flying Circus were gone. The group was merged into a large bombing organization that would not permit operation as a small strike force moving wherever current need directed. The circus was through, though the blood and spirit of its men had marked the progress of the war from El Alamein to Bizerte and from the Carpathians of Romania to the Alpine foothills of Austria.

I was glad to see my friends of the old group who had been left behind us at the base in England. I was sick and weak from dysentery and loss of weight, and there was still the pain aching inside me at the loss of Fowble and his crew. Four months before they'd been a bunch of kids, and since that time they had lost completely the youthful facade which tears so easily in combat. Now their lives were ended, but they had inflicted grievous damage on the enemy and paid a thousandfold interest on the labor and expense of their training. Circumstances had doubtless combined in similar ways many times during this war. But to me the case of this crew was different. At the least it was in the highest category of magnificent and patriotic behavior.

The days succeeding my arrival brought in the stragglers. Captain Frank Ellis and his crew had still not arrived. Frank had brought home a ship on one of the last raids in Africa that was so shot to pieces he had to leave it where it landed. Consequently, he had to depend on Air Transport Command to get him and his crew back. His old ship had borne the letter *E—E* for Ellis, we called it. It had hurt Frank to leave that ship. "Never mind," I told him. "When you get back to England you'll have a new *E* for Ellis; I promise you the next new airplane we get." When I got in there was a new Liberator waiting for delivery to my squadron. I gave the order to paint the large *E* on the tail. It was parked in Frank's old parking place, where I knew he would be glad to see it.

The other ships were cleaned up in a hurry. We had to get right into operations because bad weather for flying is the normal thing in the English winter, and we had to take fullest advantage of the remaining good weather of late fall.

In the time we had been operating in England before the group had bombed a couple of airfields in France, but we had never crossed the border of the Reich. Now we were excited and nervous about the prospect of carrying the fight home to Germany. It was just the normal feeling about getting our feet wet for the first time. We knew until we did we couldn't fully consider ourselves a part of the air war of Western Europe.

One morning just before dawn we were rolled out of our sacks to go to the briefing room. The layout as to who would fly the mission had been planned the day before. Lieutenant Colonel Miller, group air executive, was to lead as air commander and would fly in the number one plane. I would be deputy lead and fly on his right wing to take over in case anything happened to him. We were briefed to go to Vegesack, Germany. It seemed at that time a long way to go over hotly defended enemy territory. About three months later when we had friendly fighter cover it wouldn't have seemed half so far. When the target for the day was announced to the crews in the briefing room and they knew that we were really hitting Germany for the first time, there was no chorus of cheers. I have heard much about cheers from combat men upon such momentous occasions. I'm sure such responses don't come from units whose combat losses are anything like ours were. We were going to Germany and, with no support from friendly fighter planes and unlike heroes of fiction, we did not cheer. We sat in grim silence. We were all cowards at heart. We had come too far along in combat to kid ourselves about that. But we knew how to control our cowardice and, by controlling it, how to draw much blood from the enemy. There was no reason to cheer. You wouldn't fool anybody. The guy next to you knew the way you felt about it just as he knew his own feeling.

I was going to ride with Bob Wright. Bob was the last remaining pilot of my once magnificent C Flight. He was a tall, lazy looking Texan from Austin who had a broad streak of Pete Hughes and Ed Fowble running through him. His one-engine landing on Sicily the day the invasion began proved that.

There were three groups of B-24s going to Vegesack. The B-17s of the Eighth Air Force were also going out that day, but they were bombing targets in another area. They had all the friendly fighters assigned to cover their operation.

After the briefing we all went to the equipment room to get our flying gear. We collected a veritable mountain of electrically heated suits with gloves and boots which plugged into the suits. The suit was connected by a wire and plug which led to a power outlet in the ship. I always called the electric cord which joined the suit to the socket in the ship an "umbilical cord." Whenever I asked for that item of equipment by that name, the men checking out gear would be confused. Finally, they came to know what I meant, and because the cord had no particular name, my name for it was generally used as the proper one.

Besides the suits we got oxygen masks, flak suits, steel helmets, escape kits, and many other things. And with all this load of equipment we went to our ship. I chatted with the crew chief —that is, the chief ground crew mechanic assigned to our plane —until time to fire up the engines. Then Bob Wright and I donned our pile of gear and climbed laboriously through the bomb bay, past the load of big eggs all fused and ready for the Krauts, and onto the flight deck.

Sergeant Kelly Altshuler, the dark-eyed Chicagoan riding as

our engineer, yelled "clear!" as I turned switches on. One by one
the big props turned over, as one by one engines spat, hesitated,
and then broke out in a roar as they caught. We saw Colonel
Miller taxi by to take the place at the head of the takeoff runway, where he waited for the other ships to line up back of him.
There they would wait in a given order of sequence for takeoff.
As he went by us we pulled out of our hard stand and waddled
down the taxi strip behind him.

Those moments of waiting for takeoff have been called anxious, uncertain, or tense by those who write about them, and
they are all of that. When I reported to a ship before a mission
I always tried to get the serious job of checking ship and equipment done thoroughly but quickly. After that I would try to fill
any spare moment with light banter in order to get a laugh if I
could. At that moment a laugh means everything. Signs of nervousness on the part of the ranking officer immediately infect
all others, and so I tried to play clown.

After a little while we got our signal for takeoff. We rose
above the end of the runway and circled behind the lead ship as
the group formed over the field. We formed up the group and
joined with the other two groups leading on ahead of us. This
much was accomplished without incident. Then the three groups
of Libs struck out across the North Sea in the direction of the
Dutch coast. During the crossing our heavy load of bombs and
gas made our planes labor as we reached altitude. I watched the
lead ship on whose wing we were flying and also continually
checked the rest of the formation. At any time I might be called
upon to take over the lead, and I wanted to anticipate that eventuality.

When I saw the coast of Holland ahead I called the navigator, McClain. "Mac, are we hitting the coast at the briefed
point?"

"Yes, sir. Just about. Maybe a mile or two south, but it's
okay."

"Keep checking our navigation. Don't rely on the lead ship."
"Right."

Just as I finished talking with Mac I noticed the lead plane
wavering. I couldn't tell what was wrong. It was weaving about,

not behaving at all as a ship leading a formation is supposed to. I switched from interphone back to radio. Colonel Miller was calling me.

"We're having engine trouble. Don't know what it is yet. You may have to take over. Stand by."

"Roger, wilco," I said.

Just as we crossed the enemy coast the lead airplane began a series of zooms indicating it was aborting. It peeled out of formation in a diving turn to the right and passed under us heading back to England. Well, I thought, it looks like I have the honor of taking the boys on their first trip to Germany. The weather was clear and I could see the two groups ahead of us leading the way in. I got on my radio. "Attention all ships of Bourbon Blue formation. Deputy leader taking over. Stack it in."

The other ships of the formation seemed to show momentary indecision when the leader pulled out. But I told Bob to pull off some power to make it easier for them to close in on us. We slowed up until we were creeping along at a bare 150 miles per hour indicated airspeed. When the other ships closed in on us we put on a little more power. Then I switched again to interphone. "Mac, keep on the ball down there. We will follow the leading formation ahead of us, but let's know where we are." And then to the bombardier, "McSween, you are now holding the baby. Try to get as much dope set in your bombsight as you can while we're going along."

"Roger, roger," came the answers over the interphone.

The formation ahead of us turned south and we followed them at proper interval. As yet no sign of any enemy fighters. Where are they? I wondered. They know exactly where we are. The German ground sector control system plots us perfectly. They must be waiting for the perfect moment to make the "bounce." There was some scattered flak off to our left, but we would get none of it.

"Sir, the formation ahead has missed its turning point." Mac was keeping on the ball.

"That's all right," I said. "We'll follow them for a while. Maybe they will turn shortly."

On they went, not giving a sign that they knew they were off course. I switched to another radio frequency and called "Bourbon Leader" in the lead group. I got no answer, though I made several attempts to get him. Then at last they turned east. They were far south of where they should have been. Before long the lead group turned again heading northeast, which, according to our plotting, was just about the heading to take us over Vegesack. The second of the three groups, immediately ahead of us, did not make this second turn but kept going straight east.

"What do you want to do?" asked Bob in his typically casual manner.

"We'll follow the lead group. To hell with those other fellows. If they don't know which way to go to get to the target, we'll just let them go."

We turned to the northeast. The formation now ahead of us, which was the lead group of the three, was almost out of sight. We could see them obviously on their bomb run. Then they turned north, apparently having bombed and now on their route out to the North Sea. As we approached our briefed target area we saw it was covered by an extremely effective smoke screen. The wind was blowing just right to carry the smoke over the target. In those days we didn't have any real method of bombing on instruments, and so smoke constituted quite a problem. Sometimes when you make a run into a target directly up- or downwind the streamers of smoke from smoke pots function less effectively, and it is possible to see parts of a target through channels in the smoke. That day we could see nothing. A heavy haze added to the difficulty.

Finally, McSween called me: "I've got a target in the sight. Steady now. I'm not sure it's the one we are supposed to hit, but it is the only one I can see."

We held the course prescribed by the bombardier for a seeming infinity until at last we saw the indicator lights on the instrument panel flashing their message that the bombs were falling.

"Bombs away," called McSween.

We had just entered the flak defences of Vegesack and bursts were blossoming on all sides of us. Occasional shells kicked the ship around, and again I could hear the menacing "wuff, wuff, wuff" as the bursts centered close to us. The fuss over my radio was terrific, but I could hear the flak bursts. That meant we were getting hit.

We turned north and headed out of the flak area. I looked off to my high right. There red-headed Smitty was leading a flight of three ships. He was flying Frank Ellis's brand new *E* for Ellis. His own plane was in the shop, and I had to give him Frank's plane for this trip, though Frank had not yet arrived from Africa to consent to the arrangement. I saw two extremely close bursts ahead of Smitty. I saw the wing of the Lib split the black clouds of smoke left by the bursts, and then I saw it yaw and dip a little. He was hit; I hoped not hard. How I hoped! He was trying to hold position, but the plane was wallowing, and I saw a rope of greasy black smoke start from his number three engine and grow into a great, black streamer. Then Smitty called me.

"I'm hit pretty hard. Lost number three. Oxygen lines out. Can't stay with you, so I'm letting down."

"Good luck, Smitty. I'm praying for you. Take it easy."

At that time our instructions were that a leader could not jeopardize his formation for one crippled bomber. The absolute rule was not to deviate from the plan of attack or withdrawal to aid stragglers. Later it was a little different because it was proved possible for a formation to alter its plan of flight in such a way as to save some of the cripples. One factor in the change was that on later missions there was generally friendly fighter support. We had no friendly support, and were ordered not to risk an entire formation in attempting to save one or two stragglers.

Regretfully, I watched Smitty losing altitude. Then my attention was called to another ship of the formation. It was *R* for Roger, of Paul Burton's squadron. A lieutenant named Furst was flying it, and he evidently had his oxygen lines knocked out. He let down to the left and Smitty pulled his ship over in that direction.

Just then I heard a call over the interphone from one of the waist gunners. "Fighters at eight o'clock high." This meant, of course, they were coming in above us from our rear, left-hand quarter. They made one pass on the formation and then zoomed off to the left in the direction of the two cripples. Five Ju88s, the German twin-engined fighters, made repeated attacks on those two ships. Our waist gunner gave us a continuing report of the fight, since he could see what was going on in that quarter much better than we could from the cockpit.

"Gee, those Libs are catching hell," he moaned. "There goes Furst, he's on fire going down, but there are two Ju88s down." Shortly after that our gunner lost sight of Furst. It was evident R for Roger was lost. It was burning hard on the way down. Maybe the crew got out. We never knew.

Then we lost sight of Smitty, who was far to our rear still fighting like a porpoise beset by barracuda. He had all guns going, and when last we saw him he was inflicting as much sting as he could.

We were out of flak. We got two or three more halfhearted attacks by fighters, but our formation was good and the Nazis seemed to have little spirit that day to continue. We went out past the coast toward the island of Helgoland which was off to the right spewing up more flak. We were not going to go over that patch. After flying north a while we turned west toward home. All the way home I thought of Smitty, a quiet redhead and a very shy, fine person. I again recalled his wanting me to be the best man in his wedding. Smitty was gone. He hadn't had a chance. Was it my fault? I had done just as I had been instructed to do many times, but even so, could I have done otherwise than I had without risking my formation? I wondered. There was Furst, too, doubtless another fine pilot with a great crew. I had not known him well and naturally my feelings were not quite like they were about Smitty, with whom I had been closely associated for many months.

At length we sighted England and after a few minutes more we were over our own base peeling off to land. It was just getting dark and was about an hour later than the time we had been due. We had lost time when the lead group went wandering over half of Germany off course, looking for the target. As our plane pulled into its hard stand and the engines killed, a jeep pulled up. It was Bill Taylor, my squadron adjutant. He shouted at me from the jeep.

"Sure glad to see you. We were sweating you out. We've been waiting for you for over an hour."

I told Bill about Smitty and then got into the jeep to go to the interrogation room. No use to sweat Smitty out, I thought. When I walked into the interrogation room I saw Colonel Wood. "Nice work, Phil!" he said. "Miller had engine trouble and when I heard he'd had to abort I was worried. Guess you did all right."

"Well, I don't know," I replied. "I don't think we hit the briefed target. We hit some kind of an important looking factory. I guess the photographs will tell the story as soon as they are developed."

We got out pictures of the target area, and I was able to point out the spot where the bombs fell. We had no records on what the buildings were that we hit, but the intelligence people could figure it out in time.

Just then one of my men rushed in and up to where I was standing. "A ship is coming in. It may be Lieutenant Smith."

I jumped in a jeep at the door and sped to the tower. I saw the big letter *E* on the tail of a plane at the end of the runway. Its inboard engines were out, and it was taxiing with the outboards toward the hard stand assigned to it.

"Thank God!" I thought. I never had believed it possible. I drove down to where the ship parked and ran shouting to it. The bomb doors opened and out jumped Smitty. He was laughing and then in a moment so was I.

"You look worried," he said. "I knew I'd make it. I just couldn't get home as fast as you did. Furst and I got three of those Ju88s, but I'm afraid there isn't much hope for Furst. We're going to need a little help with Sergeant Lesho." The sergeant, it turned out, had taken a .50 caliber machine gun Hollywood style, when it was shot from its mount by enemy fire, and held it against his body. With the gun held in this manner he had scored a probable kill. The attacking Ju88 had been seen headed down with smoke pouring from an engine. Sergeant Lesho had received serious bruises about his chest and had to be taken to the hospital. Several of the boys had picked up splinters of 20 mm. shells, which had burst in virtually every part of the airplane, but none of them was seriously wounded. It was really a miracle. Smitty seemed so calm about it all, but he knew as well as I that he had used up more good luck than one man's ration normally allows. He was going to forget that. He was home now, and you could see he was trying to bring down the curtain on the memory of some horrible hours.

After that I found myself something of a hero with the group command for having taken over the formation and led it on the first raid into Germany. I really wondered what else I could have done. Later intelligence reported we had done considerable damage to the factory we hit. It wasn't as high-priority a target as the one we were supposed to hit and couldn't. But for a first trip into Germany and for a target of opportunity, the results looked pretty good. At least they were good enough so that the next day we got a teletype commendation from General Hodges, the division commander.

I reflected that it was fine to be considered a hero, but if that raid is any sample of the way the rest of our raids are to be, I doubt that I shall live to finish a tour. We were extremely lucky to have lost only one ship. Nearly all the planes in the formation had suffered flak damage. You could figure the losses mathematically against the number of raids in a tour and get yourself into a state of melancholia. Because, mathematically, at that time and figured from the way it went for some time after, no one had a chance to get through. Of course, those of us who were not actual combat crew members were not supposed to feel it necessary to get in a tour. Theoretically, we had administrative functions in addition to our combat work. Nevertheless, our business was bombing, not administering. The men who went out day in and day out couldn't long be expected to retain respect for their commanders if the commanders shirked their part of combat.

The fall of 1943 was terrible for flying. Mission after mission went out with poor results. It was the kind of thing that was hard on everyone, but I think it was worst for the few of us who acted as command pilots. We felt ourselves responsible for the success of the missions we led. And though a mission might fail because of bad weather, the command pilot assigned would brood over it. He was likely to get the idea that perhaps someone else thought he had done poorly or made improper decisions, or that some other commander might have done better.

Colonel Miller felt very bad about having to abort at the

enemy coast on the Vegesack mission. After that he led a couple of other missions when the weather was terrible, and those missions were fizzles, all from circumstances utterly beyond his control. I knew other commanders were suffering from bad missions, but at that time I didn't quite get their point of view. I had a lot of confidence in myself as a leader, but I had not much confidence in my ability to finish a tour alive.

Soon after Vegesack I was assigned to lead the group on a mission to an airfield near Oslo, Norway. The B-17s were going after some power stations in that area. The weather was so bad as to make it utterly impossible to go over Western Europe. Tom Conroy, the new junior squadron commander, was to be my deputy leader. The weather over base and in the direction we were going was also poor, but we were briefed to expect it to get better as we neared the coast of Norway. Again we had no fighter support, but were told that we might expect enemy defenses to be light. There was little flak in the area, and supposedly there were only a few enemy fighters.

I set up Bob Wright and crew to fly with me in the lead ship. We took off in instrument weather, ceiling nearly zero. We climbed out on the prescribed course trying to get through the overcast. Up and up we went, much higher than we had been told we would have to go to reach the top of the stuff. Then we turned back, using our radio aid to navigation to come directly over the field. The overcast at this altitude was not as dense as I have seen it, but it was dense enough so that I couldn't see another ship in the sky. I did hear all sorts of radio calls from other ships obviously as much lost as I was as far as assembling the formation was concerned. Occasionally I would see a flare signal fired, but I would either not be able to catch a glimpse of the plane from which it was fired, or would see it only for a moment and then lose it. All my crew members were searching the sky with me and reporting over interphone in an effort to help.

As the lead crew of the group, we fired many flares trying to get the other ships of the group to form on us. We called them on the radio, giving our position. We did everything we knew to do in an effort to lure someone to us. Finally we struck out on course alone to the point on the northern English coast where we were to meet the other group formation and head out over the North Sea. We got there and saw no one. It was as hazy there as it was over home base. Generally the weather was instrument weather with some spots where the haze lightened, but we could see no one.

We hadn't picked up a single wing man of a whole group formation which was supposed to be with us. We stooged around in the stuff for half an hour later than our briefed time of departure from the friendly coast. Finally, finding no one to make any part of the formation, I aborted the mission and landed. It was evident from the radio calls we had heard that nearly all the ships of our group had already returned to base after failing to make formation. Our division tactical doctrine contained in it one mandate that my mind particularly applied to this situation. It said, in effect, that under no circumstances will an air commander take a unit over the enemy coast if it were not properly formed. I had heard this doctrine many times. And yet I was uncertain. Should I have gone on? Did any of the others succeed in going on and getting to the target? Was I afraid to go on?

As soon as I got on the ground I went to group operations to find out who had landed. I found all of us had returned except Tom Conroy, the deputy leader, and one other. I was burned up. Tom was an up-and-coming young leader, and I had let him give me the slip. He would return in the blaze of glory of being the only one in a "lead" capacity who had been able to get over the target. My reaction to this situation on the spur of the moment was so typical and so narrow that I later looked back upon it with shame.

Many hours later Tom flew in. He had been to Norway. The weather had cleared somewhat en route, but never got good enough for him to bomb the primary target. He had joined with a few ships of another group that had managed to get together, and the bunch of them finally picked a target of opportunity and bombed. Bombing results were dubious, pending the developing of the bombing pictures.

I went through agony over my apparent failure to get the formation together and get over the target. At least I could have

gone on alone, but I didn't. It was almost too much for me to
bear. I found out later, to add to my misery, that General Timberlake was in one of the planes of another group that had been
able to get together and bomb. Why hadn't they told us the general was flying? They usually did. Why hadn't I gone on? What
must the others think about it? I was deeply ashamed of myself.

The final report of the bombing of the mission proved that
bombing results were generally poor. An improper target of opportunity had been bombed, but Tom was in no way to blame
because he had joined another formation having none of his
own to fly with, and was accordingly under the authority of the
other leader. He had bombed as they bombed, and they had
bombed as best they could under the limitations imposed by the
weather. There was no enemy opposition of any kind and all
of the ships returned without damage.

That evening I saw Tom at the bar in the officers' club. A
surge of feeling almost made me play the little boy, envious and
angry, but I forced it down; and painfully swallowing my pride,
I went up to him. "Tom," I said, "you did today what I should
have done. I aborted for no reason, and you went on and bombed
the target. I am ashamed of myself, but I admire you and admit
I envy your performance." He accepted my compliment with
what seemed to me to be a bit of surprise. I was never particularly close to Tom. No one was, but I knew he was a very efficient squadron commander, and I recognized the envy in my
attitude.

Though anguished, I was later relieved when reports indicated the raid was a poor one even for those crews who got to
Norway. But after that temporary relief, my brooding about the
mission began to build up again in spite of my strongest efforts
to put the thought of it behind me. The more I thought about it,
the more important it seemed. The fact that the weather had
been as it was and the fact that only a handful of ships out of the
whole combat wing had managed to get out and bomb more or
less ineffectively meant nothing. I would have given years of
my life to have been with them.

I got Colonel Wood to say that I could lead the next mission.
I had to clear my mind of this bad one. For two or three days

missions were planned and scrubbed on account of the weather. Then finally Colonel Wood said he had decided to lead the next one but that I might go as deputy lead. The next day after that announcement we were waked early to perform the same mission which had been hanging fire—the airdrome near Oslo. The weather was still bad, but we were to try it again, this time with Colonel Wood leading and me in the number two slot.

I had a suspicion that this time it might be a rough raid, but I didn't care how rough it would be. I remembered my thesis of what happens on the second raid on a new target. We had been briefed on this mission four or five times now, and there might well have been leaks in security. The fact that little opposition was met before was no indication it would be light this time. However, I was mad enough to care nothing about opposition until I had reestablished my reputation as a leader.

We took off in weather almost as bad as it had been the time before. Colonel Wood took off. I told Bob Wright, who again was my pilot, to give our ship the gun before the lead plane cleared the runway. This is bad practice for aircraft so heavily loaded. Usually more interval between takeoffs is allowed, but the weather was so bad I knew if we didn't follow close upon the leader we would lose him and perhaps never find him again.

Sure enough we tacked onto the lead ship right after takeoff. Climbing through the heavy cloud over the area, we never lost it. But for a little more than an hour our two ships circled over the field, unable to get a single other airplane in formation with us. It was the same old story of haze almost as thick as solid cloud. When the time allotted for formation of the group expired, Colonel Wood put out a radio call to say we were proceeding to the point of departure from the friendly coast. He directed any other ships of our unit to proceed there individually where they might again try to pick us up. Just after we left the coast we met one other ship. It was V for Victor, bearing the name *Vagabond King*, flown by a starry-eyed young captain named McCormick. Thus our three Libs set forth to bomb Norway. We had no fighter escort, and heavy weather intervened between us and our target.

For a while we managed to get over the overcast into rather

clear air. But farther out over the North Sea the tops of the clouds got higher and higher as we approached the line where our weather officer had told us to expect a front. When we neared the front I got a call on the radio from Colonel Wood. He told me he was having supercharger trouble. He said he would keep on going as long as he could, but if the cloud layer got much higher he didn't believe he would be able to get over it. I acknowledged his message and told him I stood ready to take over should he have to turn back.

After a while, however, the cloud level began to subside, and it was evident he was going to make it. At this point we saw a fourth Lib way out to the right of us. The pilot had evidently spotted us because he headed our way. Soon it came near enough for me to see it was *B* for Baker, and good old Mac McLaughlin. Mac came over and tacked high right on our ship, making us four in all.

We soon saw the coast of Norway. Underneath were the extremely cold waters of the Skagerrak. Under no circumstances would a man bail out over such water. It's not possible to live more than ten or fifteen minutes in it. It was early December, but the sea had the look of water that is icy cold twelve months a year. Just about that time I looked out and saw four fighter planes. Our gunners saw them at the same time. I called the other ships of the formation and told them to expect attack momentarily from fighters at two o'clock high.

The fighters were queuing up, as the British say. They drew along in line astern until they were in perfect position to make a diving, quartering attack from our right. Then one by one they peeled. I could see the first increase his speed as down, down he came. A beautiful, perfectly streamlined Focke-Wulf 190. At fairly short range he opened fire on us with the four cannons in his wings. He fired a long burst and passed very close under us. Our gunners got in only a few shots. When first I had seen his guns smoking I thought he was being hit by our fire, but then I realized he was giving it to us and the smoke along his wing was from the mouths of his own cannons. Apparently our gunners hadn't laid a thing on him.

In orderly and quick succession the other three came by.

They were not as close as the first but were easily close enough to get hits. As they passed under, my right waist gunner called me on the interphone. "The number four engine is losing oil."

I nudged Bob Wright. "I won't feather that prop unless the oil pressure begins to drop as long as we are under attack. I'll watch the oil pressure gauge and catch it if the pressure falls off." Bob nodded. You have to feather props while there is oil pressure left or else they won't feather. It is sometimes bad policy to feather or stop a prop when under fighter attack because it lets the fighters know you are a cripple and they concentrate on you. Of course they might have seen our oil leak, but oil on an engine nacelle is less prominent than a feathered prop. If an engine is dead, however, and the prop is allowed to windmill, it exerts much more drag on the plane than if it is feathered. Also a dead engine with a windmilling prop and no oil is apt to heat up and cause a fire. All these considerations work automatically in a combat pilot's mind to help him reach a conclusion.

The fighters broke away underneath us and then climbed high to our left rear and turned again to attack. Since they were behind us, I couldn't see the start of their second attack. I was kept informed by my waist gunner and tail gunner. As they got closer I could see them. This time it looked as though McCormick in the *Vagabond King* was going to bear the brunt of it. And just then they were on him. I could see the cannon shells ripping through his plane and some hitting the tail of Colonel Wood's. The second, third, and fourth fighters came in. Our waist gunners reported one fighter down in flames and another limping off with his engine smoking. But the *Vagabond King* suddenly spurted flame all over the top of its broad wing. A moment later the flames almost covered it. Then it headed down slowly and majestically toward the cold waters below. Our little formation drew away, and I never saw that plane again. My men didn't see it hit the water, but it was evident it couldn't have made shore. No chutes were seen. Fred Sayre, the copilot, stuck his head between Wright and me. I had ranked him out of his seat but told him he might go along on the mission and ride on the flight deck if he wanted to. Now Fred took a look at the *Vagabond King* going down in flames and said, "Some days it just doesn't pay to open the door." Great guy, Fred. I knew he felt just the way I did about seeing our friend McCormick go down, but he was doing his bit to raise our spirits when the going was rough. Our number four engine was leaking oil to the point that the outer part of the right wing was black with it. I called all stations on the interphone.

"We can't bail out over this water, but we're hit. Those fighters must know it. If they hit us again we're gone. We may make shore if we're lucky. Check all your equipment for an emergency." I was taking what I thought was a coldly accurate view of our situation.

But as luck would have it, the shooting down of two of the four fighters seemed to have an effect on the other two. The fact, which I hadn't discovered until that moment, that there were stragglers—single B-24s—flying behind us also had an effect. The remaining two fighters left us to attack a single Lib flying about a mile to our rear. My heart went out to the men in that ship. I don't know whether they got through the attacks or not. Our attention was diverted elsewhere when I heard the gunners say it was being attacked. At least we seemed momentarily free of the enemy.

We were still a good way offshore. I was watching the oil pressure gauge on the engine that had been hit. Pretty soon the oil pressure started a fast descent toward zero. I called to Bob that I was feathering the prop. I pushed the feathering button and at the same moment cut off the gas to the engine and switched the mags off. Nervously, I watched the prop. After a moment I saw the big fan slow up until at length it came to a standstill, with its blades turned edges into the slipstream. Thank God, there was still enough oil left for the feathering mechanism to work.

We still had problems. Here we were about half an hour from the target with a full load of bombs and only three engines. I wasn't certain whether we could continue to the target with our load and the dead engine. I put more power on the three good engines. Bob retrimmed his ship. He was concentrating on flying good formation. We didn't know when we might be attacked again, and we didn't want to take any chances on straggling. After seeing how we flew for a few minutes we decided we probably could pull enough power on our three good engines without completely burning them up to carry our bombs to the target. At that moment I remembered how I played what I considered a good game of bridge, for an hour or two drawing marvelous hands. Suddenly I would relax and completely muff a bid. When I did that I always got the feeling that my luck had run out. When I had good luck I had to play well or it quit me. I was afraid my previous good luck in combat flying had run out because I muffed the first mission on Norway. I would have to play much harder now in order to earn my luck and stay in the game.

Shortly after McCormick was shot out of the left wing position, McLaughlin, who had been flying high right on our ship slid down and under and filled in the spot left vacant. We flew on, fairly close upon our target, a three-ship flight of Libs obviously a little shot up but proceeding satisfactorily.

We finally got over our target, dropped our bombs, and then turned right. Being in the right hand seat, I got a good view of the bomb bursts—they were perfect. There were the airfield, some repair shops, and some buildings beyond that our intelligence had told us were occupied by Nazi officers. Our bombs started bursting close to the end of the airfield, holed up a good, hard-surface runway, split open the shops, and continued blossoming in great explosions in the officers' quarters. I was exultant over the damage. I hoped some of those Nazi pilots who had just been giving us such a going over were quartered in those buildings.

At the time the fighters left us I had felt we would be lucky if we made it to Sweden, where we might bail out and be interned. There have been very few times when I was as certain I would not get home. But now that we were lightened by the dropping of several tons of bombs I found I could take a different view of things. Of the three ships, ours was the worst hit; but we had three apparently good engines. They showed no ill effects from the excess power output, and now that we were rid of the bombs we could throttle them back to the point where there should be little danger of burning them up. True, we had a long distance to go across the North Sea to get back to England, but there was no reason to assume we couldn't make it. As we turned from the target, Colonel Wood called me. He suggested I take the lead and said he would drop in on my wing, since my ship was crippled. He felt he might give us better protection that way, and it would enable us to set the pace going back. I accepted the proposal, and soon we found ourselves leading a majestic formation of three B-24s headed southwest toward England.

The start of our return trip was nice enough. I was optimistic about our chances, but I somehow felt that we hadn't seen the last of the fighter planes. And as I was turning it over in my mind and we were leaving the coast of Norway, our waist gunner reported fighters coming up from the rear. This time instead of the sleek, single-engined sky sharks—the FW-190s—we had Ju88s. They were the familiar twin-engined planes, much faster and more maneuverable than a heavy bomber, but not the extreme fighter-type planes that the Focke-Wulfs were. They approached in twos, coming past us high and to the right somewhat as the 190s had done. They were higher and farther out. Finally the first one turned in. All three of our ships sent up a cone of .50 caliber fire. Just after the first attacker turned toward us we could see streaks of smoke coming from under its wings. These streaks extended themselves like lines drawn by points coming in our direction. We knew they were launching rockets. We had seen them before. After the rockets left the attacking plane Bob put the nose of our ship down and pulled off several inches of power. Since we were in such a small formation, it was not difficult for the other ships to follow us in this evasive maneuver.

In a second or two the rockets bursts. They burst short. The deterrent force of our .50 caliber guns in keeping the attacker away from us, plus the evasive maneuver, gave us a pretty safe margin of distance from where the rockets exploded. Time and again the Ju88s lined up on us. Each time we met them with heavy .50 caliber fire. Each time they turned and released their rockets. And each time Bob waited until the rocket launchers under the wings of the attacker were smoking, indicating that the rockets were away, and then he would make a turn, usually a diving turn in one direction or another. The two ships with us got on to it and stayed in formation remarkably well. All the bursts occurred short and were either to the right or the left, according to the way we turned, but always they missed us by a fairly safe margin.

Bob did a magnificent job of evasive action, and one he wouldn't have been able to do with a larger formation. During all this wavering and zigzagging we were coming with good progress upon the northern edge of the cloud bank that had carpeted our flight nearly all the way coming up. Those clouds ahead looked awfully good. We were sorry the undercast hadn't lasted right up to the time we had hit the enemy coast. But now we were over the first, patchy clouds, and in a few minutes more we were over an almost solid undercast. The last Ju88 made a pass just as we pulled off power and dived our little formation into the bank of cloud. The cloud layer was thin there and the fighters followed us down, but they never got another shot at us.

Lightened as we were with much less gas and no bombs, our plane moved along at a nice pace with the three good engines set for moderate power. We had nothing to worry about as long as we didn't lose another engine, and there was no reason to suppose we would. Just the same, we notified Air Sea Rescue Service of our position, speed, and heading in order that they could keep a check on us until we made it over land again. Two hours and a half later we landed at our home airdrome with the deep satisfaction of having done a good job against odds. We had put our bombs on the target, and we had carried them there from a considerable distance after being crippled. It almost erased the anguish I had felt because of my poor leadership on the first Norway mission.

After making that successful trip to Norway I was ready for a short rest. I had never been to London, and my last leave was one I had taken at Bengasi to go to Alexandria for two days. With a relaxed, clear conscience, I asked for three days off. I made a reservation at the Red Cross Reindeer Club. I had heard that with the aid at one's disposal at a Red Cross club it would be possible to see London, get good theater tickets, be advised about shopping, or find just about anything the town had to offer.

London I found very pleasantly quiet. I spent practically all of my visit seeing the sights—Westminster Abbey, the Tower of London, Trafalgar Square, the wax museum, and a host of places I had wanted to see. Next time, I thought, I would do what I would enjoy without regard to sight-seeing. I did go back refreshed, and with a more exalted opinion of the Red Cross than I had had before. The courtesies and benefits furnished by the Red Cross to Americans in the service, both officers and enlisted men, white and black, were a great credit to that organization.

After my return we experienced a period when our losses were depressingly heavy. I saw many new faces in my squadron. But the difficulty of getting used to the new faces was as nothing compared to the sight of the remaining old ones under the shock of losing their friends. Our sorest trial of morale came when replacements were not quickly forthcoming for the crews we lost, and the old guys had to face empty barracks for days on end. The winding up of personal affairs of those missing in action, including the packing and cataloguing of personal effects, was heartrending. If new men came in quickly the missing ones were less conspicuous.

I well remember the period before Christmas, 1943. Two things in particular stand out. First, the weather. Anyone who was asked to lead one of those midwinter forays knew the odds were greatly against his being able to complete his mission with any degree of success. We had not got our pathfinder equipment set up then—that came a few months later—and so at that time we could not bomb by instruments. Each trip out was apt to be characterized by a number of midair collisions between bombers climbing through heavy overcast. There were cases of ships loading up in freezing cloud layers and spinning in under the tremendous weight of gas, bombs, and ice. There were always men who returned with frostbitten hands, faces, and feet. Normally these were the ones who were lucky enough to get over the target. We were short of the proper number of electric flying suits with electric gloves and boots. Every time some men would have to go without and would have to be hospitalized because of frostbite.

The other thing I particularly remember was about Christmas itself. At the Government's urging, most of the folks back home had mailed our Christmas packages early. Many of the packages arrived in late November. I was taught to make quite a holiday out of opening Christmas packages, and I had come to feel it a kind of sin to open them before Christmas. Kind friends and members of my family saw to it that I had many packages to open. My problem each time I was up for a mission was to decide whether or not to open my presents. I always felt there was a pretty fair chance I wouldn't come back, and it seemed stupid to leave the packages laying around unopened. I had seen the unopened Christmas packages of many of my missing friends marked "Return to Sender." I went through that indecision many times. Each time I would go to bed leaving the packages unopened. In the icy cold of the black morning when I was called out to fly I would wonder again whether I would be back to see them once more. Strange that a man my age should spend as much time as I did debating the matter of Christmas packages!

The truth, I guess, was that those packages were the most recent tie between me and loved ones back home. It was not what was in them, but that they represented so much time and effort and affection that caused me to make almost a fetish of them. Whatever they contained they were expressions straight from the hearts of those dearest to me; and to open them before Christmas was to destroy their magic. I was true to my principle, and the Lord rewarded me by bringing me home on all those occasions. The end of that dilemma was that on Christmas morning I found myself alone in my room sitting on the floor opening presents. I don't remember what I got, but I felt closer to those at home at that moment than I had since I left the States.

Our station had been selected for a Christmas broadcast over CBS which afforded excitement. I was particularly interested in the broadcast because Edward R. Murrow and Larry LeSueur came up to run it. I had met Larry some time before. He had come up a month early for a short visit to make advance arrangements. I had cornered him and got him on the subject of politics, the war, and Russia. Larry had spent a long time in Russia and was the best authority I ever had a chance to talk to. LeSueur and Murrow were too busy on that occasion for me to see much of them, but after I renewed my old acquaintance with Larry he invited me to stay with him next time I came to London. I was pleased at the prospect of having a chance to talk about things I hadn't discussed in a long time.

The Christmas broadcast was a huge success. Many officers and enlisted men had an opportunity to say a few words to reassure their families back home that they were well and as happy as Americans ever can be so far from home. I was convinced of the dedication of the American newsmen. They performed an immensely important role, and the ones I saw had a conscientiousness about their work which was quite impressive. When the newsmen left the day after the broadcast I was on hand to say goodbye and to tell Larry I would see him on my next trip to London. Already I was planning to ask for a few days' leave.

After Christmas I knew the group was in for great changes. I had seen in our briefing room on numerous occasions a newcomer to our wing. He was Colonel Milton W. Arnold, an officer I remembered who had graciously said "sir" to me on a badminton court at Kelly Field back in 1941. At that time I was a flying cadet and he was a captain clearly mistaking me for a civilian. The keen-eyed, wavy-haired Colonel Arnold was now at wing headquarters as General Timberlake's chief-of-staff. He was only recently out of the Air Transport Command. We heard he had fought so vigorously to get out and get into combat as to make himself a nuisance, and we admired that. Since he had been in the wing he had led several of our missions and had clearly demonstrated his ability to lead. He was a regular officer and a West Pointer who quite obviously felt it his duty to come to grips with the enemy in the closest and most direct manner possible.

Colonel Wood, according to the report I heard, would soon move to take command of a new wing, and Colonel Arnold would take over our group. The switch affected me because there was the shadow of a rumor that in all the changes to follow I was going to be taken away from my beloved squadron to be put in the place occupied by John A. Brooks III, the job of group operations officer. I had cussed group operations for nearly everything I conceived to be wrong with the group. It was a little ironic that now I was to be passed the platter to see what I could do with it, and the prospect didn't make me happy because I loved my squadron. There was something about having my own command that was a lot better than the best staff job. I made no bones about my dislike of the prospect of being group operations officer.

Very soon the changes came. Colonel Wood moved out to his new command, taking Major Brooks with him. Colonel Arnold moved in. Colonel Miller remained in his position as air executive and I went into the operations office. Major Ken Caldwell took over my squadron. He was the first pilot who had flown lead ship on many of our early missions. Ken was a Kansas City boy, very strong-willed and opinionated. He was a hard worker, bull necked and square jawed, with a temperament in keeping with his looks; a pilot who was generally liked, and admired by the few who didn't like him.

A few days after he took over the squadron, Ken was acting as group command pilot on a mission to an airfield in the south of France. He was flying with Captain Dave Wilhite from Owensboro, Kentucky. Wilhite was a pilot out of Conroy's squadron and was the one man of all the other squadrons whom I had most wished to have in mine. Dave was undoubtedly one of the great pilots of the group, as of course was Ken. Coming away from the target for some unexplained reason our group got separated from the rest of the division formation. The fighter planes which were supposed to give support to the heavy bombers maintained cover over the main part of the division. Our group, being separated from the main unit, invited and got heavy fighter attacks just a few miles from the coast of France.

Evidently the group was hit by the Abbeyville Kids. That was the name we gave the Nazi pilots flying the yellow-nosed Focke-Wulf 190s based near Abbeyville. They were part of what was commonly known as the Goering Squadron. In a matter of seconds several Liberators were shot right out of the lead of our formation. Major Caldwell's and Wilhite's airplane was seen going down, with many cannon holes in the fuselage and fire burning in the cockpit. Soon after that news came through that

Ken had been killed in action. I never heard about Dave. Ken was as game as any airman I've known. If he had a serious fault it was a smaller capacity for fear than the ordinary man has, giving him a tendency to lack caution.

After Ken went down Frank Ellis took over the squadron. Frank was a grimly determined officer of great capability. When he took over the squadron Bob Wright became squadron operations officer. They both became majors and if ever two men had earned their rank, they were the two.

Colonel Arnold turned out to be a man to gain even more of my admiration than I had had at first. He possessed boundless nervous energy. Nothing he saw when he arrived was good enough; he turned over everything and looked under it, and generally demanded that something new and better be put in its place. And so I lived to rue the day that I had ever criticized group operations. For every criticism I had ever made resulted in a great deal of work. The physical layout of the operations office was greatly changed. I brought the assistant operations officer, Major Dan Minnick, back into the main office. He had been given a little cubbyhole down the hall in which to work as training officer. I shoved and shifted. I got carpenters in to put up new status boards, tables, pictures, etc. I got the communications men to put in new telephones and work on the teletype service. And in all this I had Colonel Arnold prodding me with an uncomfortably sharp prodder.

Before I got my new system halfway started, General Hodges, the division commander, came in on an inspection trip with a whole staff of inspectors. I was caught absolutely flat-footed. I had all the things in the way of records and evidence of training of lead crews in my mind, but only a little of it on paper at that time. General Hodges, an extremely stern man, took the hide off me in the few places where Colonel Arnold, by sheer oversight, had left any. I started to take refuge in the explanation that I felt I had been left a chaotic situation which I hadn't had time to straighten out. But I knew that would not do, so I took the criticism without comment. I understood what General Hodges expected to find in a group operations office and agreed with him. I didn't have it, and so I just shut up and tried not to flinch as he let go. There was a devilish gleam in Colonel Arnold's eye as he saw me sweat and squirm. I could picture him relating particulars of my moment of misery later to some of our friends as a high point of comedy in the inspection.

Behind all the changes that came to the group and that I thought were real improvements stood not only Colonel Arnold, but less directly General Timberlake. He was between the group headquarters and the division—the CO between Colonel Arnold and General Hodges. General Ted was one I had come to know much better in the last few months and to esteem more. He and Colonel Arnold had been classmates at the academy. At the time of his promotion to general he had been the youngest officer to achieve that rank since the Civil War. He came of an Army family, being the son of a prominent regular Army officer and having two brothers who were also generals. He knew more men in his three groups by their full names than most of his group commanders did. He was apt to pop up in a squadron operations office any time "just looking around." He had a pleasant way on these trips. He wouldn't make anyone uncomfortable at the time, but he would elicit all the information obtainable from anyone he talked to, and his sharp blue eyes would see everything worth seeing. Upon his departure he would have an impeccably accurate estimate of the efficiency of whatever outfit he'd seen. He would not tolerate inefficiency. He was bighearted, but if he thought a man needed removing, he would see it done quickly. And because of the speed of such movements he inflicted a minimum of pain.

Colonel Arnold and General Timberlake completely erased my remaining prejudice against West Pointers. They were, by far, the two greatest officers I had ever been close enough to really to know. Their energy was unlimited, their wit and intellect admirable, and their manner graceful. Their methods of approach to problems were slightly different, and their ways of handling men were different, but the results of their efforts were nearly identical.

Shortly after Colonel Arnold took command our group had a party. It was the custom to have one party a month. That party came after a series of particularly rough raids. Several crews were missing from the raids of the previous few days, and numerous others had returned only by the skin of their teeth. The boys had been fighting hard and were ready to play hard.

Colonel Arnold had moved me into a small building near the officers' club where he and Colonel Miller lived. There, before the party, he had General Timberlake, Colonel Miller, and me in for drinks. By the time we got over to the club the party was going strong. The floor was littered with bits of cloth which, after a moment's notice, were identifiable as the ends of neckties. As we entered the door—our group led by General Timberlake and proceeding in order of rank to myself in the rear—some lieutenant in high spirit grabbed the general by his tie and shouted, "What're you doin' with that tie on?" And with one wide sweep of his arm, he swung a knife blade within a fraction of an inch of the general's throat, cutting off his tie just below the knot.

The general turned with cool dignity to Colonel Arnold behind him. "God, Milt, what have you got here?"

"Go on in and enjoy yourself, Ted, but don't annoy the boys." Colonel Arnold was chuckling.

We went in. It was obvious that for a long time no one noticed that one of the guests was wearing the star insignia of a brigadier general. No offense meant; they just didn't notice it. Finally, however, proper note was taken. We were standing at the bar when a very young second lieutenant reeled up to the general. He looked again to be sure that really was a general he saw and then turned around and motioned to two or three of his friends to come on over. Turning again to General Timberlake, he said, "You know, general, I'm a second lieutenant. I been in this man's Army two years now. One as a GI and another as a secon' lieutenant. And this is the firs' time I ever got a chance to talk to a general." And then with real supplication in his gaze he looked up to the general and pleaded, "Say something, general!"

General Ted's blue eyes twinkled. "What shall I say?"

"Tha's all right! Tha's fine—now—say something else!"

We were holding our sides and bending over laughing with tears coming down our cheeks. It was a real tribute to our Army. General Ted bore himself with such dignity without stiffness on that occasion that it was a matter of comment for a long time to come. He was no officer to permit indignity to his rank. But like Colonel Arnold, he apparently realized that if the boys were going to fight a hard war, they might also be expected to play hard. We left a little early, feeling it was evident no one would be hurt in the merrymaking and that seemed to be the only line drawn.

Missions came and went. In time I was lead or deputy lead of several of the great air battles. In one raid on Emden we were intercepted after missing a rendezvous with our friendly fighters. Our bombers alone knocked down 117 enemy fighter planes. The air was so full of parachutes for a while that it looked more like a paratrooper landing than a bombing mission. During the height of the battle there were several bombers in various stages of disintegration everywhere I looked. But the heavy decks of clouds under us were sewn with threads of black smoke where stricken Nazi fighter planes dived earthward. Finally our fighters arrived. They accounted for 21 more German fighters, bringing our total of enemy destroyed to 138. My Liberator was credited with two sure kills.

These missions were hours of horrifying screaming in our headphones, mixed with sounds of voices calling "bombs away," "fighters at two o'clock high, coming in," "K King is hit hard and is leaving formation on fire, crew bailing out—."

After several such missions, I usually asked Colonel Arnold for two or three days off to go to London. After my first visit I always stayed with Larry LeSueur. That happened as a result of his invitation to me at Christmas time. I had hoped I might find other accommodations than those of the Red Cross, but the difficulty of getting hotel rooms was extreme.

According to Larry's suggestion, when I got to town I went to the offices of CBS on Hallam Street. Larry wasn't in, but I was welcomed and told to make myself comfortable by George Moorad, one of Larry's associates. George was searching for material to make up his next night's broadcast, which was for the "Report to the Nation" program. He wanted to know about recent bombardment missions and, when he found I had been on the big Emden raid, he asked me if I would be interviewed on his program. I thought immediately that this was an opportunity of getting the news to Anne that I was well. Her receipt of my airmail letters was delayed a minimum of ten days, and her papers carried news of many heavy air battles in the last two weeks. "You know, Columbia in New York will send your wife and parents a wire telling them you are to be on the air," George said. That decided me and I gladly accepted. I gave George a number of the details of the mission, and he went merrily off to get the story checked with the censors. That was on Monday. He told me to meet him at 2:00 A.M. Wednesday at the BBC Building. The broadcast was set for 2:30 A.M. Wednesday, London time, which would be 8:30 Tuesday evening in New York Eastern War Time.

After George left I had a long chat with the darkly immaculate Ed Murrow. I had heard from some of the other members of the staff that Ed had been on a recent raid over Berlin with the RAF and I was very much interested because at that time the American Eighth Air Force bombers hadn't started making runs over The Big B in daylight. I asked Ed about his mission, but he seemed reluctant to talk about it. I think he performed the mission solely in order to keep faith with his listeners. He didn't seem particularly proud of it, though I think he had every right to be. Seeing his extreme modesty about it, I decided I would kid him a little. I told him of a column I had read by Ernie Pyle some months before. Ernie Pyle told how he had been offered a chance to go on a bombing mission and had turned it down. "That was one of the most impressive columns I ever read," I said. "You don't know what an added burden an extra man is on a bombing raid." I continued, "One more man might consume enough oxygen so that if an oxygen line is out it might make the difference of whether that plane would get back or have to be abandoned in enemy territory." I had set out to pull his leg a little, but immediately I was ashamed of what I had done because I could see he was genuinely distressed.

Larry came in then and shouted a cheery welcome to me. Both he and Ed, in their grimly formal clothes, looked like men who might have stepped in from Number 10 Downing Street.

In England Larry sought only to be a straight reporter. Only seldom would he branch out editorially. Ed, on the other hand, had done a great deal of editorializing. He performed magnificent work in explaining the British to the Americans in those early days of the war when that problem was much more crucial than it was upon my arrival. I felt he was a little too favorable to the British government, but there was a strong need for what he was doing. I also would have liked him to be more critical of the governments in exile, then resting comfortably in London. I'm sure he felt there was plenty of criticism without any from him. Ed remained the somber voice periodically intoning "This is London" to millions of Americans. J. P. Marquand drew a wonderful picture of the projection of Ed's personality on the American public in that beautiful book *So Little Time.*

Of course it was natural that Larry would leave interpretations of the British to Murrow. Larry had been in Moscow for a long time before he came to London and was almost as much of an authority on the Russians as anyone could be. He had just written a book about Russia which was published simultaneously in the United States and Great Britain, as well as in several other countries. It was called *The Twelve Months That Changed the World.*

Chatting there with the "voices," I spent the rest of that day getting caught up on the big picture of the war, which I so sorely missed at my bomber base. I talked with nearly all the men on the CBS staff either during the afternoon or at dinner that evening.

Next day Larry had to go to work early, and he left me to shift for myself. I went window-shopping down Regent Street toward Picadilly. As I walked along with my mind idly wandering, I stopped in front of a bookshop. There in the window I saw a copy of *The Twelve Months That Changed the World.* I had an idea for another leg-pull. I went into a nearby telephone booth and called CBS. At length I got Ed Murrow on the phone. "Ed," I said, "I've got something of utmost importance to Larry I want to let you know about. I was just walking off Picadilly when I came upon a bookshop offering Larry's new book at a special cut-rate price. I was disturbed and I went in to question the proprietor about it. His only explanation was that it seemed they had overstocked with that volume and were trying to take their loss quickly and clear out of the investment as best they could."

I could hear Ed laughing. "Wait a minute, Phil. Larry's just come in. I'll tell him about it." Then in a minute he returned chuckling to the phone. "Larry's got his hat and coat on and is coming right down. Thanks a million."

Actually Larry's book was very much of a success in London. All books there were severely limited by the paper ration, and his was sold out very quickly. I bought a copy and found a few days later the book was impossible to buy.

That evening Larry told me he had accepted an invitation for us to attend a cocktail party where he thought I might meet some people I would enjoy knowing. I don't remember where the party was or who gave it, but I do remember being in a great room filled with people particularly suited to make me feel uncomfortable. I remember Larry taking me over to T. S. Eliot to introduce me. Eliot looked like he did in photographs I had seen —a reasonably good-looking man with a nose and chin I didn't like. After the introduction Larry said to him, "I just finished reading your last book, Mr. Eliot."

The great poet smiled a little grimly and expanded in anticipation of a compliment. "I do hope you don't feel any the worse for it," he said.

"Well, to tell you the truth," Larry replied, "I don't feel very good about it."

That threw Eliot a little off his stride. For a moment he spluttered and then with some irritation threw back, "I didn't intend that you should." Then he was called away.

Larry laughed. "I felt regardless of what you think of the guy, you'd like to meet him."

Later I went back to the flat to catch a nap before the broadcast I was to do. In the tense hush of the BBC studio, at 2:29 A.M. I saw the hand on the big clock speeding around, and I heard George Moorad say, "Hello, New York, hello, New York. Do you get me? This is George."

The Lincoln Flying School, Lincoln, Nebraska.

From left, Jake Greenwell, Charles Hainline with dog Washout, James Lewers, Charles Back, John Petot, and Philip Ardery at the Lincoln Flying School, Lincoln, Nebraska.

Bombing of harbor installations at Reggio, Italy, on July 11, 1943, by planes of the Second Bomb Division of the Eighth Air Force.

Bombing of harbor installations at Reggio, Italy.

Mrs. Ardery with son Peter Brooks at San Angelo, Texas.

President Franklin Delano Roosevelt visits Lowry Field, Denver, Colorado, spring, 1943.

Setting up camp in Libya near Bengasi, July, 1943.

Ardery and Majors Cross and Burton at Bengasi.

Lieutenant Ardery's last class of student fliers at Goodfellow Field, San Angelo, Texas.

First Captain Ardery and Second Captain Charles Kruck with General George C. Marshall at Kelly Field, San Antonio, Texas, March, 1941.

Formation of BC-1s over Kelly Field, April, 1941.

Men attending a briefing before a bombing raid.

Father Beck performing communion service for members of the 389th
Bomb Group before a mission over enemy territory.

Burning boiler house and power house after bombing at Steaua Romana refinery.

Oil storage tanks in flames at Columbia Aquila refinery near Ploesti. In background a wave of fourteen Liberators continues the bombing attack.

Liberators bombing Astra Romana refinery.

Flames erupting from distillation plant at Steaua Romana refinery near Ploesti, Romania, August 1, 1943.

Liberators pass into the Ploesti, Romania, target area at extremely low level.

Liberators bombing Astra Romana refinery, Ploesti, Romania, August 1, 1943.

Colonel Edward J. "Ted" Timberlake at base near Norwich, England, in August, 1943.

Brigadier General Timberlake presents Colonel Philip Ardery with his second Distinguished Flying Cross at base near Norwich.

Colonel Bob Terrill, General Hodges, Colonel Larry Thomas, Brigadier General Timberlake, Colonel Miller, Colonel George Bronson, Bombardier Johnnie Fino, and Colonel Ardery at base near Norwich.

Brigadier General Timberlake and Colonel Ardery stand before a Liberator at base near Norwich.

Bombs falling over Kjeller, Norway, near Oslo, during raid by the Eighth
Air Force on November 18, 1943.

Smoke rises over German repair and maintenance base at Kjeller after
raid on November 18, 1943.

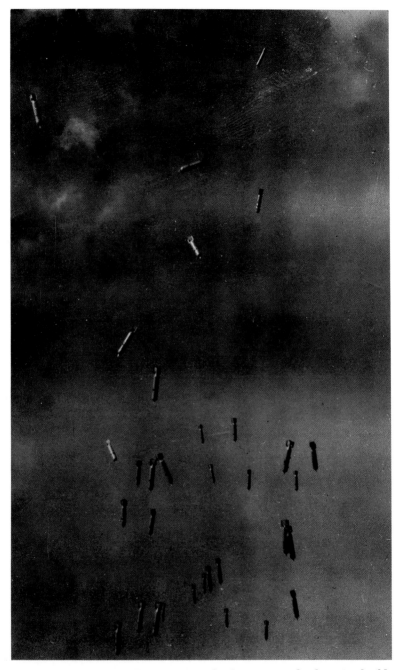

Blind bombing over Emden, Germany, leading port and submarine building yard on the Ruhr River, September 27, 1943.

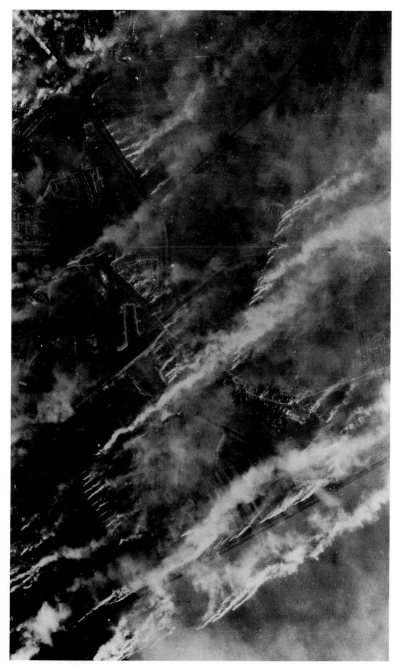

Smoke rising from Emden after bombing raid of September 27, 1943.

Enlisted men at opening of an officers' club at an Eighth Air Force base in England on October 25, 1943.

Combat crew of the 389th Bomb Group beside a Liberator at base in England.

Crew of *Old Blister Butt* at Eighth Air Force base in England.

Crew of *Ole Irish* stand before their plane at base in England on August 27, 1943.

Lieutenant Colonel James M. Stewart interrogating a crew of the 453rd Bomb Group after their return to base in England from a mission over enemy territory.

Wreckage of a crashed Liberator at base near Norwich.

Liberators flying formation en route to bombing raid over enemy territory.

Firemen spraying wreckage of a bomber at base near Norwich.

General "Tooey" Spaatz reviews Colonel Wood and the staff of the 389th Bomb Group at an Eighth Air Force base in England.

The 389th Bomb Group of the Eighth Air Force receives a citation for
their participation in the Ploesti raids from Lieutenant General Carl
Spaatz, May 6, 1944.

Wing and group commanders of the Second Bomb Division, Eighth Air
Force, England, meeting on September 19, 1944. Seated far left, Colonel
Jack W. Wood; fifth from left, Brigadier General Timberlake; far right,
Colonel Milton W. Arnold. Standing, first row, fourth from left, Colonel
Frederic H. Miller. Standing, second row, fourth from left, Colonel
Lawrence M. Thomas.

Liberators on a mission over the Pas de Calais sometime before D day in 1944.

First row (from left): Captain Johnnie Fino, wing bombardier, and Colonel Ardery. Second row: Mike Phipps; Captain Sam Ross, communications officer; Captain Alba, adjutant; Lieutenant Gene Porter. Third row: Lieutenant Jarecki; Captain McClain, wing navigator; other unknown. Photo taken at base near Norwich.

Major Ardery after completing his combat mission tour on March 23, 1944.

Liberators dropping bombs over the Erkner ball bearing factory near
Berlin on March 8, 1944.

Smoke rises from Erkner suburb of Berlin after bombing raid by the
Eighth Air Force.

Smoke rises from Erkner factory after raid by Flying Fortresses and Liberators on March 8, 1944.

From left, Capt. W.T. "Temp" Cumiskey, Lt. Col. Philip Ardery, and Gen. "Ted" Timberlake on D-Day, June 6, 1944, in Norwich, England.

"Sure, George," shot back the answer. "You go on at plus five. All set?"

"Right."

I read my script in the measured tones of a country boy who is uncertain of his act and suffering from mike fright. I didn't care how it sounded as long as Anne could tell it was I. With every word of that script, which told of the Emden raid, I was saying to her, "Anne, I'm all right. I'm well. I'm here talking to you and giving you news about me that is ten days fresher than that in the letter you'll get in tomorrow's mail. I love you and I'll be back soon." The broadcast over, I caught the early morning train back to base.

Upon my return, I dived into the business of group operations officer almost viciously. There was much to be done to improve the training of the lead crews, and directing their training was primarily my responsibility. Since our type of bombing required putting all the eggs in one basket, the lead crews who carried that basket had to be exceptional. The aircraft they flew had to be exceptional. Breakdowns in the system were breakdowns of the functioning of group operations. I stood or fell on their record.

In those days just prior to the spring of 1944 many of the raids were long and hard. The heavy bombers had just begun to go all the way into the Berlin area. When the weather was bad it usually meant that formations which did get over enemy territory were leaner. Of the ships which took off, fewer were able to climb through the heavy cloud and find the designated point where the various units formed up before going out. And, generally, to fail to make formation was to fail to make the mission. Frequently, in this bad weather the bombers and fighters would fail to meet at the assigned rendezvous. Sometimes only a handful of escorting fighters would make it through the weather to give cover. These circumstances combined to make losses heavy and bombing accuracy poor.

Nearly every time we went out one group and, sometimes, one combat wing out of the three divisions would be hit hard. Experience had taught the masterminds of the Luftwaffe that the way to inflict maximum damage and suffer minimum losses was to have all their available attacking fighters hit one or two small units—usually units for one reason or another less protected than the rest. It might be that the friendly support was spread particularly thin at one point or another, or one group might be flying poorer formation than another. Whenever we took off we knew some unit in the day's mass of bombers had a bad card to draw, and we hoped it wouldn't be ours.

Our group was fairly lucky. There were times after two or three hard raids in a row when our ranks were pitifully thinned out. But we had no times as bad as some of the traditionally unlucky groups. Some groups lost almost their entire force on a single raid. There were five days in February when the Eighth Air Force lost 244 heavy bombers and 33 fighters. Those were five days of clearing skies after many weeks of weather so bad as to make pinpoint bombing impossible. On one of those five days Colonel Arnold led a very successful mission to Gotha, and I flew on his wing as deputy lead. Our group lost more crews and airplanes on that raid than on any raid in its previous history, including the low-level attack on Ploesti. The next day Colonel Miller led our group out on a brilliant mission against the aircraft factory at Fürth. Those raids cost us sorely, but they nearly bled the enemy to death. Their fighter plane production never recovered from what the Air Force did that week.

When a group lost heavily on one or two raids there was a natural strain on the morale of the remaining combat crews. It was hard for the boys coming back to go to quarters that were practically vacant, quarters which had been full a few hours before. It wore on their nerves to go to the club and find the place more filled with the ghosts of those who had gone than the presence of the few who remained. General Doolittle was a savvy guy about this particular hardship. I heard a story about a visit he made to one of the groups that had lost nearly everyone on a single raid. The incident happened just after the unit had been filled up with replacements following a similar occurrence only a few weeks before. The general, as was his custom, flew his own fighter plane to the base and went unannounced to pay a visit to the officers' club.

It was late evening and the bar was open. A lone lieutenant was solemnly drinking a beer. The general stepped up beside him and ordered one. The lieutenant, noticing who the newcomer was, turned to the star-bearing little flier and said, "What're you doing up here, general? Lookin' over our mo-ralle?"

The general smiled. "Not at all. I try to get around to visit all my groups every now and then. I didn't have much to do in headquarters this afternoon, so I decided I'd fly up and pay you a call."

"You know, general," the lieutenant continued, "Funny thing, mo-ralle. Ours is okay till the high-ranking generals start coming around lookin' it over. Then it just goes all to hell."

The general laughed, chatted with the officer a while, went out, climbed in his ship, and flew off. Yes, General Doolittle was a savvy guy. He was hard when the situation called for that, but when he left that group that day he knew that there was enough fighting spirit in the handful of flying men left to give proper inspiration to the new bunch of replacements he was sending in.

In these hard raids, I took mine as they came. For those qualified to act as command pilot in the lead ship of our group there was a system. They rotated in a regular schedule, and with few exceptions when a man's name came up he took the mission, wherever it was.

The first few daylight raids on Berlin were run by the B-17s. The Libs hit other targets concurrently with these Fortress raids. The theory was that the Libs, fully loaded, couldn't fly as high as the Forts and thus would be more vulnerable to the intense flak barrage over the city. The RAF high command had said it would be impossible ever to hit Berlin in a daylight raid and sustain for any length of time the losses that would result. But then, as we knew would happen, calls came for the B-24s to take the trip over The Big B.

On one of the earliest of these I drew the lead. The mission was really supposed to bomb a ball bearing works on the southeast edge of the Nazi capital. That was to be our target if the weather was clear. Our forecast had it, however, that the area would likely be covered with cloud, so that the ball bearing works was designated as a secondary target. The primary target, given under the assumption that weather would prevent pin-point bombing, was the center of Berlin. In case of cloud cover-age preventing visual bombing we would bomb the center of the town on instruments. At that time our instrument bombing was accurate enough for a wide area like the city of Berlin, but not accurate enough for a single factory.

The way the mission was planned, I would fly in a pathfinder airplane to be brought in by a special pathfinder crew a few hours before briefing. We were leery about allowing our group, and as in this case our whole combat wing of three groups, to be led by a strange crew. The deputy command pilot was Major Jack Dieterle, a new squadron commander. Jack was a tall, dark-eyed young fellow from Toledo, Ohio, and one of the excellent younger leaders. He was flying with one of the best lead crews we had. According to the plan, if the target did happen to be clear, my plane would shift places with Jack's in sufficient time before reaching the target to allow him to make an unhampered visual bombing run. After bombing we would shift back and I would lead the wing home. If, of course, it was blind bombing I would merely hold my place in the lead, and we would bomb the center of town on instruments.

We were up several hours before dawn. If the fellows ever felt like breaking into loud cheers upon having an important tar-get announced in the briefing room, that morning they might have. But when the curtain was lifted from the big map, reveal-ing the long route in, the target, and the long route out, there were no cheers. I knew where the target was, and so when the map was uncovered I didn't look at the board. Instead I watched the faces of the crews. They became a shade more grave, but were otherwise unmoved.

When the main briefing was over the briefing officer called on me as the lead commander to give any final comments I wished. I remember saying, "Today let's win the contest of for-mation flying. You all know the poorest formation is the one that gets ripped. It won't be us! Now, if the target should be open we will know it in plenty of time for me to shift the lead to you, Jack. And if I do shift to you, and after that you have a mal-function of a bombsight or for any reason fail to drop on the factory, there will be no use to shift leads back. We will be right on the southern outskirts of Berlin. You will simply turn north and fly over the center of town and let them have it. Good luck, fellows. I'll see you here tonight."

There was the usual sickening hour before takeoff. The hour of getting into heavy, smelly clothes; fitting oxygen masks; checking the ships; checking the bomb loading, fusing, gas loading, oxygen, guns, ammunition; and the million other things. On that occasion, as on others, I got to myself for a moment and prayed that I be given the courage to do my best and that whatever happened I would fight as long as I could. Before takeoff I nervously whistled a tune. It was "Room with a View." It brought back to my mind that most unusual wedding trip to Kentucky. I loved it and now it helped to calm me.

We started engines and taxied to the head of the runway and then cut them to wait for the rest of the ships to marshall behind us. I chatted with my crew, the pathfinder boys. I soon discovered they had nothing like the total number of missions which our crews were required to accomplish to become lead crews. They were nervous and showed it. I tried to affect an air of casualness about the mission to calm them down, but I was worried.

On the dot of that moment of anticipation which had been set for takeoff we got a green signal light from the tower. The darkness prior to early morning was just beginning to break as the pilot pushed the throttles open. I followed them up with my hands behind his and locked them. I concentrated on the engine instruments in order to catch a runaway prop or supercharger should one need catching, and stood by for the raised thumb signal from the pilot indicating "landing gear up." The overweight Liberator waddled down the runway gathering speed very slowly at first, but at last picking up enough to struggle into the air at the end of the concrete strip.

We circled our airdrome in weather which was not nearly as bad as that to which we were accustomed, and at the designated time we had our group fairly well formed and in position to pick up the other two groups of our combat wing. We were leading the wing, and ours was the last wing of the three divisions all going over the same target that day—the eighth of March, 1944.

Within reasonable bounds our mission went as briefed until we got far into Germany. At a well-defined checkpoint the whole flotilla of bombers was supposed to turn from its easterly heading to about forty degrees southeast of the original course. After we held this heading for a while we planned to turn again due east and continue past the longitude of Berlin. Then we would turn north and swing back around to the west. We were to fly over our target and drop bombs heading west. From that heading we would be more or less on course home, and if the plan were followed we would pass just south of the main defenses of the city.

When we came to the point where we were supposed to turn southeast, the great chain of formation of bombers kept flying directly east. Our navigator called me on the interphone, telling me that the division leader had passed up the turning point. What did I want to do? Should we turn as briefed, or should we follow the leader?

I was in a little bit of a quandary. The weather was moderately clear, I had my maps in my lap, and I could plainly identify the spot the navigator pointed out as the place where we were supposed to turn. But all the fighter support, thin as it was that far into Germany, would remain over the main formation if we turned. If we got out from under our fighter cover we would certainly find ourselves elected.

At this point it might be well to explain a few things about the method the Jerries used in planning attacks on us. From the time we entered the continental coast on a raid, until a good while after we left it, we were shadowed by a German monitoring aircraft. This would be a light, fast craft that flew far above us and off to one side enough to be out of danger from our guns and away from attack by our fighter cover. This ship would maintain constant radio contact with the Nazi Ground Sector Control. The Ground Sector Control by reports from the monitor plane, plus information gained from the German radar, would get a complete picture of the condition, heading, speed, and altitude of our bomber formations. The Germans knew constantly which formations within the larger formation were the most vulnerable to attack because of poor flying, lack of friendly fighter cover, or whatever. They kept their own fighters alerted and were able to hit any part of our attacking force according to precise plan in a matter of seconds after the order was given.

I knew all this. I recalled how my friend Fearless Ken Caldwell had been killed and his formation shot to pieces because he withdrew from the division formation coming out of France that evening several months before. But then, there is also the mission to be accomplished. If everyone else missed the target it would be many times more necessary that I hit it. I looked at the formation ahead. They were still headed due east with no sign of a turn. I tried unsuccessfully to get the division leader on the radio.

Finally, of course, I thought of Anne and Pete back home and how near I was to the completion of my combat tour. If I could get home from this raid I had only one more to go. Usually they gave you an easy one for the last one. But while that thought was turning over I already knew I had made up my mind that the right thing to do was to pull out of the division formation. If others failed to fly the mission as briefed and I knew they were wrong and I was unable to raise anyone on the radio to correct the error, there was only one logical avenue of action open to me.

I called the navigator and told him to give us a heading to get us back on the briefed course. I got it almost immediately and gave the order to turn. At that moment, one of two or three such moments in my flying career, I thought I had given up my last good chance to get home. I decided we would try our best to do a good job of bombing and then fight our way out. If my airplane were shot down I determined I would get all the men out, then hit the silk. From there on it would be a question of escape from Germany. I felt equal to the attempt, though I sensed a tiredness unlike any I ever had before.

As we turned southeast we were not very far from our target. The weather cleared until it was the clearest I ever saw that far into Germany. There wasn't even any haze in the air. I called Jack Dieterle, my deputy leader, to ask him if he had himself properly spotted. He replied that he did. I told him it was evident the bombing would be visual and ordered him to prepare to shift places with me so that his crew could lead on the bomb run. He acknowledged.

Just about that time I noticed the bombers ahead, which were now only specks in the distance. They were turning to the southeast. There was no doubt about their being far off course. Evidently something had messed up in the lead and everyone else elected to follow. Just now the leader of the column was plainly trying to get back on course. The fact that we had turned southeast before the head of the column turned put us now almost abreast of them flying a parallel course. Of course they were pretty far off to our left, but it would make it difficult for us to get the proper interval to bomb without getting in someone's way. We would simply have to give ourselves margin enough to be sure we would not fly through another formation when we turned on the target. Else we might get ourselves mixed up and miss the aiming point after these long hours of work and worry.

Soon we turned due east again preparatory to doubling back to the left on our bomb run. I shifted the lead temporarily to Dieterle. The maneuver was awkwardly completed chiefly because of the high altitude at which we were flying and the fact that the pathfinder pilot in the seat beside me was not used to flying wing position. In his meager experience he was used to leading, and it was evident he was a poor wing man. I flew the ship part of the time, though I wasn't very good either.

As we turned left to head toward the target, I noticed the last units of the other bombers had made their turn and were now very far in advance. We were just about completely snapped off the end of the long string of bomber formations of the three divisions. Anyway, I thought, we should have a good clear bomb run.

Just about that moment I got a call from Dieterle. "My navigator says he isn't sure where we are," he said. "What position do you make us?"

Hastily consulting with my navigator, I reported to him that we were just about directly on course to our target, after having gone a little farther east and south than briefed. We could look out to the right front and see the vast, sprawling city of Berlin through the quartz-like air. Ahead and slightly to our right was a towering column of smoke. I watched it intermittently until suddenly it occurred to me that the navigator in Dieterle's ship apparently still hadn't found himself. He was just slightly south of the proper course and nearing the bomb release line. But as yet the bomb bay doors of the ship had not opened. It was apparent the navigator still had not spotted the target. I looked for the ball bearing factory, and like a flash it occurred to me: that column of smoke, which I could now see was an inky black cloud covering a large area, was what was left of our target. It would be impossible to pick any aiming point out of that inky blotch. Evidently in the clear visibility the first bombers had hit and the ones behind had hit again until now the factory was a completely leveled, flaming, smoking mass. The bombs of at least eight hundred heavy bombers had hit an area as big as a few city blocks.

"That black smoke is the target," I shouted over the radio.

"I know it," came back the reply. "We're past where we could make a good run on it now. If we hit it we'll have to circle to take a second run. What are your orders?"

We had been specifically briefed according to the division field order that no second runs would be made. I remembered that. Besides, though sometimes such appearance is deceptive, it was evident to my mind that there had already been many more than sufficient bombers over that target to do the job.

"Turn right and we'll fly over the center of town and make the delivery," I yelled. The radio jamming at this point was terrible. My radio was dinning into my headphones the most horrible cacophony I had ever heard. I was afraid Jack might not get the message, but he did.

My pilot turned to me and said, "We're not supposed to fly over the center of Berlin unless it is overcast. We are a pathfinder crew. That's what we're here for. If we go over there now we'll be shot to hell by the flak and then ripped to pieces by fighters coming out."

That was the only experience I ever had of reluctance on the part of a lead pilot. He was no more frightened than I. We had met a situation where there was only one thing left to do, and we would do it. In a few minutes we were within range of the outer circle of the heavy guns guarding Berlin. The first few score of bursts were surprisingly low. Then they crept up on us. On in we went. Berlin seemed the biggest city in the world. We flew on for terribly long minutes until finally we were passing over some large buildings almost in the middle of town. The formation was completely haywire. The flak bursts were so thick it seemed to me some of the shells must be colliding with each other. A couple of bombers I could see were already heavily hit. But being in the airplane next to the lead, I couldn't see far enough back into our disordered formation to gauge well the overall effect of this devastating fire.

We kept flying over heavily built-up areas. Why didn't the bombardier in Dieterle's ship let go? We knew now we were only bombing the city, and one place was about as good as another. What were they holding their bombs for? I called Dieterle.

"Why the hell don't you let them go? We'll be past the city in another hour of this kind of flying."

"Sorry, the bombardier wants to bomb the railroad yards. Bomb line almost here."

A few seconds later the bombs were away from the lead ship and in quick succession from every other ship of the gangling formation. We turned sharp left to head out to the west side of town. The flak was all around us, and we could see the sheets of flame in the explosion of many shell bursts. The ships kicked around in the air like canoes in a Lake Superior storm.

I took over the flying of our plane for a moment. I put on enough power to pull ahead a little and slid to the left and under Dieterle, then dropped down a hundred feet or so and headed straight west waggling my wings furiously. Then I pulled off some power and slowed up. Many of the pilots by this time had doubtless become confused as to who was leading. But immediately Dieterle pulled up on my right wing. I kept waggling my wings for a moment, and held a reduced power setting. Soon the others began forming on me in a good, tight formation. About that time we saw the edge of the field of flak just ahead. We flew through the last black bursts and out into the clear, clean air beyond. I held reduced power so the plane kept going as slowly as it could and be stable. Then I told the pilot not to put on any more throttle until I ordered it.

Once out of the flak, I looked around to take stock of our situation. Many airplanes showed gaping holes; many had feathered propellers marking dead engines. Some were smoking as if they were about to burst into flames, and a couple had gone down. I called all the aircraft in the formation and told them I would use as little power as possible so the cripples could stay with me, and I would let down slowly to 15,000 feet for those whose oxygen lines were out. Some had already dropped below us, but were staying abreast of us underneath. I knew as we let down they would be able to resume positions in the formation. I looked for friendly fighters and saw none. I looked for the other bomber formations, but they were long gone out of sight. I listened for calls from ships of our formation reporting enemy fighters about, and here I was not disappointed. But after listening for a few minutes to the calls of our crippled ships too far to my rear for me to see them from the cockpit, I was convinced there were really very few German fighters attacking. Our tail gunner reported moderate enemy activity, but that was all. I thanked goodness for what we had done in February to the German fighter production.

I did my best to keep the formation well grouped and fly it in such a manner that the cripples could stay up. Many of the cripples did manage to stay with us, but there were reports of two ships falling back. One of these had three good engines, and I couldn't imagine why it couldn't hold on. Had I flown any slower it would have been to the detriment of the main formation, because our planes would have been unstable flying so close to the stalling point. That makes formation flying much more difficult. The way the main formation was moving, several ships with only three engines seemed to have little difficulty staying up. We kept getting reports of attack after attack on the two that dropped back until at last their calls were heard no more. From one I picked up that familiar last call: "Ship on fire, crew bailing out." At rather frequent intervals I called our Ground Sector Control to tell them we were a lone formation of bombers considerably behind the rest of the formations, without friendly fighter support and under enemy attack.

When our wing first left the Berlin area I still felt we wouldn't make it home. But it finally dawned on me that for some peculiar reason there were only a few Jerries left to attack us. My hopes continued to rise by the minute for the next three-quarters of an hour. In that time we would have been gutted, had there been any reasonable force of enemy fighters about. To me it looked like a bad guess on the part of the German Ground Sector Control. It was evident they were much weaker than they had been only a week or so before, and they had spent most of their available force attacking the formations ahead. After all, we had been at least in the area of the other bombing units until we made that last turn north to go over the center of Berlin. It was only then that we got too far behind for any support from friendly planes.

It was likely that many of the Jerries had been used to stop the first attacking units which started in on their bomb run. Many times that was their plan—to blunt the head of the column. And by the time we came over the majority of them were either shot down, damaged, or on the ground refueling. Their short range wouldn't permit them to fly long without landing for fuel.

Coming out we went three-quarters of an hour without friendly fighter support. Each minute was an agony, but finally my calls for help began to bear fruit. At length we saw a few ships headed toward us in the distance; they looked like our fighters. Two formations of four were coming our way, and they were flying just like the boys from the tall corn fly them. They slid in from an angle, flipping up their wings in a saucy-looking maneuver whose purpose is to let us see the white stars on their undersides. They don't want the combined turrets of a bomber unit to let loose on them. As soon as we were sure who they were the relief we felt was something beyond explanation. I took the formation on down to 12,000 feet upon getting the support. I knew the pilots who had been flying without oxygen at 15,000 must be tired. We could risk a slightly lower altitude with friendly fighter cover.

I sat back in my seat, unbuckled my safety belt, and took off my oxygen mask to give my face a rest. I called the boys in the back of the airplane to tell them our altitude so that they could take off their masks if they wanted to. We felt ourselves as good as home now that we could look up at those big, beautiful Thunderbolts in pairs crisscrossing over our heads. A song was running like a continuing nervous tremor through my mind, though until this moment of relaxation I had taken little note of it. It was "Room with a View."

· During the remainder of the trip home we met a few patches of moderate flak, but we didn't suffer from them. In that last hour and a half of the flight my eased mind covered many things. I felt this would be the last hard raid of my tour, and now I believed I would live to see the show out. I had felt that at the moment I saw that first Thunderbolt a hundred miles back. Here was a life not ended, but before me.

Soon, through a few bursts of flak from the coastal defense guns, we passed out over the beaches of France. Those few flak bursts looked downright funny compared to the ones we saw over Berlin. And then there was the lovely coast of England followed shortly by the familiar, wooded surroundings of our home station. I called the engineer and told him to make a careful inspection of the plane. We had felt many shell bursts close to the ship. We hadn't noticed anything wrong with the way it flew, but I didn't want to take any chances. If a plane is crippled it's good to know it before landing. After we had put the landing gear down I told the engineer to check the tires carefully.

Soon he returned to the cockpit and said all was well. No evidence of any real damage, just a lot of small holes all over. I relaxed. You can tell to look at a tire when a bomber is in the air whether it is punctured or not. If it has been holed by flak or fighter shells it will assume an unusual configuration in the slipstream. So we were okay. We led the formation over the field and peeled off. The pilot set a nice glide on his final approach to the runway and we touched down easily. It seemed almost a perfect landing for the first hundred and fifty feet. Then the ship began to wobble peculiarly. It was going down on the right wheel and had a strong tendency to pull off the runway to the right. The pilot didn't seem to be making the proper effort to stop it, so I took over.

I jammed on the left brake and threw on power on the number four—right outboard—engine. It was evident our engineer had been wrong. We had a flat right tire. As the Lib slowed down and the wings lost their lift it came down hard on the rim. We could feel the grinding of the tire as it buckled under the weight and finally tore off. I knew we had to get the ship clear of the runway. Had I known we had a flat tire, I would have waited for the others to land. We couldn't afford to let our ship jam traffic. There were other runways, but none so long as the one we were on. If we got off the runway we would bog down immediately and doubtless other ships would be coming in in worse condition than we.

As our plane careened down the strip, the left brake smoking and the right tire gone, it slowed up quickly. We were approaching the crossway intersection of another runway. Just as we came abreast of it I released the brake pressure on the left brake and pulled off the throttle to let the ship spin around in a sharp right turn of slightly more than ninety degrees. Then I hit the left brake again for a moment and gave the right outboard engine another blast of power. It straightened us out and pulled us clear of the path of other ships coming in behind. As soon as we were well away from the long runway I cut the engines. We were right in front of the tower. Sweat was running down my forehead in such volume that it was getting in my eyes. My clothes were made for the freezing cold of high altitude, not for such exertion on the ground. I looked toward the railed balcony of the control tower and saw Colonel Arnold and General Timberlake waving to me.

I climbed out of the sad-looking bomber; it was listing at a steep tilt with its right wing down. I gave it a hasty once-over and noticed gas dripping from a hole in the wing. We had fuel cells punctured. I saw a lot of holes; they were everywhere, though most of them were small. The ship had taken quite a beating to carry out its mission. Before I left it to walk over to the tower, I told the crew chief standing by to save me a sample of the flak.

I knew he would find some in it, and I thought a piece of that flak would be a proper memento of an ordeal which someday I might not mind remembering. I walked over to the tower and climbed the stairs to be greeted by the broad smile and sparkling eyes of Colonel Arnold. "Hope you had fun today, Phil."

General Ted was smiling, too. They were naturally too rapt in attention to the landing progress of the other airplanes to want a full account of the mission at that time. Together we watched the rest of the landings. Some ships were okay and some were crippled in different degrees of seriousness. Finally, the last one expected in had landed, and then the general, Colonel Arnold, and I piled in the general's big Packard and drove to the wing headquarters to go over the results of the mission. Dieterle and his navigator and bombardier joined us there. With those three aiding me I tried to piece together the way things went. I covered every detail as well as I could. When all of us got through I think we had given a pretty accurate and detailed picture.

My pathfinder crew left to eat, and I never saw them again. I was frankly disappointed in the way that crew functioned, but perhaps it was not their fault. I felt the injustice of the situation applied to them as well as to our wing. Someone in authority had designated that crew of clearly inadequate combat experience to lead a combat wing on a very intricate mission. The crew had done the best it could. One thing which remained in my mind was the fact that the engineer who had inspected the tire wasn't even able to tell it was punctured.

The mission was considered a great success. The bombers ahead of us were credited with 100 percent destruction of the ball bearing factory. Thus our scattering of bombs on Berlin resulted in more damage than we could have expected had we bombed the bomb craters of units ahead of us. The Air Force lost thirty-eight bombers and sixteen fighters on the mission, and that was less than expected.

My mind was relaxed, but I was tired, and the feeling of satisfaction permitted my tiredness to descend upon me with appalling suddenness. As I left the operations office of the wing, General Ted complimented me and Colonel Arnold slapped me on the shoulder, laughed and said, "My God, you must have had a time of it today. Go get something to eat and see if you can find a sack to crawl into. I'll see you tomorrow."

After that mission I walked about the station with more general confidence than I'd had since the day of my abort on the first Norway raid. From a strictly objective assessment of results, maybe my decision on that sad occasion was right. Nevertheless I had done injury to myself by that decision. For a while after my trip to Berlin I didn't fly operationally. But in my job as group operations officer I had found that there were other duties to perform which were just about as trying. Once or twice I found these other duties almost more than I could take. It was my job to visit the scenes of accidents in order to be able to make the necessary reports. Sometimes that meant I had to view the remains of my friends strewn across the English countryside. One such occasion particularly stays in my mind.

I could have committed murder when I saw that macabre display. The ambulance had visited the scene of the accident when I got there, but the attendants had missed some of the remains of the crew members. I tramped over a tremendous barley field in which small bits of a great Liberator were scattered like seeds from the hand of Satan. I had seen half of a pink hand, upturned and mysteriously unbleeding. It looked like something out of a landscape by Dali, except in this case it was part of someone I knew. As soon as I had seen enough to make a report I met an Englishman who had the land under lease. He had planted the barley in the field and was obviously a farmer of considerable holdings. He became annoyed when he found we had not brought the proper forms with us for him to fill out his claim of damage to the barley crop. He was impatient at a delay of twenty-four hours in getting the form, and clearly indicated he thought that the payment of his claim should be given immediate precedence over all else. Two officers who were with me placed themselves one on one side and one on the other and drew me away from him. If they hadn't I might have scattered him about to keep company with the remains of our crew.

But again we had an accident. One of our ships returned

from a raid hideously crippled. At an altitude too low to permit the crew to jump out, it began to go to pieces. It was headed down toward a small village. The pilot, from undeniable evidence, made a superhuman effort and forced his plane over the inhabited area. It crashed just past the last house and burned with all personnel aboard. The next day a beautiful wreath arrived. It was sent by the villagers with a card bearing these words: "With heartfelt sympathy and as a token of sincere appreciation from the residents of Taverham, Norfolk, for self-sacrifice made by this crew of our American Allies."

Another of the nonflying but sometimes harrowing duties of the group operations officer was occasional tower control. When the boys were coming back from missions that were rated at all difficult, or if the weather was as questionable as it generally was, it was necessary for a special traffic controller to be in the tower before and during landing. Colonel Arnold did this himself much of the time, but it was a duty which sometimes he would delegate to Colonel Miller or me. It has happened that I have been on the microphone in the tower and have been asked to make decisions for the crew of a stricken bomber in the air that might well mean the difference of life or death.

I was in the tower one evening as it began to grow dark, when the boys came back from a rough one. One after another of our available runways was blocked by bombers crash-landing when, just as the dark became complete, I got a call from a straggler. The late Lib was piloted by my own boy of the old days when I had the squadron. It was Mac McLaughlin flying *B* for Baker, *Ole Irish*. Mac's voice was calm as he called in for a landing. He told me he had only three engines, his landing gear wasn't functioning right, he had no flaps and no brakes. I had two of my three runways blocked, and the third, a very short one had just been cleared of a partly wrecked ship. I told him he couldn't use the long runway. I gave him directions to land on the short runway crosswind. Mac came in so low over the trees he almost took the tops out of the last two or three of them. He touched down perfectly, took the full length of the runway, but finally managed to get the plane stopped by dragging the tail.

When he was announced safe Earl Widen, our new and sterling Protestant chaplain, came to me and announced, "Now I'm going to stop this praying and go to bed."

That night after I left the tower and repaired to the bar to have a few beers to help me sleep, I saw Major John Berger, our group surgeon. John had been at the end of the runway in an ambulance picking up the wounded. He didn't know how I felt, and so he told me about one boy he had cared for. A gunner, he was, who had caught a 20 mm. shell from an attacking fighter plane. The shell went through the back part of his head, but for some uncanny reason it hadn't exploded. It took part of the head away, but not enough to kill him. It just left him permanently blind. Peculiarly, there was no pain. The boy insisted on helping himself get out of the plane and into the waiting ambulance. He couldn't understand what had happened to him, and he didn't know he would never see again.

The things which hit me hard seemed to come in strings, and just a little while after that rough evening was over I found myself again in the tower trying to help the boys in. I didn't think I would have very much to do this time, because the raid was not calculated to have been a very tough one and there was comparatively good weather. But the group had evidently encountered very heavy flak.

The first call I got from one of our ships was not from the formation leader. It was from a young pilot, new to the group and home early. He was shot up and was able to get one main landing gear and the nose wheel down by the emergency manual procedure. The other main wheel was stuck in the up position. Flak had cut the cable which was used to lower the wheel. Having put the one main wheel and the nose wheel down, he could not now retract them. It would have been better to make a belly landing with all wheels up than to land as it appeared he would now have to.

He was giving out of gas and he called me to make a decision for him. Should he head the ship out to sea and jump, or should he try to land it? He had no wounded aboard. I told him to land. I was a major then, and a lieutenant colonel from our division headquarters who was visiting in the tower at the time told me

I was crazy. He voiced the opinion that the crew should bail out. I was acting on the delegated authority of Colonel Arnold, and I let that officer know that I would run the traffic at the tower with no interference from anyone but my group commander.

As the ship turned in from the base leg of the traffic pattern, I saw our fire truck spurt exhaust. Its crew was hastily donning asbestos suits. The airplane was now on its final approach. Then it touched down on the one main wheel, held level for a moment and began to go down on the right side. Finally it touched the right wing and slid along partly on, partly off the runway for what seemed an incredible distance. The props on the right side dug in and broke off, and fire flew from under the ship where it scraped the concrete runway. At length the plane went into a giant ground loop and stopped. The fire truck dashed out as the flames licked upward from the bottom of the crashed Lib. I was abreast of the fire truck in my galloping jeep. We were almost on the wreck by the time it came to a full stop. Fire had already begun in the nacelle of the right outboard engine as well as in the center section underneath the fuselage. The next moment after the skidding hulk stopped the top hatch opened and men started jumping out. They were also jumping from the waist windows. I knew in two or three seconds the flames might ignite gas fumes and convert the wreck into an uncontrollable pyre. But in those seconds the firemen were pointing their hoses and squirting chemical spray everywhere there was evidence of fire. The white foam spat into the engine nacelle and under the ship, and the flames crackled and died.

There were other duties of the group operations officer which at that time were almost as harrowing as the duty of flying combat. But they were all in the routine of war, and proper performance of them brought a genuine sense of satisfaction.

One day shortly after my completion of the Berlin trip Colonel Arnold took me aside and asked me what plans I had made for the time when I had completed my tour. I told him I knew it was impossible for one in my position to plan and that I would do what I was assigned to do. But if I had my choice I would go back to the States as soon as possible. My aching to get a glimpse of Anne and Pete grew more acute with each day that passed.

The colonel told me he thought I would, without a doubt, be able to go back to the States within three or four months of the time I had the tour complete. However, he let me know that owing to the fact that replacements were coming through slowly, everyone was expected to do a little extra work before going home. I replied that if I had to stay in England I would as soon be in the command I was in as any I could possibly think of. Then he mentioned the fact that General Ted had said he had a place for me in the wing. That ended our conversation of that day. But for days afterwards I continued to consider what had been said about the job at the wing. It was a job others had asked for, and I was vastly flattered that it might be offered to me. Just about that time my promotion to the rank of lieutenant colonel came through. I was very glad, but I felt a little ashamed about it. I had been such a continual beneficiary of good luck that I felt it quite possible my qualities had been overrated. I felt the best way to get along in my job was not to let myself get overrated. At the time the prospects of my future were presented to me I was not confronted with the necessity of making any decision, nor was I given to understand the matter had been finally decided by others. It was something to think about during the days I had remaining.

The last mission seemed almost automatic. I can recall few details about it. It was not hard and was made easier by the fact that, from some indescribable source, I had gained complete confidence that I would come back. This last mission was one deep into southern France. Colonel Arnold and General Ted also made it. Neither of those officers let much time elapse between their missions, nor did they pick missions. They flew on some of the toughest we had. They always maintained a spirit of levity and half-seriousness which made me quite ashamed of the moody way in which I took my hard ones. I felt it was just the difference between two real soldiers—West Pointers, God bless them—and a civilian covered with a uniform such as I. I used to hate the academy product, but in these last few months I had met too many good soldiers who were academy men to keep that misconception.

The main thing that I remember about the last mission was

that when I got back to the interrogation room I was met by the newly promoted Lieutenant Colonel Paul Burton. It was the same soft-voiced Paul who had gone out with me from Tucson on the original cadre of the group. Paul still had his squadron. He was a few missions behind me and had a little way to go to complete his tour. Paul and I had always liked each other. We were the only two left in the group of the original four squadron commanders who had shared the tent together in Bengasi. Hank Yaeger had been shot down and Del Cross had left the command. Paul rejoiced with me over my finishing the tour. Soon after that when he set out leading the group and was shot down over Germany, I remembered his charming manner that day. I missed him as a very material part of the group I had known in the beginning. And again I felt as though fate had been almost unfair.

I had had two truly efficient assistants in my old job to whom I owed most of whatever credit the office had earned. They were moving along as I moved. Major Dan Minnick, my first assistant, was slated to go to Division Headquarters as the division training officer. The other assistant, Captain Don Westerbeke, was going to take over my job of group operations officer. Some short days after taking over my job Westy fell victim of the trail of bad luck I always seemed to leave behind me. He was shot down over Holland and after a time was reported a prisoner of the Germans. I could not help but put Westy's case together with that of Ken Caldwell, who took over my command of the squadron and was almost immediately killed in action. The old group was greatly changed by the loss of those men, and so was I.

6

The Wing

On March 24, 1944, I completed my tour in the prophetically named Liberator *Round Trip Ticket*. Almost at once I was given orders transferring me to the wing. I felt a strong attachment to my old group and was glad the wing headquarters were located on the same airdrome where I'd been. Our wing included, of course, my old group and two others at bases only a few miles away.

When I arrived in the new command I reported directly to General Timberlake, who then told me he anticipated using me as his A-3 staff officer. A-3 is military for operations officer. The job had previously been filled by Major Morton Macks, the funniest man I ever knew in the Army. Besides Mort's quality as a clown he was an extremely smart and efficient operations man. I think the only reason General Ted was willing to replace him was that he had been overseas a long time, had completed a combat tour of operations, and wanted to go home. The general was letting him go purely out of compassion.

As was customary, the first thing I did after reporting was to ask for a day or two of leave to go to London. The general approved my request and immediately I got on the telephone to LeSueur, who had told me to be sure to come down when I could. He wanted to help me celebrate my last mission. "Come on down," Larry said. "I have a new flat and a nice room for you. I may have to leave town before you're ready to go back, but I'll give you the run of the place."

This trip to London would be a much nicer one than those past. I wouldn't have to return to sweat out any more missions, and I would return to one of the best jobs in the Air Corps. Still, when I got to London, to my own surprise I guess as much as to Larry's, I didn't feel much in the mood for hilarity. I wanted to talk with the boys about war and politics and see some people I had tried to see and missed on my previous trips. I was tired and I wanted to relax. At the CBS offices I talked to Messrs. Shaw and Collingwood and some of the other fellows while I waited for LeSueur to return from lunch. While we were in the midst of a loud controversy Larry, sleek and dark in his ultra-conservative pinstripes, strode in looking the part of a key international operator. He greeted me with, "Hiyah, jerk!"

That afternoon we chatted in the office for a while and then started wandering about town. Our first stop was the flat of Robert Capa, a thick-voiced, swarthy photographer for *Life*. Capa had asked Larry to come by and give him some advice about flats for rent. The stocky little photographer made a strong impression on me as another fearless journalist.

That evening we had dinner with Davidson Taylor of the Office of War Information, Charles Wertenbaker of *Time*, and some others. Dave Taylor had previously worked on the Louisville *Courier-Journal* and had a lot to say about Kentucky that was of particular interest to me.

As a result of the days I spent in London, I confirmed my already strong conviction that American reporters were doing a whale of a job. It was a job the American people had come to take for granted. Larry and Capa were both qualified parachutists hoping for a chance to jump somewhere behind enemy lines. All the rest of them spent many waking hours of each day planning how they might establish themselves personally in the war—not to make headlines, but merely to make themselves feel they were being fair to the public.

The day after my arrival Larry had to leave town. He left

me with the keys to his sumptuous flat. I had been hoping for some time to be able to see Stanley Reed, Jr., an old law school classmate of mine, and now with Larry gone I decided to try again to find him. Stanley was the son of a Supreme Court justice, and a naval officer in one of the headquarters in London. He was a Kentuckian by birth, but because of his long separation from Kentucky he had come to look, talk, and act like a native of Long Island. We had a point of common interest in our acquaintance with Harold Laski, professor of economics at the University of London. Stanley knew Laski rather better than I did, though we had both met him at the same time when he came to Harvard to give talks to the law students. After several telephone calls I located Stanley and arranged to have dinner with him the next evening. Stanley told me that after dinner he would take me to Laski's house. He had been there before and assured me I would be welcome. That was to be a Thursday evening, and he said on Thursday nights Laski opened his doors to friends for discussions of currently interesting topics.

After I hung up I remembered an incident that happened some months before when I met a conversative M.P. on the train to London. I asked the M.P. what he thought of Laski. As I recall, he termed the professor something of a "crazy man." I had then asked to what the honorable M.P. attributed the power of Laski's views. I remember the reply: "Oh, there are always people to listen to someone like that. And then, too, he writes those books, you know!"

I was very pleased to have a chance to see Laski again. I had read two of his recent essays, "Reflections on the Revolution of Our Times" and "Faith, Reason, and Civilization," and was impressed by both. For clarity of thought and mastery of presentation I thought I had never seen a contemporary who could approach Laski in his field. I did, however, find myself in disagreement with him on some points. He drew parallels between the beginnings of Christianity and the incipient political forces of today. I disagreed with his concept that there are forces which may supplant religion. I have heard many times that religion "is the opium of the people," but I saw its force among men who fought some of the greatest air battles the world has ever known.

It did not serve to reconcile them to their shortcomings, their failures, or their unanswerable needs. It seemed to me that the religion given them by their chaplains, Protestant, Catholic, and Jewish alike, was no sanctuary for a pilot who quit combat. It was the strength of a pilot who might have had to quit without it.

Stanley and I had dinner and took a bus to Laski's house on the edge of London. The little man with the big glasses and the funny moustache met us at the door. "Mr. Laski," Reed said, "you may not remember my friend Colonel Ardery."

Laski's face brightened. "Oh, yes. He was with you in law school; of course I remember. Come in, Ardery. Glad to have you and Reed drop in."

From the entrance hall we stepped down into a small library which held more books than any other room its size I ever saw. Several others arrived—most of them American Army officers. Laski started talking about Churchill's recent issue in Parliament over increased pay for schoolteachers. The prime minister's action in the case had been subject to many interpretations. Churchill had chosen to make a petty fuss over teachers' pay the subject of a vote of confidence on which his government would stand or fall. Did he do it to demonstrate to Roosevelt and Stalin his power over the government? Did he do it because he really wanted to know how his government stood? Or did he do it just from sheer cussedness? Though he gave no direct answer, I believe Laski thought the latter. I remember the long discussion better than I remember the conclusions. It seems to me it was the general view that Churchill had got his Churchillian temper up and decided to give the opposition a bit of a hosing. Laski impressed me as a man who, above all, possessed in abundance the qualities of a gentleman. He was supersensitive to injustice and tyranny. I think, if he had faults, one was that his intellectual capability caused him to overestimate people.

Next morning I rose early, threw my few things into my Air Corps B-4 bag, and caught the train.

The new job was even bigger and better than I had imagined it would be. Never in my life had I found myself so surrounded with such superior people as I did in that headquarters. A fine officer of Italian extraction by the name of Carmelo Alba, then a captain, was the S-1 (adjutant). Major Mike Phipps, ten goals at polo and just as good at the work of an intelligence officer, was the S-2 (intelligence). I became the S-3 (operations). Among the other figures in the headquarters was Colonel Larry Thomas, the chief of staff. He had come in to take the job previously filled by Colonel Arnold when the latter left to take his group command. Some time after my arrival Colonel Thomas went out to take command of a group; and the Hollywood idol, Lieutenant Colonel Jimmy Stewart, came in to take his place.

Then there was Fred Jarecki, Mike's assistant in intelligence. Soon after I came in Major Vic Sieverding also entered the intelligence branch. He was a delightful, older officer who had been a practicing lawyer in Des Moines, Iowa. Captain Fred Willis, my old squadron intelligence officer, had worked in this headquarters after leaving the squadron; but about the time of my arrival he went back to work in a group.

In my own department I had Captain Bill Selvidge of Ardmore, Oklahoma. He was my first assistant operations officer and chief controller. Bill was a great wit, a pilot who had completed a tour in my old group, a lawyer and former state legislator. He was a good-looking, slightly balding fellow, with a straight-line moustache.

As my wing bombardier there was the small, hyperfunctioning John Fino, a captain who soon became a major. My navigator was Mac McClain, the Waterloo, Iowa, redhead who had guided the ship I was in on many rough missions, including the group's first raid into Germany and the shoot-fest we attended in Norway. Mac had been on Wright's crew. He was made a captain toward the end of his tour and brought into this headquarters to supervise the work of the navigators of the three groups.

And then there was our general. For many, many months my opinion of General Ted had gradually been taking shape. I remembered well the first time I ever saw him. He was a full colonel then, standing outside the group operations tent at Bengasi. It was just before he took off to lead the long, first raid on Wiener Neustadt in Austria. His powerful face made a great impression on me. I thought it the type of face that should be carved on the side of a mountain somewhere.

That face was a good representation of what was behind it. Once, when I was a group operations officer at a critique of one of our missions, I challenged the whole system of bombing used by the Eighth Air Force. General Ted was there. I proposed a radical plan which would completely change the mode of flying of the strategic bombers. Of course, I knew it wouldn't get anywhere, but as a proposal it at least precipitated argument which threw some light on questions not previously discussed. The general surprised me by his eager participation in the discussion, for then I realized he was no hidebound follower of tradition. He was quite willing to accept any innovation based on sound logic and to be a trailblazer. His horizons were not the limits of his West Point texts. He had the imagination necessary for the ingenious operation of a military command.

General Timberlake, like his academy classmate Colonel Arnold, was a great commanding officer. They were the only two officers whom I knew well over a period of some time who never showed the slightest evidence of low morale. Both of them had officers under them coming periodically to seek bolstering of their spirits by airing real or fancied complaints. Neither of them, so far as I could ever see, went to anyone higher up to seek such assistance, nor did either show any visible evidence of periodic depression. From my experience in the combat zone, I consider such forbearance to be one of the greatest assets a commander can have. His command will love him if he can carry the gripes of all those under him with never a complaint of his own. In the combat zone, as elsewhere, there are injustices done everyone at times—chiefly in matters of promotion or comparative recognition passed out among several officers who may deserve equal credit, but who actually get very different rewards. Under the pressure of the continued strain of war and in the face of two or three successive injustices, though the points involved may be minor, an officer's mettle can be sorely tested.

Another side of the general was revealed by the feeling of those under him that it was a pleasure to render him the courtesy and respect that he was entitled to demand. He never demanded it, but he always got it. He had an air of levity about him that made him seem quite informal, but all of us under him knew he would not respect an officer who failed in matters of normal military courtesy, whether it directly involved himself or other officers within his command.

All the officers of the wing headquarters ate meals together at one big table. Dinner was the high point of the day. Normally the chief of staff sat on the general's right and I sat on his left. Sometimes the discussions got a little boisterous, though never too much so. All closets were opened and all skeletons dragged out for what laughs they might produce. Major Morton Macks, my predecessor who stayed in the headquarters for a few weeks after my arrival, was high man at getting laughs. The moment anyone got too serious Mort would step in. He could be the overbearing cad, the dumb guy just trying to get along, or the utter maniac. We never knew how he would meet a situation. Carmelo Alba and Johnnie Fino caught their share of comment. The general once fondly said he was going to have to call his command Little Italy if he got in one more character of their type.

During one phase of our lives together it became more or less customary for everyone to go to extremes in granting courtesy to the general. This, I think, sprang from the fact that there were a few very obsequious officers in another local headquarters who continually groveled before their commanding general. And so some of our officers enjoyed burlesquing them in their behavior toward General Ted.

In regard to the source of the burlesque, Mike Phipps had a story about a full colonel who each morning would walk in and stand in front of his commanding general's desk. According to Mike, the colonel would say, "Sir!" whereupon the general would look up with some irritation from the mass of papers in front of him and ask, "Well, what do you want?"

"Oh, nothing, sir—just sir, sir."

And so Mike sometimes addressed General Timberlake as "sir, general, sir."

I was happy in these surroundings. The associations I made there were a large part of my happiness. Another large part of it was the fact that I felt I would soon be going back to Anne and Pete.

When I first arrived in the wing there was a shortage of qualified people to do the work of controller. As a result I had to work almost every night for a while. Mort Macks was fine at the job, but since he hadn't been off for a long time, he went on leave. Bill Selvidge was sick in the hospital for a time and there was no one else to do the work but me. It required my being in or very near the operations office from late in the afternoon until after the ships took off in the morning.

The job worked something like this. Usually about four in the afternoon we would get a call from the division which would give us a "stand by until 2300." That means that more than likely we would have a mission, but that the field order might not start coming in on the teletypes until eleven that night. This warning would come in by way of a conference call from the division operations officer or division controller to all wing controllers or operations officers on a simultaneous telephone plug-in. I would immediately call the information to the groups.

There would not be much to do from that time until after dinner. When dinner was over I would go to the operations office to sweat out the arrival of the field order. Usually a field order would begin coming in on the teletypes about 10 or 11 p.m. Sometimes after coming in it would be canceled; sometimes it would be changed completely at a later hour; sometimes it would be changed only slightly. Sometimes—though rarely—we would be notified that no operations were anticipated for the next day. On those rare occasions I would leave a skeleton crew in the office and go to bed.

According to the normal procedure, the division field order would start coming in sometime between ten and eleven in the evening. As fast as it rattled off our teletypes I would begin preparing the wing field order. The wing would be called on for a designated number of aircraft. Sometimes we used only two groups to supply them when it was possible to do so, and sometimes all three would have to go to make up the required strength. I would decide that matter. I would decide which of our groups would lead and which would carry one type of bomb and which would carry another if the bomb load was diversified. I would also designate the gas load to be carried, and all the other details division left to us to determine.

I decided these matters, but tentatively, because almost without exception General Ted would stride in just about the time our field order was complete and go over it to the minutest detail. He was more careful of these details when I was new to the wing than he was later. But after a month or so of this kind of work, it became standard procedure for all controllers to make up the order just the way the general wanted. Then he would glance over the order and okay it to go out with practically no changes.

The operations office at eleven o'clock at night was alive and businesslike, but there was an air about it of convivial excitement. Everyone was keyed up by the suspense and joy of knowing that we were cooking up a lethal surprise for the Krauts.

When the field order was approved, I would put it on the wire. Then I could take off to get a cup of hot coffee and some bread and butter or whatever was available. After that there would be little doing for several hours. Frequently the groups would brief about 2:30 or 3:00 A.M. I would usually give a conference call to the group operations officers or whoever the groups had put in charge of running the mission and designated to do the briefings. The purpose of that call was to insure that each of the briefing officers understood all the field order and that each knew what the other groups were going to do in matters of assembling the wing formation, uncovering to make the bomb run, reassembly after leaving the target, etc. At this time any officer of one of the groups had a chance to clear up points he might have to discuss with me or with any other group.

After the conference call I could usually take a catnap in my chair at the desk. Sometimes I would read some of Mike Phipps's intelligence reports and, as often as I could, I read a pony issue of *Time* or some other American magazine. New issues of *Time* always caused excitement in the headquarters; sometimes we got them within eight days of their date of sale in the States.

The time between the last conference call and breakfast always seemed momentary. That was because it was filled with naps, sometimes interrupted by telephone calls, but rarely anything to occasion much mental effort. Of course the next memorable point would be breakfast. Often the general would be first in the mess, well ahead of the deadline at eight o'clock. Then I would give him a résumé of the way the mission had gone since midnight. I would eat and go to bed, sometimes to get up for lunch and sometimes to sleep until almost dinner time. While I was asleep the office would be looked after by an assistant controller.

That was the routine of the "normal" mission. If the current operation were of unusual importance the general would be in the office much later in the evening, sometimes all night long. On my nights on there was usually someone out of intelligence working with me—Mike, Fred Jarecki, or Vic Sieverding. The intelligence officer on duty was there to catch an occasional important problem. Such a problem might arise if one of the groups didn't have full information in its files on the target to be hit. In that case, whoever was working from intelligence would get out the necessary information by direct courier. On occasions when the matter was not determined by the division, our intelligence officer gave us very good advice about the way to make the best run in to the target from the standpoint of flak defenses. We had a sharp bunch on that subject and several times successfully went to bat with the division on the way they planned the run in or route out.

Several times a week members of the general's staff who didn't stay up all night working up the mission would have themselves awakened at 1:30 or 2:00 in the morning to drive to one or more of our airfields and attend the briefings. The general felt the importance of keeping close tab on the groups, so that we might be sure the crews got all the information available before going out. At least once a week General Ted attended a briefing, and once, in the case of an exceptionally sad situation, he took over and did a briefing himself. He covered instructions which usually come from the operations, intelligence, communications, and weather sections of the group.

The work at the wing was exciting and never ending, though

there were brief letups. Sometimes there was a letup when the
ships took off. That letup might last until they came home again
but often it didn't. If the weather was bad or as questionable as
it usually was, someone had to keep close check, so that the formation plan might be changed to facilitate quicker forming of
the airplanes. Such changes in plan would be radioed to the
leader. This job, again, was the responsibility of the controller
on duty.

To the end of effecting better formations the general got a
P-47 Thunderbolt fighter for the wing staff. As operations officer
I considered it my personal ship. Shortly after our groups were
airborne someone from the wing would take off in the Thunderbolt. Often he would fly through hazy weather and help the leader of one formation to find another. Always he herded in the
stragglers and made note of anyone not maintaining proper position. This monitoring aircraft would follow the group formations until the wing was formed, and continue until our wing
fell into its proper position in the division column. It would continue with the bombers until the point of departure from the
friendly coast and then it would return and land. Sometimes the
general flew it, sometimes I did but when we didn't, whoever
did would report to him on landing.

The duty controller who took over in the morning had a good
deal to do, though rarely as much as the one who set up the mission the night before. During the mission the wing operations
office would get reports on all ships returning early. These abor-
tive aircraft had to be carefully checked, though there was very
rarely any evidence of lack of courage on the part of the aircrews. It naturally discouraged abortions for the men to know
that an intensive engineering report was given on any aircraft
coming in early after failing to accomplish its mission.

As the day wore on and a mission progressed, control point
messages would come in from the formation leaders. These messages would enable our headquarters to keep track of the progress of our ships over enemy territory. Finally at a climax of
the waiting a strike message would arrive. It would be a brief
report that the target had been attacked and it would give the
first estimate of results. The controller on duty had to make

continued checks on the weather as the planes were on their route home. If conditions were expected to be bad at the bases there were all sorts of special measures to be taken to aid in getting the ships in. The various group operations offices had to be informed and checked to see that they had taken proper action to meet the situation.

Before the ships were due, three groups of officers of wing headquarters would depart, one for each of the different fields. The general would always go to one and other representatives would go to others to be on hand when the crews arrived for interrogation. Thus the wing representatives would get the picture firsthand from the forming up of the groups, wings, and divisions, the route out, uncovering at the initial point, bombing, rally, and route back. A careful check would be made of all enemy activity by flak or fighters and of our own bombing accuracy and the quality of formation flying. The wing representatives would usually go from one table to another in the interrogation rooms trying to get an accurate overall picture. Generally the best story of how the mission ran would be obtained from the command pilots and their lead crews. Frequently the wing representatives would wait for the developed bombing pictures, unless circumstances indicated the necessity for an immediate return to wing headquarters to report. After the verbal report it took only about half an hour more to get the pictures. All this activity of wing officers was in addition to the usual intelligence interrogation of crews. Our purpose was to get a flash report quickly to enable us to ascertain enough of the results to aid in planning the next mission, usually already taking shape. The more detailed report resulting from a complete interrogation would come in later on the teletypes and hit every headquarters up to Air Force.

If the wing representatives decided not to wait for the bomb strike photos, the groups would deliver them to the control towers of the various fields. At a set time very soon after the last ships had landed we would send someone in a cub airplane assigned to our headquarters to pick up this film. If I had been the controller on duty the night before, the job was likely to fall to me. I would drive my jeep down the line of the central airdrome, having arranged by a telephone call for the little ship to be ready to go and for the tower clearance on the triangular flight to the other two fields. I would hop in the plane, a mechanic would spin the prop, and I would take off a very few minutes after leaving headquarters. I could take off in a few hundred feet and seldom went to the trouble of taxiing out to a runway. I would give the plane the throttle and fly it right out of the end of the hangar; then I would dip by the tower so that the tower control officer would be sure to see me and call the other fields to tell them to have the pictures ready. When I got over one of the fields I would make my landing so that the plane would stop its roll at the foot of the tower. I would leave the engine running, and a man would come running out to hand me the pictures. In an instant I would be off again to the other field, where the process would be repeated. Then I would fly back to the central airdrome with the first photo record of the day's bombing results. It was a very good system, and we prided ourselves on having our bombing pictures before any other wing headquarters in the division. It was just one small peculiarity typical of General Ted.

All this reporting of the results didn't end a mission. If the day were not too far along by this time, a critique would be held at the wing operations office about three hours after all the ships had landed. This would be attended by all the command pilots and the lead first pilots, bombardiers, and navigators of the three groups. At the critiques someone of my force would take extensive notes. This job generally fell to Bill Selvidge or me.

In all three proceedings Mike Phipps figured prominently. Mike was not only an intelligence officer, but also a wing gunnery officer. That gave him another avenue of interest. Johnnie Fino and Mac McClain helped everywhere. Johnnie, with his quick mind, was very good at attending interrogations and bringing back an angle or two which might have been missed by others. Mac would spend hours pouring over the navigators' logs. He always knew where all the ships were every minute of each mission, even though many of the navigators who had flown the mission might have been lost. By analyzing all the navigators' logs he could spot the causes of error in the few which messed up.

Frequently the critique of one mission had to be held the morning after, while the next mission was in progress. And so it can be seen that the work at the wing was continuous. Mission overlapped mission, so that for us it was a life with no clearcut periods of time. Day merged into day to a degree that sometimes, for weeks at a time, I wouldn't know what day of the week it was. I would sleep in the daytime for several days in a row, and then maybe sleep at night for one or two, only to get up at 1:00 or 2:00 A.M. There was work to be done at all hours of the day or night, and someone had always to be on duty in operations. Somehow the general managed to get the whole story of all details which happened in the endless flood of events. I worked to the limit of my capacity and thoroughly enjoyed it.

From my position in the wing I had a perfect chance to observe the men in the groups under us who were then going through the same difficulties I had encountered months before. One of these was Major Jimmy Stewart. Jim had come over as a squadron commander in one of our groups and later had been taken out of that group to take the job of group operations officer in another group of the wing. During most of the time that I was the wing operations officer he was the group operations officer of the other unit. I heard the famous voice of *Mr. Smith Goes to Washington* over the conference telephone countless numbers of times at 1:00 or 2:00 A.M. Jim was an excellent combat officer by any standards. He was modest, quiet, and so deadly serious it sometimes almost made me ache to see him grieve over situations for which he felt responsible but about which he could do nothing. He led many excellent missions and some difficult ones. He led some heartbreakers that failed because of conditions beyond his control.

Particularly I recall one long mission he led that was destined for a target deep into Germany. The weather—the bugaboo of every command pilot in the theater—had done him the same trick at one time or another that it did to all of us who had been fighting the air war. He failed to hit the target; the formation flown was poor, and that, too, was because his planes had been unable to effect any proper assembly before going out. There were losses that were undeniably due either directly or indirect-

ly to weather. I had taken one of our staff cars, the sad old British
Humber, to drive down to Jim's field when I heard the ships
were returning early. I got to the tower in time to see his ship
land, and I drove out to the hard stand where it was taxied for
parking. As the airplane stopped and the engines killed, the
bomb bay doors slid open and Mr. Smith, wrapped in his high-
altitude paraphernalia, got out. He was trailing his umbilical
cord and his disconnected oxygen line. I never saw a sadder face
than his—dirty and ringed from long wearing of his oxygen
mask.

"Cheer up, Jim," I said. "If you'd led some of the missions
I've led, you'd be proud of this one today. What can you expect
when the weather is like it is?"

"I know," he drawled. "Wouldn't be so bad if this weren't
about the third one in a row. If I get one more like this they're
going to arrest me as a German spy."

The days at the wing were not 100 percent work, though
when I look back on them, they seem to have been almost that.
Through my friend Mike Phipps I had the opportunity of meeting an Englishman who lived near our headquarters; that acquaintance did a lot to afford relaxation and also build up my
esteem for the English. I needed such an acquaintance, for I had
been annoyed on occasions by hearing various uncomplimentary
British opinions about Americans. One, I recall as an example,
was an opinion that the American foot soldier did not compare
well with foot soldiers of other countries. The time was a month
or so before the landing at Normandy. The case in point was the
breakthrough at Kasserine Pass during the Battle of Africa. I
knew little about the battle, but I believe the breakthrough was
a reflection of many things other than the basic quality of our
ground troops. I heard from some sources that at that time our
troops were relying on British Intelligence, which had given
them to expect a breakthrough in another sector. Our troops,
according to that report, had regrouped to meet an expected
thrust that never came, and consequently they were unprepared
to meet the attack in the location where it was actually launched.
Another consideration, of course, was the matter of the greenness
of our troops. They simply hadn't had time to learn the ropes.

That comment about the American foot soldier tended to draw me away from the British. Doubtless it was made to me as an American airman in an effort to flatter the Air Corps, since it was coupled with high praise of American fliers.

I found in Mike's friend the proof that to jump from particulars to generalities about people is a serious mistake. Vivian Lockett was a colonel of the home guard, and in some ways almost a typical member of the British upper class. He would not have made such comments as the one about our ground troops. In one way he was not typical, for he was completely indifferent to politics, or at least seemed so. So far as I knew he was not and had not been "in government," and I couldn't picture his caring to be. He loved good horses and in years past had been captain of Britain's International Polo Team. He enjoyed shooting; he liked to putter around in his garden. He had a friendly outlook on life and a spirit which neither gave nor took offense. On several occasions I was present in his home for dinner, and I always found him charming.

A few days before the Derby I got a call from him. Knowing I came from the heart of the Bluegrass country in Kentucky, the colonel said he thought I might enjoy going to the "Daahby" with him. He had arranged "transport," and if I could go he would be delighted. I was pleased to accept. Colonel Lockett had had to put his big car in storage because of the "petrol shortage," but he had a friend who ran a van line to London. He had asked this friend to delay the regular run past Newmarket several days until Derby day so that we might ride in the truck. The friend had obliged. And so on Derby day he and I found ourselves rocking along the road to Newmarket in a furniture van. The weather was beautiful and the thrill of racing was in the air. I marveled at how, in spite of anything, the English always seem to manage to keep open avenues of escape from war.

I had a great day observing how different racing in England is from racing in the States. The track was a rolling stretch of ground with heavy green turf. It was not the regular track normally used in racing at Newmarket but a substitute course; the main course had been converted into an airstrip. On the track used this day the horses started from a little offshoot, ran about a quarter of a mile, and then made a right turn to run the remaining distance straightaway up and down several little hills. One of the stands was built looking towards the starting barrier, which made it very difficult from that position to tell which horse was leading as the whole pack thundered directly at you.

Not only did I find the layout of the track peculiar, but I met many racing figures who, to put it mildly, were not like my cronies at home. I met Lord Rosebery, owner of the winner, Ocean Swell. I also was introduced to Lord Derby and the Maharajah of Kashmir. The latter, a dark man with a flamboyant uniform, I had spotted and wondered about for some time. I thought he might be in His Majesty's fire service because of the amount of red he wore.

At least it was not a day of racing such as I used to enjoy as a kid—like the days when I used to climb over the fence at Churchill Downs, run across the infield, and jump the barrier into the Club House. Here I didn't need constantly to take care of guards with clubs seeking to do me in.

After the day's racing on the way home the colonel and I chatted about the horses. I reflected that the horses seemed of finer build than those at home, but many of them appeared to be little more than pretty. I didn't see anything like the number of rough looking horses I might see in a day of racing in the States, and the time turned in by the winners was not impressive. Maybe it was the result of their running on turf and starting from an old-fashioned spring barrier instead of a modern starting gate.

As the spring came on in 1944 our imaginations hung hair-triggered, guessing when the invasion of France would start. We knew the big show was imminent. Our aircrews felt they had borne the whole war in Western Europe for a long time, and they longed for assistance on the ground to speed things up. They had come home—those who survived—to almost empty barracks on occasions when the raids were rough, to mourn their late comrades, and to wonder whether the next foggy dawn would mark their last takeoff. Misery does love company, and the tragedy of our airmen at that time lay in their aloneness. They read in the papers stories of prophets who voiced the wish that there might not be any second front, so that there might be a chance to prove that Germany could be broken by strategic air power alone. The bomber crews were interested in winning the war and winning it as quickly as possible. They were not interested in proving the possibility of "victory through air power."

In May we began to construct plans about how to form up a maximum number of heavy bombers in darkness. It had been demonstrated time and time again that large units of bombers could not fly close formation at night. The British, for example, in all their night flying had never tried to fly close formation. But we knew the invasion would force us to fly our type of formation at night.

We were intensely worried lest we send the boys out to attempt a type of night flying that would be more hazardous than the effect of enemy action. Each time we sent the groups out in extremely heavy weather we could normally expect a few losses of crews from midair collisions of our own bombers. These losses sorely tried the morale of the men, because they were not encountered as a direct result of enemy action. Though they were unavoidable, they seemed quite purposeless.

In planning a night formation we were concerned about a sad experience which had occurred a few months earlier when our ships were late coming home. They came in well after dark and the Jerries sent a fighter or two in with the formation. In the cover of darkness several of our bombers had been shot down in the traffic pattern of the home airdromes. Our staunch little General Jimmy Hodges had almost been killed standing on our control tower trying to supervise the landing of a stricken plane. Why, then, might we not expect intruder action almost anytime we put such formations in the air in darkness?

And so for days and weeks on end we planned and argued, proved and disproved, how to get the units up in the dark with minimum hazard. Only a few in the wing knew enough of the invasion plan to know that our ground troops would be getting out of their boats to walk up those starkly forbidding beaches at the first break of day. It was absolutely necessary that we be formed up enough to hit our assigned targets just a minute or two ahead of the landing. Thus all the forming up procedure and the trip to the targets had to be done in the dark. This would have been easy had we been able to fly the same sort of easy patchwork formation the British use for night operations. But we were doing pattern precision bombing—not area bombing—and in such operations we used our special crews to lead closely grouped units, so that many crews could drop bombs with the perfection of the best. There was no alternative.

One governing point was that we had to anticipate cloud cover of the targets. It might be clear, but we could take no chances. We had at that time an increasing number of ships equipped to bomb on instruments with personnel specially trained to operate them. These ships would have to lead each formation so that, regardless of whether the targets were overcast, we could hit them. If we threw our bombs short they would get the men in the boats—our men. If they went long they wouldn't help any to soften up the beaches. They had to be on the nose regardless of the weather. Of course it would be the effort of those concerned to select proper weather, but who can predict the weather in England or France?

At length we had the plan we thought the most practicable. It fit our need of getting the groups formed into the number of units which our limited numbers of instrument-bombing lead ships and crews permitted. It also took into account the narrow confines within which we were limited by consideration of the operation simultaneously of combat wings of all of the three divisions of the Eighth Air Force. In other words, in a rather narrow part of a small island we had to count on every available aircraft being in the air at night, possibly in bad weather.

While we were selecting the plan we finally proposed to our division headquarters, General Ted would argue first for one plan and then for another. I gave vigorous support to the plan I liked; and Colonel Thomas, to one of his choosing. Variations were offered by McClain and Fino. It was evident the general was trying to get a thorough testing by argument of all the plans proposed. Sometimes at the thought of it all I would put my head in my hands and moan. I imagined the episode starting with a series of bright explosions of the first few planes blowing up in midair collisions. After that it seemed to me the whole sky might be covered by flame and smoke and combed by falling bits of bombers.

When I became depressed the general would laugh and say, "calm down, Phil. We'll make it all right. All you are supposed to do is to give a little aid in setting up a plan. If we had to we would take any plan and make it work." My theory that many British civilians and American ground soldiers would be killed by falling debris from disintegrated bombers was discarded in view of the necessity to get something worked out.

The group commanders were at length called in and presented the plan we chose as the most nearly possible of a number of nearly impossible ones open to us. They met the plan with admirable calm and suggested only a few minor changes.

The big day came on. We didn't know which day it would be until a comparatively few hours before the plan was to be put into effect. For some time I had already been worrying about who was going to lead our wing on the mission. I hadn't flown operationally for about two months. I had taken a rest after my tour was complete, but I hadn't intended permanently to quit flying combat. I don't think General Ted ever considered any of his flying personnel nonoperational. He was certainly very operational himself, with many hard missions to his credit. I knew he would be flying combat as long as the war lasted, and so would the pilots on his staff.

In short, my conscience began working on me. I didn't think there would be any enemy opposition to make the mission hard, but I was definitely worried about how the forming up procedure would go. I knew those in the groups who might be called upon to lead would also be worried about it. If the whole thing messed up royally, as well it might, it wouldn't be too unlikely for a scapegoat to be found. That person would most likely be the lead command pilot. Since I had played a part in drawing up the plan for the wing, it seemed right that I have the responsibility of putting it into effect.

My old group had been selected to lead the wing. Colonel

Arnold had moved up to division headquarters as a member of General Hodges's staff, and Colonel Miller had taken over the group. In the morning before D day, when we were first alerted for the invasion, I went down to Colonel Miller's office. I volunteered my services to lead. I almost hoped that I would be turned down, but I was taken up on the spot. After all, the pilots of the group were pretty weary from heavy, sustained action, and I hadn't had any for a long time.

We went over the plan carefully with key flying personnel several times. The lead crews had flown a simulated assembly plan, but the groups as a whole had not. We were briefed about eleven that night for takeoff at 1:30 A.M. At that briefing I saw the first reaction of the crews—a show of genuine enthusiasm. When it was announced that at last the invasion was beginning, a cheer stopped the briefing officer for almost a minute. The crews were cheering as they might have cheered the end of the war. As a matter of fact, this was the end of the purely strategic air war of Western Europe, and they knew it.

The pilot of the ship I was set up to fly in was the highly qualified "Temp" Cumiskey. The squadron I used to have had been completely converted to instrument bombing, and "Temp's" crew was now in it. They were a good bunch of fellows and a team in which I had complete confidence. Before I quite realized it, I was waiting in my ship at the end of the runway. At the appointed moment I saw a signal light from the tower, and in another instant my ship was roaring down the strip into the night. The sky above was overcast, as we were told it would be. We expected to fly a very precise pattern on instruments so that the other ships could take off behind at intervals of one minute and, flying the same pattern as we flew, be in minimum danger of collision. Then we were supposed to turn and come back over the field at 12,000 feet. According to what we expected of the weather, we thought that would put us on top of the overcast.

As we flew out I noticed the cloud was heavier than I had thought it would be. At about eight thousand feet I saw by the free air temperature gauge on the instrument panel that the air

in which we were flying was below freezing. I took a flashlight
I carried and shined it out the window by my seat and onto the
engine nacelles. Just as I thought, there was a coating of ice
forming over the nacelles and frosting up the propeller hubs.
We were pretty heavily loaded with bombs. I hoped we wouldn't
pick up much ice before we broke cloud because I knew the ship
was carrying near its load limit at takeoff.

As we came back over the field we were beginning to break
out. There were scattered bits of cloud which we flew into occasionally, but we could see the stars above. Our radio compass
needle indicated we were directly over the field, and our waist
gunners reported they could see the navigation lights of two
other ships pulling up on our wings. That was encouraging. All
the boys were making a superhuman effort because they knew
this was as important as any operation they would ever be called
on to perform. In a moment I could look out and see the dull
red, left wing light of the ship on my right and the dull green,
right wing light of the ship on my left. I was pleased.

Then we turned out on course to effect the next phase of the
complicated assembly plan. We had to climb higher to keep
out of the cloud. We were then over an area that another wing
was using for takeoffs, and once when we dipped a little into
the undercast below I saw the navigation lights of a bomber
flash by only a few feet below our flight level. If we didn't want
to smash into someone we knew we'd better climb and keep out
of that bomber-filled undercast. And so we climbed.

Finally we reached the next point, where we were to accomplish a series of turns to close up the space between the various
small formations. I had five ships with me at that time. I thought
we might pick up four or five more when the dawn approached,
and I was satisfied with the way our formation looked. We now
wanted to close the interval so that, whatever the size of the
various formations, they would be in position when they struck
out across the Channel to hit the enemy coast almost at the same
instant. The plan was followed with great precision. Our navigator had to change the briefed course a little to keep our small
unit clear of some thick cloud in which the wing men wouldn't

have been able to maintain their position. But when we came upon the next designated point to make good at a certain time we hit it perfectly.

Perhaps the most amazing part of our flight thus far was that there was no enemy opposition at all. Of course we were still over the British Isles, but I had greatly feared intruder action that would render completely chaotic the intricate plan we were trying to follow. Even though we were over Britain, the German radar would have let the enemy know all three air divisions had taken off and were forming up. They would have been over to stop us in a matter of a few minutes after we started takeoffs had they desired. Much later I learned what I should have guessed: our intruders had done a wonderful job of smashing their radar just before we took off. The absence of enemy intruders, plus the progress of the mission thus far, had just about dissipated the qualms I had had about what might come of our mighty effort to support the boys in the barges. My experience in combat flying told me we were through what might have been the roughest part of the mission.

Dawn crept closer as we reached the proper point in the pattern where we were to strike out directly for the south coast of England. Now we were firing green flares one after another. Abreast of us heading due south far to our right and left were other comparatively small formations, none larger than twelve planes. The leaders of all these also were firing green flares which showed up prominently in the first gray light of dawn. These pathfinders, like ourselves, were signaling to any stray ships in the area a message which said, "I am an instrument bomber. If you haven't attached yourself to a formation yet, join me and I will lead you to the proper bomb release point."

At that instant I counted two or three straggling airplanes which joined the nearest formations. Just then we drew off the friendly coast and headed south toward Normandy. Our plan was set. There would be no more changes and no more flares fired. A tidal wave of formations abreast headed south over the Channel waters separating England from Normandy. The weather over the Channel was spotty. We had in the beginning of this mission flown through some rather heavy clouds. On our final run down to the English coast we had found clearer skies. Now heading over the Channel waters toward France, we saw the clouds building up again ahead of us, but they were below our level of flight.

There were some breaks in the clouds as we neared the enemy coast. Through them I saw masses of boats of all sizes on the water; the flash of the guns of several warships as they shelled coastal installations; the white, curling wakes of the fast patrol boats as they darted about. Through one hole in the cloud ahead I saw a coastal battery firing, but shells from our ships seemed to be bursting all around it. Then the cloud below us thickened. We couldn't see the coastline at all.

It was evident we were going to have to bomb by instruments. I called the eight other ships I now was leading and told them to "stack it in." We wanted a good pattern of bombs and to get it, the formation had to be good. The bombardier and navigator were working together as a perfectly coordinated team. I switched to interphone from time to time to be sure they hadn't fumbled the ball. It is the terror of all command pilots to have a bombardier or a navigator indicate he is inextricably messed up when the bomb release line is a matter of seconds away. I listened to them talking back and forth; finding them in good control of the situation, I switched back to radio.

A few seconds later the bomb release indicator lights on the instrument panel began blinking, and I felt the ship shift balance slightly as the load of explosives trained out of the bomb bay. I looked out and saw the planes in our formation were releasing with us. The light in the east let me know that the sun was probably on its way up at that moment, though I couldn't see the horizon for the clouds. I prayed for the men in the boats.

I called the bombardier to ask him whether he thought he had a good run. Of course we could see nothing below us but the deck of clouds into which our bombs disappeared. "Sir," he replied, "if that wasn't a good run I'd never count on one being good. I think we dropped them right in the bucket."

Thank God! I thought. No intruders, no midair collisions, no fuss, no bother—just a push-button mission and on instruments! There was only one question in my mind. I had noticed that the ship which according to the briefed plan was supposed to fly on our right wing wasn't actually the ship filling that slot. Perhaps that plane filled in with another formation. It was okay as far as my losing my deputy lead, because no deputy was needed this trip.

As we proceeded over the French coast we saw several ground-fired rockets bursting with such inaccuracy that they were good for the first laugh of the day. Not one burst was near any plane. We turned right and flew out over the west coast of the Cherbourg peninsula. For a time we flew due west and then turned north. We did not fly over the lanes of water traffic heading toward the landing beach, for we had been told that the Navy would fire on any aircraft seen in that area going north. We could fly over their heads to the target, but we'd better not fly back the same way.

I was overjoyed by the prospect of the mission's success. Of course, I would have to wait until the Navy and ground forces observation reports of the bombing accuracy came through before I would really know how well it had gone. But I was particularly elated that in spite of heavy cloud to begin with, icing conditions, and darkness, our plan of formation had been good. The units did group themselves and proceed in a most orderly manner to the beach, all hitting almost simultaneously and within a minute and a half of the briefed time. We had been given three minutes' leeway—and only three minutes. That was precision in both planning and execution.

When we landed and taxied to the hard stand I saw the general's Packard pull up. Out stepped General Ted. A photographer who had been waiting advanced behind him and began snapping pictures. When I got out the great man accosted me.

"How'd it go, Phil?"

"Fine, I think and I certainly hope."

"Well, I believe you are right. We already have the report from the Navy that the bombing was excellent. They were amazed by the accuracy, considering the total cloud cover."

That was all I needed to make my joy about the bombing complete. But there was one other item to be noted. We went from the parking area to the tower to check on returning airplanes. One failed to return. It was my deputy lead ship. Hours later we got the report that bits of the wreckage of that plane had been found about twenty miles north of the field. It was evident something had happened during the first part of the assembly. At first we thought it was a midair collision, but there was no evidence of any other ship having been hit. Finally we guessed that airplane must have picked up a load of ice and spun in. It was a real tragedy. In my flier's fatalistic credo I told myself the Lord must have wanted that crew. All the others managed to get through that blanket of ice but this one.

The rest of D day the ships were shuttling in and out carrying loads of bombs to the bomb line just ahead of our troops. I spent the time in our operations office helping with these successive missions and giving rapt attention to the advance of the thin thread across our map used to designate our ground forces' position on the beach.

That evening late, after dinner but a little before dark in the long twilight of the English summer evening, I got on my bicycle to take a ride. I wanted to think of home and all those things which seemed so much nearer now that the second front had begun. I rode down to the airdrome and out to the main runway. All the ships were in from the last mission of the day and the runway was closed off for repairs. Our field had been almost in condition to stop operation some months before because of the cracking up of the concrete strip.

The field was built by the British for their type of landing on soft, almost marshy soil. The concrete of the runways was not thick enough to carry the weight of our fully loaded planes, and small cracks had appeared and quickly expanded into large breaks. It got so bad landings and takeoffs had to be made with great care to avoid collapsing a ship's landing gear or blowing a tire.

We had a company of British engineers who puttered around the problem of repairing the concrete, but the damage was keeping well ahead of the repair when we managed to release the British help and get in a company of American Negro engineers. Those men really knew how to handle their concrete mixers.

The pavement of the longest runway was made up of big

squares about thirty feet on a side. The engineers would pick a square with serious breaks in it, completely dig it up and replace it with quick-drying concrete. This work would always be done between the time the last ship landed in the evening and the first took off the next morning. Our operations were not slowed up at all by the work, and after three or four months almost our entire runway system had been renewed.

Whenever I wanted to feel a little nearer to the States I would ride down to where the men were working. They worked quickly and efficiently with a coordination rarely seen among construction crews in England. That evening, happy from the success of the day's mission and in the knowledge that the second front was under way, I found myself in quite a chatty mood. Most of the engineers were too busy to waste more than a moment talking to me.

Sometimes I worried that there wasn't enough indication to them of our appreciation for their indispensable efforts. They were doing something the folks back home might never know about, but they didn't seem to care. They did a good job and they knew it. They were winning their part of the war so that they could get home. They felt just like I did, I guess, except that had I been in their place I might have bothered more about getting proper recognition.

A few nights after D day when our war in the West was progressing acceptably, the people of London were awakened by the most terrific barrage of antiaircraft they had ever heard. Shells were bursting low over the roofs of the houses, and many people were injured by splinters of shrapnel intended to bring down attacking planes.

A few of the people looked out their windows and saw a new type of small plane go over. The ones seen trailed small comets behind them. They flew singly in straight lines from southeast to northwest over the city. At a special point the flame trailing one would quit and the plane would dive earthward. In a matter of seconds after this happened a tremendous explosion would occur which would sometimes wreck almost a whole city block, depending upon the type of housing. The blast effect was worse than any of the previous explosions during the blitz.

The news of this first robot bomb attack on London took us with some surprise in spite of the fact that we had been expecting it for a long time. We had run many raids which were at first reported in the papers as "attacks on the Pas de Calais area," but were later termed "blows at the rocket coast." Our intelligence had a pretty good idea of the sort of activity going on at the sites whence these weird missiles came. The greater surprise was that they had not been launched in large masses to stop the invasion. They could have dealt a devastating blow.

I never knew the answer to that one. Perhaps the sites weren't ready. Perhaps they were only accurate enough at long range to hit London. I don't know. I do know that when we flew over that coast to bomb the launching sites we received the most accurate antiaircraft fire we got anywhere. There was not as much flak as there was in some other places. But at two of the larger "diggin's" which were obviously sites prepared for a larger weapon than the first robot bomb, or V-1, the defensive fire was lethal. On two or three occasions our units would come back with a whole group formation showing a 100 percent flak damage. The sheet metal men in our maintenance shops used to moan when the ships returned from the rocket coast. They had to work overtime almost continually after these raids started.

Though the antiaircraft fire was very accurate, the raids were never considered as hard as raids deep into Germany for two reasons. One was that the bombers practically never suffered from German fighter attacks. The other was that the targets in that area were close enough to friendly territory to make it possible to get a ship back which had suffered very heavy damage. Nevertheless, it was not uncommon for a formation to report one or two ships blown up in midair from direct flak hits. And it was also not uncommon for the returning planes to carry in them a few dead and some seriously wounded crew members.

We had done great damage to some of the emplacements and had measurably delayed the preparation of others. Once sites were complete they were almost invulnerable to bombing. They were well camouflaged, hard to hit, and, if hit, still harder to destroy. The larger sites were still under construction, though certainly it was not possible for work gangs to maintain intensive construction under the almost incessant rain of bombs we gave them.

Nevertheless, either from some of the installations we had been bombing, or from others of more temporary construction in the area, the Nazis were now making life hard for Londoners. Those people who suffered so bitterly during the first great blitz awakened to find that there were newer horrors to face. It was a bitter pill coming at a time when they thought terror bombing from the Germans was at an end.

I heard so many of the English people talk of the shock of this earlier bombing of London that I wanted to go there immediately to spend a day or two and see how the town was weathering this new storm. True, I had been there one night when London endured a raid by a hundred planes. On that occasion all the town's defenses, including the great rocket throwers in Hyde Park, cut loose. I hadn't panicked, perhaps only because I never woke up. I had gone to bed quite late and tired, and read about the raid in the morning's papers. It struck about two hours after I went to bed and lasted about an hour. The fact that I slept through the whole thing led me to believe it wasn't much of a show.

Once or twice I saw the puny efforts of the Nazis attempting a raid on our airdrome. We would hear frantic calls over the public address system for all personnel to report to the shelters. It was only a cue for us to go outside to see the sight. Several times we were alerted by lone raiders, and twice I watched the enemy planes get shot down.

I wondered how the Yanks, who were now so thick in London, would bear this trial. A British saying familiar to my ears was in effect, "You may say what you like about the British. But after all is said and done you must admit they're a pretty steady lot. You take the conduct of the people of London, for example: if the blitz had happened in New York instead of London it would have wrought utter panic. Oh, yes, you Americans are clever and quick. The British are slow and stolid. But in the blitz the true character and spirit of London came out."

I believed at least part of that. It came as a frequent comment and was somewhat in the same vein as the British reasoning that

Americans were poor foot soldiers; that they had not the stolidity, the tenacity of the British. Here was an opportunity for me to see Americans and British side-by-side enduring the same terror weapon. I couldn't resist it.

Many of my friends of earlier visits were now over on the beachhead. Larry LeSueur was in the very front line of troops fighting in Normandy. Instead of having his lavish quarters put at my disposal, this time I felt myself lucky to be able to find a room in a hotel. I had been told getting rooms in the hotels was a lot easier since the buzz bombs started, but I found it quite the opposite. The hotels are of a more solid construction than many of the buildings containing the most comfortable of London's flats. Consequently many flat-dwellers had moved out of their residences and into hotels.

This time there was a car from our headquarters going to London to spare me the burden of the trip by rail. I had quite a comfortable drive down. When I reached the outskirts of London it seemed to me I could notice already the difference between this and the London of my last visit. There was evidently an alert on at the time of my arrival.

The streets were almost bare. Those people who could be seen seemed to be persons who had unavoidable business. There were no window-shoppers or casual strollers, and most everyone wore a slightly worried expression. It was about noon. Then I heard for the first time that noise unfamiliar to me but obviously well known to those on the street. It sounded more like a Model T Ford than anything else I could compare it to. The noise grew. Thrr, rhrr, rhrr, rhrr, rhrr—it went with a sort of spasmodic rhythm. The driver came to a stop. I was looking out of the car window to try to get a glimpse of the "doodlebug" at this moment and so missed a chance to see what the pedestrians were doing.

The noise stopped suddenly. There was absolute silence for a number of seconds and then the explosion. It evidently wasn't very near us, but down the street and through a cut in the skyline of buildings I could see a cloud of black smoke with some small bits of debris floating around. The explosion was quite loud, and my driver and I felt a slight bit of the concussion. It was obvious we weren't close enough to that one to get the proper effect of it.

We drove on. The driver admitted that he wished he hadn't come to London. After all, he had been on a nice quiet bomber station out of all this mess only a little while ago. Just then the all clear sounded. The expressions of the pedestrians seemed to brighten up a bit and a small part of the old gaiety and life returned to London. Throughout the rest of that day hot on the heels of each all clear came the sirens screaming out the next alert. It was easy to see how this disruption could impair the total effort of a great city. I certainly felt the strain myself.

After locating my room at the Park Lane Hotel, I went into the lobby to check at the ticket agent's office to see what shows I might find with seats available. I wasn't much surprised to discover I was able to get the best seat in the house, or very nearly the best, at any show in town. I wasn't so thoroughly imbued with the fear of the robomb as those who had been longer subjected to its horror. Consequently, I went to two movies that in earlier days were continually sold out. In the afternoon I saw *The Song of Bernadette* and in the evening, *For Whom the Bell Tolls*. As I went up to the ticket window of the theater where the latter was showing, a buzz bomb went over quite close. It grew suddenly silent for a space and let out a roaring explosion not far away. I did get a fair glimmer of the stolidity of the British as the girl in the window smiled at me and said, "I don't believe he likes us."

As I went back to my hotel I thought a good deal about these missiles. They seemed to embody the superiority of the Germans as military technicians. I loathed Nazis, but in loathing them I regretted the fact that we had failed to push development of jet and rocket propulsion. This had long been so obviously the next great development in motive power that its importance seemed utterly inescapable. At least it was to the Germans.

I noticed as I walked in the door of the hotel that the clouds were lower on the tops of the buildings than when I went out. It was very dark, but the fog dipped down into the streets and I could see that that night London was like the city of Sherlock

Holmes. In these conditions the buzz bombs were at their worst. The countermeasures the British had taken against them, chiefly antiaircraft fire and fighter planes, were pretty successful in good weather. They prevented a large number of the missiles from reaching their targets. But in bad weather there was very little to stop them. Some would still fall to radar-directed antiaircraft fire or snarl up in barrage balloon cables. But many more would get through to blast large parts of London.

I went up to my room, turned the light out, and went to the window. Throwing back the blackout curtain, for the first time I saw the frightful weapons flying over. Two passed within plain view of the window. When I had seen them I went to bed. But I admit that my pulse leaped high every time I heard a bomb go over, and the closer it came the harder was the pounding of my temples.

The next day the fog was heavy most of the daylight hours. The bombs came with only brief respite—an all clear for twenty minutes maybe—then another alert. One of the sirens was very near my hotel room. It jarred my nerves much more than sirens I had previously heard at a distance. I don't know why. Both carried the same warning.

That day I talked to people and walked about in the streets. I found a number of officers and other persons with whom Hitler's newest weapon was a ready and catching topic of conversation. I found it considered foolhardy to stand in a window, as I had done the night before. It seems there are two effects of the blast. The first, a positive effect, is an outward push of air from the spot where the explosion occurs. This covers a narrower radius than the second, negative thrust. This is a suction formed by air rushing in to fill the partial vacuum caused by the initial blast. In this secondary thrust many gawpers in windows had been pulled out into the street. Clothes had even been torn off pedestrians. The route of the most intensive effect of the blast was unpredictable. On one street leading from a corner which had been hit windows might be out for blocks. On another street leading from the same corner the effect of the bomb might carry a much shorter distance. Why? I never got the answer. Apparently it had something to do with the configuration of the buildings, though it was difficult to predict avenues of blast effect from an advance look at an area.

I found that many of the people of London spent every night in shelters where their rest was inadequate to prepare them for a normal day's work. Many others, for pride or some other reason, wouldn't go to the shelters but lay in sleepless terror in their beds. Many people slept in their clothes because they wanted to spare themselves the embarrassment of being seen on the street in nightclothes in case a bomb blew them out the window. Many were afraid to take a bath except during an all clear. If an alert were sounded they would get out of the tub in a hurry to avoid any risk of being taken at a crisis in the nude.

The afternoon after I arrived I was walking along Berkeley Street near Berkeley Square. I could hear a buzz bomb approach closer and closer. It sounded as though it were coming directly toward the spot where I was. There were a half dozen people on the street near me, among them a couple of American GIs. An elderly man dashed for the entrance of a nearby shelter. The bomb came closer—closer than any I'd ever heard. The two GIs walked on looking nervously upward. A lone woman stepped back to place herself up against the wall of a substantial looking building and shut her eyes. Yes, she was praying; there was no mistake about that. The others appeared to continue down the street a little more quickly than normally. The bomb passed over. Just as it did, its engine stopped. Poor someone, I thought. I knew when it got almost directly overhead with its engine still going it wouldn't harm us. Then there was a great explosion. The breeze of the concussion was very sharp on my cheek.

That night the air cleared a little. There were one or two bombs over early in the evening and one alert close to dawn during which I heard a few bombs. But that was nothing like it had been. I had planned the next day to return to my station and I knew I would be glad when the time of departure arrived. I'd seen the people of London show the same courage which they showed in the face of many severe trials. This time they had the Americans as their guests to face the same hardship, and their guests also bore it well. From what I heard and from my own personal observation the Americans bore the bombing as well as everyone else. There were many cases reported of American soldiers being the first to the scene of an incident to help with the rescue work. Frequently, there were cases where they labored to the point of exhaustion to assist in saving trapped victims. But in fairness I must admit the Americans made much less than the British of pretending to be unmoved by the bombs. When an American doesn't like something, especially an American GI, you can expect to hear him sound off about it. An Englishman won't. I have seen two types of hound dogs in my time. One bays to the scent and another hunts mute. Both have sporting hearts. It is in their background and the way they are trained that they behave differently.

I took the train for the base the next morning. I was glad to be taking it. I left the people of London my sympathy in their hardship and heroism.

7

Something
to Believe In

When I got back to the base I took an early opportunity to go to General Ted with something that had been on my mind ever since June 13, 1943, over a year before, on the day I landed in Prestwick, Scotland. When I went to the wing to be operations officer, Colonel Arnold had indicated I had reason to hope that I might stay in England only about three months after the completion of my tour.

The concept of a combat tour seemed to be peculiar to the Air Corps, and I was aware of the fairness of complaints from the ground forces that there was no combat tour for them. But only a very small number of the combat people of my old group lived to the end of such a tour. When I sought to go home it was not with the firm conviction that I had fought as much of the war as anyone else. It was simply that apparently there was an avenue open, and I was less of a soldier than I was a husband and a father. Anne knew of a few combat airmen who had gone home immediately after completing their last mission. She had heard from their wives, and she naturally wondered why I couldn't come home.

Though I was told that there were great opportunities to be

had by those who stayed on overseas, I didn't want another promotion: I felt it an act of generosity that I had received the last one.

I wanted to do a good job wherever the Army assigned me, but now more than anything else in the world I wanted to see my wife and child. The job I had I knew could be filled as satisfactorily by any one of a dozen possible candidates within the command. The general was generous enough to offer me an opportunity to stay with him. He also said that if I wished, there was a chance I might be returned to the States.

About that time Colonel Larry Thomas left the wing to take command of one of the groups and the general brought Lieutenant Colonel Jimmy Stewart up to the wing as his chief of staff. The fellows in the wing were delighted to get Stewart, though of course they all missed Larry. We all had seen enough of Jim to know that he was the kind of person who would quietly and efficiently do a good job.

A few days after these changes General Ted told me he had asked for orders returning me to the States. After that I worked under great difficulty. Anyone does who looks forward to something not connected with his current assignment. For many days after my conference with General Ted there was no definite news. I never failed to seek information. One time when I had asked the same question a number of times in a row he turned to me and said quietly, "Phil, you have many qualities." And then he shouted, "One of which is not *patience!*" From that time on I approached the subject indirectly.

Before much time had passed I was presented with orders —the most precious I had ever seen—directing me to London for the purpose of returning to the "Zone of Interior." Several days later I said goodbye to my friends at the base. Though I am poor at goodbyes, that one seemed particularly hard in spite of my longing to be off.

Entering London as on my last trip, I experienced an alert. I heard an explosion some distance ahead and a few minutes later came upon an apartment building cut in half. From where it stood and to the end of the block every other building was demolished. I looked up to a third-story flat cut right through the middle. There hanging over the distance of three floors to the rubble below was a closet whose door stood open, showing some small dresses hanging inside. My driver stopped without any word from me, and together we gaped at the scene. Rescue workers were digging in the ruins. An old English gentleman was walking up and down the sidewalk. His hands were placidly folded behind his back and his face was a picture of grief. I didn't realize how we, two curious Americans, must have impressed him until he stopped beside the car and quietly asked, "Can I help you?"

I was stung by the remark. Obviously that man had lost someone dear to him. I was sincerely sorry—I hadn't realized. Quickly I said what I suppose was on my mind when we stopped. "Can we help?"

"No, thank you. I believe we are being taken care of," he replied.

We drove on.

That was another rough day in London. When I got my priority on the plane it was about noon. I was told the bus for the airport would leave at 2:30. Would I leave an address where I might be called? I explained I was not registered anywhere. I would go to the Dorchester to have lunch and come back shortly.

"Why," I asked, "do you have to have a place where you can call me?"

The girl behind the counter shrugged her shoulders. "Maybe the building won't be here at 2:30."

Our plane was ready on time at an airport not far from the center of town. As we took off I could see dust from the explosion of another bomb over the tops of the buildings.

When we dropped down at Scotland the sun was lying low in the sea. Scotland was at peace as much as London was at war. By the time we landed I had struck up an acquaintance with Elmer Lower of the Office of War Information. He had known my brother in the prewar newspaper world. We dined together, got quarters, and turned in. The next day we boarded a fine, big C-54 that took us out to Iceland and on to the United States.

While I flew along on the hop from Scotland to Iceland, and then from Iceland to America, I had a few much-needed hours for reflection. I thought of Pete Hughes. I thought of Ed Fowble and his fine crew. I thought of Bill Young, my colleague at the Franklin County Bar, then a German prisoner. I thought of Don Buck, my first squadron operations officer, who was reported missing and later declared killed in action. I thought of Westerbeke, of Caldwell, of Lighter, and the scores of others who proudly had gone forth and were not returning. They would leave many homes and hearts broken. Many wives and parents would be denied the last wish to have the remains of a loved one given burial.

As far as the air war of Europe was concerned, I knew I had seen it at its toughest. Later General Arnold, in his report to the secretary of war, expressed my thoughts about one small part of it when he said, "The week of 20–26 February 1944 may well be classed by future historians as marking a decisive battle of history, one as decisive and of greater world importance than Gettysburg." I had seen bad weather cover our operations until the German fighter production reached a peak we never dreamed of, and I had been on hand as a command pilot in the process of doing a tour when the weather cleared. The call went out for us to break the back of that German fighter production. During that week I went out twice, and I saw many a gallant friend go down. I recalled that the trip to Gotha that week cost us more heavily than our bloody, low-level Ploesti raid had. These two were easily the roughest raids in the history of our group, and yet my good luck or someone else's bad luck had brought me home from both.

We did break the back of the Luftwaffe that winter. There was bitter, bloody fighting for the ground forces from D day on. But the biggest job of the strategic bomber force was done. The job of winning the air war was not over, but the great crisis in the air had clearly passed.

I knew I was luckier than I deserved to be.

As the plane carried me across I remembered many things in my childhood. I remembered many evenings being curled up under the kitchen table in our Bourbon County farmhouse listening to our cook Clara and friends of hers preparing dinner. Or, as we would have said then, "getting supper." There were often two or three women and maybe a man in the kitchen, and the patois of their voices was a delight. They sang beautiful songs, but their language was what most impressed me. The blacks talked among themselves with an accent most whites couldn't understand but which I had learned well. I frequently heard slightly risque remarks about the whites in earshot of "the house" that went entirely unnoticed. There was a humor, a sentimentality, a high morality of some, and a Rabelaisian raunchiness of others that taught me early that all of us are pretty much alike.

The greatest of all my heroes as a little boy, aside from my father, was an old black man named Willis Barton. He had been in his youth a slave belonging to my great-grandfather Lafayette Ardery. Cap'n, we called him. I thought him very handsome. He was extremely wise. He couldn't read or write, but there were many things he knew about how to operate our farm, so that his word on a subject was rarely challenged.

On wintry mornings when I was too young to go to school, and later during days out of school, I would go with him to the back of the farm to load bright, golden fodder shocks onto a slide to bring to the front of the farm, where we would throw it out to the cattle. A slide was a sort of low-slung sled pulled by two mules. The bed of it was just high enough for me to sit on and let my shoes occasionally touch the frosty earth gliding under the runners.

Cap'n was full of history and told me many stories about old Lafayette Ardery and about his own recollections of the soldiers coming home from "the war." He must have been about seven years old at the time of the surrender at Appomattox.

Of all the influences on me as a young boy, aside from that of my parents, Cap'n was undoubtedly the greatest. He was a Calvinist as much as they were, and he left me in no doubt about the superiority of that certain set of values.

Dogs chasing rabbits; pigeons flying around high up among the tier rails inside the tobacco barn; the faint and sometimes not so faint smell of a skunk on an early, frosty morning; muskrats building their homes on the banks of the spring branch; the loading of brown gravel from the creek into the wagon to put on our driveway; sometimes finding a nest of turtle eggs as our shovels hurried to make a load for the mules, Pete and Jane, to pull back to the house. Such things characterized my life as a boy, and they crowded my memory as I flew along.

I realized that as a child I had really had something to believe in. I believed that people were basically decent and honest—with a few exceptions. I believed in my father and my mother and Cap'n. I had a strong view of the rightness of things like work and saving money. I was convinced that the road ahead might be rough in spots, but it always pointed up to better things and times.

As our plane skimmed over the American suburban countryside north of New York, I kept my nose flattened against the window. The bigness of everything was overpowering—the highways, the broad expanses of fields, the spacious lawns of houses. Such bigness must be part of an explanation of the people. Space enough for all. Wealth enough for all to share. Those attributes of wealth, the automobiles, the houses, the refrigerators, the radios were better and finer than they might have been had they belonged only to a privileged few. Give opportunities to all and the privileges of the wealthiest are not lessened. That is America.

When I got to my room in the Biltmore I put in a call to Texas. It was ten in the morning of July 6, 1944. The call went through in less than five minutes. After yelling in almost frenzied excitement at Anne for a few minutes, I told her I would see her as soon as I could get there. Then I called mother and dad in Kentucky. It must have taken all of five minutes more for that call to go through. I spent the next hours taking a hot bath and getting to the airport. And then within a very short time I was in the air flying to Texas.

As I came lugging my bags at an awkward gallop up the walk to the little white house in San Angelo, I heard the sound of squeals from inside. The door swung open. It was the face I had imagined every day since I left. It hadn't changed. And as she stood a moment in the door her skirt was brushed aside and a little blond head popped up beside her.

Anne looked down at him.

"It's your daddy, Pete. He's come back."

Index

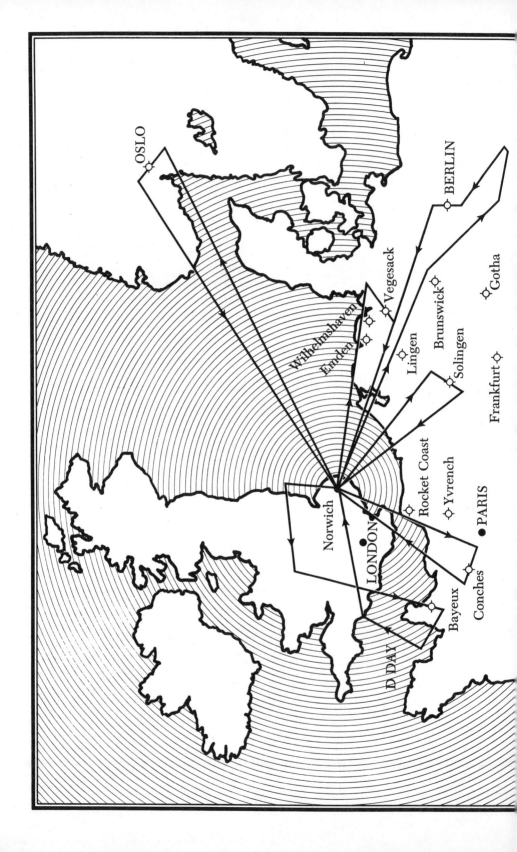